NON SANZ DROICT.

THE
TEMPEST.

Actus primus, Scena prima.

William Shakespeare

The Tempest

With New and Updated
Critical Essays
and a Revised Bibliography

Edited by Robert Langbaum

THE SIGNET CLASSICS SHAKESPEARE
General Editor: Sylvan Barnet

SIGNET CLASSICS

SIGNET CLASSICS
Published by New American Library, a division of
Penguin Group (USA) Inc., 375 Hudson Street,
New York, New York 10014, USA
Penguin Group (Canada), 90 Eglinton Avenue East, Suite 700, Toronto,
Ontario M4P 2Y3, Canada (a division of Pearson Penguin Canada Inc.)
Penguin Books Ltd., 80 Strand, London WC2R 0RL, England
Penguin Ireland, 25 St. Stephen's Green, Dublin 2,
Ireland (a division of Penguin Books Ltd.)
Penguin Group (Australia), 250 Camberwell Road, Camberwell, Victoria 3124,
Australia (a division of Pearson Australia Group Pty. Ltd.)
Penguin Books India Pvt. Ltd., 11 Community Centre, Panchsheel Park,
New Delhi - 110 017, India
Penguin Group (NZ), 67 Apollo Drive, Rosedale, North Shore,
Auckland 1311, New Zealand (a division of Pearson New Zealand Ltd.)
Penguin Books (South Africa) (Pty.) Ltd., 24 Sturdee Avenue,
Rosebank, Johannesburg 2196, South Africa

Penguin Books Ltd., Registered Offices:
80 Strand, London WC2R 0RL, England

Published by Signet Classics, an imprint of New American Library, a division
of Penguin Group (USA) Inc. The Signet Classics edition of *The Tempest*
was first published in March 1964, and an updated edition was published
in 1987.

First Signet Classics Printing (Second Revised Edition), September 1998
40 39 38

Copyright © Robert Langbaum, 1964, 1987, 1998
Copyright © Sylvan Barnet, 1964, 1987, 1998
All rights reserved

REGISTERED TRADEMARK—MARCA REGISTRADA

Printed in the United States of America

Contents

Shakespeare: An Overview

Biographical Sketch

Between the record of his baptism in Stratford on 26 April 1564 and the record of his burial in Stratford on 25 April 1616, some forty official documents name Shakespeare, and many others name his parents, his children, and his grandchildren. Further, there are at least fifty literary references to him in the works of his contemporaries. More facts are known about William Shakespeare than about any other playwright of the period except Ben Jonson. The facts should, however, be distinguished from the legends. The latter, inevitably more engaging and better known, tell us that the Stratford boy killed a calf in high style, poached deer and rabbits, and was forced to flee to London, where he held horses outside a playhouse. These traditions are only traditions; they may be true, but no evidence supports them, and it is well to stick to the facts.

Mary Arden, the dramatist's mother, was the daughter of a substantial landowner; about 1557 she married John Shakespeare, a tanner, glove-maker, and trader in wool, grain, and other farm commodities. In 1557 John Shakespeare was a member of the council (the governing body of Stratford), in 1558 a constable of the borough, in 1561 one of the two town chamberlains, in 1565 an alderman (entitling him to the appellation of "Mr."), in 1568 high bailiff—the town's highest political office, equivalent to mayor. After 1577, for an unknown reason he drops out of local politics. What *is* known is that he had to mortgage his wife's property, and that he was involved in serious litigation.

The birthday of William Shakespeare, the third child and the eldest son of this locally prominent man, is unrecorded, but the Stratford parish register records that the infant was baptized on 26 April 1564. (It is quite possible that he was born on 23 April, but this date has probably been assigned by tradition because it is the date on which, fifty-two years later, he died, and perhaps because it is the feast day of St. George, patron saint of England.) The attendance records of the Stratford grammar school of the period are not extant, but it is reasonable to assume that the son of a prominent local official attended the free school—it had been established for the purpose of educating males precisely of his class—and received substantial training in Latin. The masters of the school from Shakespeare's seventh to fifteenth years held Oxford degrees; the Elizabethan curriculum excluded mathematics and the natural sciences but taught a good deal of Latin rhetoric, logic, and literature, including plays by Plautus, Terence, and Seneca.

On 27 November 1582 a marriage license was issued for the marriage of Shakespeare and Anne Hathaway, eight years his senior. The couple had a daughter, Susanna, in May 1583. Perhaps the marriage was necessary, but perhaps the couple had earlier engaged, in the presence of witnesses, in a formal "troth plight" which would render their children legitimate even if no further ceremony were performed. In February 1585, Anne Hathaway bore Shakespeare twins, Hamnet and Judith.

That Shakespeare was born is excellent; that he married and had children is pleasant; but that we know nothing about his departure from Stratford to London or about the beginning of his theatrical career is lamentable and must be admitted. We would gladly sacrifice details about his children's baptism for details about his earliest days in the theater. Perhaps the poaching episode is true (but it is first reported almost a century after Shakespeare's death), or perhaps he left Stratford to be a schoolmaster, as another tradition holds; perhaps he was moved (like Petruchio in *The Taming of the Shrew*) by

> Such wind as scatters young men through the world,
> To seek their fortunes farther than at home
> Where small experience grows.   (1.2.49–51)

In 1592, thanks to the cantankerousness of Robert Greene, we have our first reference, a snarling one, to Shakespeare as an actor and playwright. Greene, a graduate of St. John's College, Cambridge, had become a playwright and a pamphleteer in London, and in one of his pamphlets he warns three university-educated playwrights against an actor who has presumed to turn playwright:

> There is an upstart crow, beautified with our feathers, that with his *tiger's heart wrapped in a player's hide* supposes he is as well able to bombast out a blank verse as the best of you, and being an absolute Johannes-factotum [i.e., jack-of-all-trades] is in his own conceit the only Shake-scene in a country.

The reference to the player, as well as the allusion to Aesop's crow (who strutted in borrowed plumage, as an actor struts in fine words not his own), makes it clear that by this date Shakespeare had both acted and written. That Shakespeare is meant is indicated not only by *Shake-scene* but also by the parody of a line from one of Shakespeare's plays, *3 Henry VI*: "O, tiger's heart wrapped in a woman's hide" (1.4.137). If in 1592 Shakespeare was prominent enough to be attacked by an envious dramatist, he probably had served an apprenticeship in the theater for at least a few years.

In any case, although there are no extant references to Shakespeare between the record of the baptism of his twins in 1585 and Greene's hostile comment about "Shake-scene" in 1592, it is evident that during some of these "dark years" or "lost years" Shakespeare had acted and written. There are a number of subsequent references to him as an actor. Documents indicate that in 1598 he is a "principal comedian," in 1603 a "principal tragedian," in 1608 he is one of the "men players." (We do not have, however, any solid information about which roles he may have played; later traditions say he played Adam in *As You Like It* and the ghost in *Hamlet*, but nothing supports the assertions. Probably his role as dramatist came to supersede his role as actor.) The profession of actor was not for a gentleman, and it occasionally drew the scorn of university men like Greene who resented writing speeches for persons less educated than themselves, but it was respectable enough; players, if prosperous, were in effect members of the bourgeoisie, and there is nothing to suggest that Stratford considered William Shakespeare less than a solid citizen. When, in 1596, the Shakespeares were granted a coat of arms—i.e., the right to be considered gentlemen— the grant was made to Shakespeare's father, but probably William Shakespeare had arranged the matter on his own behalf. In subsequent transactions he is occasionally styled a gentleman.

Although in 1593 and 1594 Shakespeare published two narrative poems dedicated to the Earl of Southampton, *Venus and Adonis* and *The Rape of Lucrece*, and may well have written most or all of his sonnets in the middle nineties, Shakespeare's literary activity seems to have been almost entirely devoted to the theater. (It may be significant that the two narrative poems were written in years when the plague closed the theaters for several months.) In 1594 he was a charter member of a theatrical company called the Chamberlain's Men, which in 1603 became the royal company, the King's Men, making Shakespeare the king's playwright. Until he retired to Stratford (about 1611, apparently), he was with this remarkably stable company. From 1599 the company acted primarily at the Globe theater, in which Shakespeare held a one-tenth interest. Other Elizabethan dramatists are known to have acted, but no other is known also to have been entitled to a share of the profits.

Shakespeare's first eight published plays did not have his name on them, but this is not remarkable; the most popular play of the period, Thomas Kyd's *The Spanish Tragedy*, went through many editions without naming Kyd, and Kyd's authorship is known only because a book on the profession of acting happens to quote (and attribute to Kyd) some lines on the interest of Roman emperors in the drama. What is remarkable is that after 1598 Shakespeare's name commonly appears on printed plays—some of which are not his. Presumably his name was a drawing card, and publishers used it to attract potential buyers. Another indication of his popularity comes from Francis Meres, author of *Palladis Tamia: Wit's Treasury* (1598). In this anthology of snippets accompanied by an essay on literature, many playwrights are mentioned, but Shakespeare's name occurs more often than any other, and Shakespeare is the only playwright whose plays are listed.

From his acting, his play writing, and his share in a playhouse, Shakespeare seems to have made considerable money. He put it to work, making substantial investments in Stratford real estate. As early as 1597 he bought New Place, the second-largest house in Stratford. His family moved in soon afterward, and the house remained in the family until a granddaughter died in 1670. When Shakespeare made his will in 1616, less than a month before he died, he sought to leave his property intact to his descendants. Of small bequests to relatives and to friends (including three actors, Richard Burbage, John Heminges, and Henry Condell), that to his wife of the second-best bed has provoked the most comment. It has sometimes been taken as a sign of an unhappy marriage (other supposed signs are the apparently hasty marriage, his wife's seniority of eight years, and his residence in London without his family). Perhaps the second-best bed was the bed the couple had slept in, the best bed being reserved for visitors. In any case, had Shakespeare not excepted it, the bed would have gone (with the rest of his household possessions) to his daughter and her husband.

On 25 April 1616 Shakespeare was buried within the chancel of the church at Stratford. An unattractive monument to his memory, placed on a wall near the grave, says that he died on 23 April. Over the grave itself are the lines, perhaps by Shakespeare, that (more than his literary fame) have kept his bones undisturbed in the crowded burial ground where old bones were often dislodged to make way for new:

> Good friend, for Jesus' sake forbear
> To dig the dust enclosed here.
> Blessed be the man that spares these stones
> And cursed be he that moves my bones.

A Note on the Anti-Stratfordians, Especially Baconians and Oxfordians

Not until 1769—more than a hundred and fifty years after Shakespeare's death—is there any record of anyone expressing doubt about Shakespeare's authorship of the plays and poems. In 1769, however, Herbert Lawrence nominated Francis Bacon (1561–1626) in *The Life and Adventures of Common Sense*. Since then, at least two dozen other nominees have been offered, including Christopher Marlowe, Sir Walter Raleigh, Queen Elizabeth I, and Edward de Vere, 17th earl of Oxford. The impulse behind all anti-Stratfordian movements is the scarcely concealed snobbish opinion that "the man from Stratford" simply could not have written the plays because he was a country fellow without a university education and without access to high society. Anyone, the argument goes, who used so many legal terms, medical terms, nautical terms, and so forth, and who showed some familiarity with classical writing, must have attended a university, and anyone who knew so much about courtly elegance and courtly deceit must himself have moved among courtiers. The plays do indeed reveal an author whose interests were exceptionally broad, but specialists in any given field—law, medicine, arms and armor, and so on—soon find that the plays do not reveal deep knowledge in specialized matters; indeed, the playwright often gets technical details wrong.

The claim on behalf of Bacon, forgotten almost as soon as it was put forth in 1769, was independently reasserted by Joseph C. Hart in 1848. In 1856 it was reaffirmed by W. H. Smith in a book, and also by Delia Bacon in an article; in 1857 Delia Bacon published a book, arguing that Francis Bacon had directed a group of intellectuals who wrote the plays.

Francis Bacon's claim has largely faded, perhaps because it was advanced with such evident craziness by Ignatius Donnelly, who in *The Great Cryptogram* (1888) claimed to break a code in the plays that proved Bacon had written not only the plays attributed to Shakespeare but also other Renaissance works, for instance the plays of Christopher Marlowe and the essays of Montaigne.

Consider the last two lines of the Epilogue in *The Tempest*:

As you from crimes would pardoned be,
Let your indulgence set me free.

What was Shakespeare—sorry, Francis Bacon, Baron Verulam—*really* saying in these two lines? According to Baconians, the lines are an anagram reading, "Tempest of
Francis Bacon, Lord Verulam; do ye ne'er divulge me, ye
words." Ingenious, and it is a pity that in the quotation the
letter *a* appears only twice in the cryptogram, whereas in the
deciphered message it appears three times. Oh, no problem;
just alter "Verulam" to "Verul'm" and it works out very
nicely.

Most people understand that with sufficient ingenuity one
can torture any text and find in it what one wishes. For instance: Did Shakespeare have a hand in the King James Version of the Bible? It was nearing completion in 1610, when
Shakespeare was forty-six years old. If you look at the 46th
Psalm and count forward for forty-six words, you will find
the word *shake*. Now if you go to the end of the psalm and
count backward forty-six words, you will find the word
spear. Clear evidence, according to some, that Shakespeare
slyly left his mark in the book.

Bacon's candidacy has largely been replaced in the twentieth century by the candidacy of Edward de Vere (1550–
1604), 17th earl of Oxford. The basic ideas behind the
Oxford theory, advanced at greatest length by Dorothy and
Charlton Ogburn in *This Star of England* (1952, rev. 1955),
a book of 1297 pages, and by Charlton Ogburn in *The Mysterious William Shakespeare* (1984), a book of 892 pages, are
these: (1) The man from Stratford could not possibly have
had the mental equipment and the experience to have written
the plays—only a courtier could have written them; (2) Oxford had the requisite background (social position, education,
years at Queen Elizabeth's court); (3) Oxford did not wish
his authorship to be known for two basic reasons: writing for
the public theater was a vulgar pursuit, and the plays show
so much courtly and royal disreputable behavior that they
would have compromised Oxford's position at court. Oxfordians offer countless details to support the claim. For example,
Hamlet's phrase "that ever I was born to set it right" (1.5.89)
barely conceals "E. Ver, I was born to set it right," an unam-
biguous announcement of de Vere's authorship, according to
This Star of England (p. 654). A second example: Consider

Ben Jonson's poem entitled "To the Memory of My Beloved Master William Shakespeare," prefixed to the first collected edition of Shakespeare's plays in 1623. According to Oxfordians, when Jonson in this poem speaks of the author of the plays as the "swan of Avon," he is alluding not to William Shakespeare, who was born and died in Stratford-on-Avon and who throughout his adult life owned property there; rather, he is alluding to Oxford, who, the Ogburns say, used "William Shakespeare" as his pen name, and whose manor at Bilton was on the Avon River. Oxfordians do not offer any evidence that Oxford took a pen name, and they do not mention that Oxford had sold the manor in 1581, forty-two years before Jonson wrote his poem. Surely a reference to the Shakespeare who was born in Stratford, who had returned to Stratford, and who had died there only seven years before Jonson wrote the poem is more plausible. And exactly why Jonson, who elsewhere also spoke of Shakespeare as a playwright, and why Heminges and Condell, who had acted with Shakespeare for about twenty years, should speak of Shakespeare as the author in their dedication in the 1623 volume of collected plays is never adequately explained by Oxfordians. Either Jonson, Heminges and Condell, and numerous others were in on the conspiracy, or they were all duped—equally unlikely alternatives. Another difficulty in the Oxford theory is that Oxford died in 1604, and some of the plays are clearly indebted to works and events later than 1604. Among the Oxfordian responses are: At his death Oxford left some plays, and in later years these were touched up by hacks, who added the material that points to later dates. *The Tempest*, almost universally regarded as one of Shakespeare's greatest plays and pretty clearly dated to 1611, does indeed date from a period after the death of Oxford, but it is a crude piece of work that should not be included in the canon of works by Oxford.

The anti-Stratfordians, in addition to assuming that the author must have been a man of rank and a university man, usually assume two conspiracies: (1) a conspiracy in Elizabethan and Jacobean times, in which a surprisingly large number of persons connected with the theater knew that the actor Shakespeare did not write the plays attributed to him but for some reason or other pretended that he did; (2) a conspiracy of today's Stratfordians, the professors who teach Shakespeare in the colleges and universities, who are said to have a vested interest in preserving Shakespeare as the author of the plays they teach. In fact, (1) it is inconceivable that the secret of Shakespeare's non-authorship could have been preserved by all of the people who supposedly were in on the conspiracy, and (2) academic fame awaits any scholar today who can disprove Shakespeare's authorship.

The Stratfordian case is convincing not only because hundreds or even thousands of anti-Stratford arguments—of the sort that say "ever I was born"—has the secret double meaning "E. Ver, I was born"—add up to nothing at all but also because irrefutable evidence connects the man from Stratford with the London theater and with the authorship of particular plays. The anti-Stratfordians do not seem to understand that it is not enough to dismiss the Stratford case by saying that a fellow from the provinces simply couldn't have written the plays. Nor do they understand that it is not enough to dismiss all of the evidence connecting Shakespeare with the plays by asserting that it is perjured.

The Shakespeare Canon

We return to William Shakespeare. Thirty-seven plays as well as some nondramatic poems are generally held to constitute the Shakespeare canon, the body of authentic works. The exact dates of composition of most of the works are highly uncertain, but evidence of a starting point and/or of a final limiting point often provides a framework for informed guessing. For example, *Richard II* cannot be earlier than 1595, the publication date of some material to which it is indebted; *The Merchant of Venice* cannot be later than 1598, the year Francis Meres mentioned it. Sometimes arguments for a date hang on an alleged topical allusion, such as the lines about the unseasonable weather in *A Midsummer Night's Dream*, 2.1.81–117, but such an allusion, if indeed it is an allusion to an event in the real world, can be variously interpreted, and in any case there is always the possibility that a topical allusion was inserted years later, to bring the play up to date. (The issue of alterations in a text between the time that Shakespeare drafted it and the time that it was printed—alterations due to censorship or playhouse practice or Shakespeare's own second thoughts—will be discussed in "The Play Text as a Collaboration" later in this overview.) Dates are often attributed on the basis of style, and although conjectures about style usually rest on other conjectures (such as Shakespeare's development as a playwright, or the appropriateness of lines to character), sooner or later one must rely on one's literary sense. There is no documentary proof, for example, that *Othello* is not as early as *Romeo and Juliet*, but one feels that *Othello* is a later, more mature work, and because the first record of its performance is 1604, one is glad enough to set its composition at that date and not push it back into Shakespeare's early years. (*Romeo and Juliet* was first published in 1597, but evidence suggests that it was written a little earlier.) The following chronology, then, is indebted not only to facts but also to informed guesswork and sensitivity. The dates, necessarily imprecise for some works, indicate something like a scholarly consensus concerning the time of original composition. Some plays show evidence of later revision.

Plays. The first collected edition of Shakespeare, published in 1623, included thirty-six plays. These are all accepted as Shakespeare's, though for one of them, *Henry VIII*, he is thought to have had a collaborator. A thirty-seventh play, *Pericles*, published in 1609 and attributed to Shakespeare on the title page, is also widely accepted as being partly by Shakespeare even though it is not included in the 1623 volume. Still another play not in the 1623 volume, *The Two Noble Kinsmen*, was first published in 1634, with a title page attributing it to John Fletcher and Shakespeare. Probably most students of the subject now believe that Shakespeare did indeed have a hand in it. Of the remaining plays attributed at one time or another to Shakespeare, only one, *Edward III*, anonymously published in 1596, is now regarded by some scholars as a serious candidate. The prevailing opinion, however, is that this rather simpleminded play is not

Shakespeare's; at most he may have revised some passages, chiefly scenes with the Countess of Salisbury. We include *The Two Noble Kinsmen* but do not include *Edward III* in the following list.

1588–94	*The Comedy of Errors*
1588–94	*Love's Labor's Lost*
1589–91	*2 Henry VI*
1590–91	*3 Henry VI*
1589–92	*1 Henry VI*
1592–93	*Richard III*
1589–94	*Titus Andronicus*
1593–94	*The Taming of the Shrew*
1592–94	*The Two Gentlemen of Verona*
1594–96	*Romeo and Juliet*
1595	*Richard II*
1595–96	*A Midsummer Night's Dream*
1596–97	*King John*
1594–96	*The Merchant of Venice*
1596–97	*1 Henry IV*
1597	*The Merry Wives of Windsor*
1597–98	*2 Henry IV*
1598–99	*Much Ado About Nothing*
1598–99	*Henry V*
1599	*Julius Caesar*
1599–1600	*As You Like It*
1599–1600	*Twelfth Night*
1600–1601	*Hamlet*
1601–1602	*Troilus and Cressida*
1602–1604	*All's Well That Ends Well*
1603–1604	*Othello*
1604	*Measure for Measure*
1605–1606	*King Lear*
1605–1606	*Macbeth*
1606–1607	*Antony and Cleopatra*
1605–1608	*Timon of Athens*
1607–1608	*Coriolanus*
1607–1608	*Pericles*
1609–10	*Cymbeline*

1610–11	*The Winter's Tale*
1611	*The Tempest*
1612–13	*Henry VIII*
1613	*The Two Noble Kinsmen*

Poems. In 1989 Donald W. Foster published a book in which he argued that "A Funeral Elegy for Master William Peter," published in 1612, ascribed only to the initials W.S., *may* be by Shakespeare. Foster later published an article in a scholarly journal, *PMLA* 111 (1996), in which he asserted the claim more positively. The evidence begins with the initials, and includes the fact that the publisher and the printer of the elegy had published Shakespeare's *Sonnets* in 1609. But such facts add up to rather little, especially because no one has found any connection between Shakespeare and William Peter (an Oxford graduate about whom little is known, who was murdered at the age of twenty-nine). The argument is based chiefly on statistical examinations of word patterns, which are said to correlate with Shakespeare's known work. Despite such correlations, however, many readers feel that the poem does not sound like Shakespeare. True, Shakespeare has a great range of styles, but consistently his work is imaginative and interesting. Many readers find neither of these qualities in "A Funeral Elegy."

1592–93	*Venus and Adonis*
1593–94	*The Rape of Lucrece*
1593–1600	*Sonnets*
1600–1601	*The Phoenix and the Turtle*

Shakespeare's English

1. Spelling and Pronunciation. From the philologist's point of view, Shakespeare's English is modern English. It requires footnotes, but the inexperienced reader can comprehend substantial passages with very little help, whereas for the same reader Chaucer's Middle English is a foreign language. By the beginning of the fifteenth century the chief grammatical changes in English had taken place, and the final unaccented

-*e* of Middle English had been lost (though it survives even today in spelling, as in *name*); during the fifteenth century the dialect of London, the commercial and political center, gradually displaced the provincial dialects, at least in writing; by the end of the century, printing had helped to regularize and stabilize the language, especially spelling. Elizabethan spelling may seem erratic to us (there were dozens of spellings of *Shakespeare*, and a simple word like *been* was also spelled *beene* and *bin*), but it had much in common with our spelling. Elizabethan spelling was conservative in that for the most part it reflected an older pronunciation (Middle English) rather than the sound of the language as it was then spoken, just as our spelling continues to reflect medieval pronunciation—most obviously in the now silent but formerly pronounced letters in a word such as *knight*. Elizabethan pronunciation, though not identical with ours, was much closer to ours than to that of the Middle Ages. Incidentally, though no one can be certain about what Elizabethan English sounded like, specialists tend to believe it was rather like the speech of a modern stage Irishman (*time* apparently was pronounced *toime*, *old* pronounced *awld*, *day* pronounced *die*, and *join* pronounced *jine*) and not at all like the Oxford speech that most of us think it was.

An awareness of the difference between our pronunciation and Shakespeare's is crucial in three areas—in accent, or number of syllables (many metrically regular lines may look irregular to us); in rhymes (which may not look like rhymes); and in puns (which may not look like puns). Examples will be useful. Some words that were at least on occasion stressed differently from today are *aspèct*, *còmplete*, *fòrlorn*, *revènue*, and *sepùlcher*. Words that sometimes had an additional syllable are *emp[e]ress*, *Hen[e]ry*, *mon[e]th*, and *villain* (three syllables, *vil-lay-in*). An additional syllable is often found in possessives, like *moon*'s (pronounced *moones*) and in words ending in -*tion* or -*sion*. Words that had one less syllable than they now have are *needle* (pronounced *neel*) and *violet* (pronounced *vilet*). Among rhymes now lost are *one* with *loan*, *love* with *prove*, *beast* with *jest*, *eat* with *great*. (In reading, trust your sense of metrics and your ear, more than your eye.) An example of a pun that has become obliterated by a

change in pronunciation is Falstaff's reply to Prince Hal's
"Come, tell us your reason" in *1 Henry IV*: "Give you a reason on compulsion? If reasons were as plentiful as blackberries, I would give no man a reason upon compulsion, I"
(2.4.237–40). The *ea* in *reason* was pronounced rather like a
long *a,* like the *ai* in *raisin,* hence the comparison with
blackberries.

Puns are not merely attempts to be funny; like metaphors
they often involve bringing into a meaningful relationship
areas of experience normally seen as remote. In *2 Henry IV,*
when Feeble is conscripted, he stoically says, "I care not. A
man can die but once. We owe God a death" (3.2.242–43),
punning on *debt,* which was the way *death* was pronounced.
Here an enormously significant fact of life is put into simple
commercial imagery, suggesting its commonplace quality.
Shakespeare used the same pun earlier in *1 Henry IV,* when
Prince Hal says to Falstaff, "Why, thou owest God a death,"
and Falstaff replies, " 'Tis not due yet: I would be loath to
pay him before his day. What need I be so forward with him
that calls not on me?" (5.1.126–29).

Sometimes the puns reveal a delightful playfulness; sometimes they reveal aggressiveness, as when, replying to
Claudius's "But now, my cousin Hamlet, and my son," Hamlet says, "A little more than kin, and less than kind!"
(1.2.64–65). These are Hamlet's first words in the play, and
we already hear him warring verbally against Claudius.
Hamlet's "less than kind" probably means (1) Hamlet is not
of Claudius's family or nature, *kind* having the sense it still
has in our word *mankind*; (2) Hamlet is not kindly (affection-
ately) disposed toward Claudius; (3) Claudius is not naturally
(but rather unnaturally, in a legal sense incestuously) Hamlet's father. The puns evidently were not put in as sops to the
groundlings; they are an important way of communicating a
complex meaning.

2. *Vocabulary.* A conspicuous difficulty in reading Shakespeare is rooted in the fact that some of his words are no
longer in common use—for example, words concerned with
armor, astrology, clothing, coinage, hawking, horsemanship,
law, medicine, sailing, and war. Shakespeare had a large

vocabulary—something near thirty thousand words—but it was not so much a vocabulary of big words as a vocabulary drawn from a wide range of life, and it is partly his ability to call upon a great body of concrete language that gives his plays the sense of being in close contact with life. When the right word did not already exist, he made it up. Among words thought to be his coinages are _accommodation, allknowing, amazement, bare-faced, countless, dexterously, dislocate, dwindle, fancy-free, frugal, indistinguishable, lackluster, laughable, overawe, premeditated, sea change, star-crossed_. Among those that have not survived are the verb _convive_, meaning to feast together, and _smilet_, a little smile.

Less overtly troublesome than the technical words but more treacherous are the words that seem readily intelligible to us but whose Elizabethan meanings differ from their modern ones. When Horatio describes the Ghost as an "erring spirit," he is saying not that the ghost has sinned or made an error but that it is wandering. Here is a short list of some of the most common words in Shakespeare's plays that often (but not always) have a meaning other than their most usual modern meaning:

_'a_	he
abuse	deceive
accident	occurrence
advertise	inform
an, and	if
annoy	harm
appeal	accuse
artificial	skillful
brave	fine, splendid
censure	opinion
cheer	(1) face (2) frame of mind
chorus	a single person who comments on the events
closet	small private room
competitor	partner
conceit	idea, imagination
cousin	kinsman

cunning	skillful
disaster	evil astrological influence
doom	judgment
entertain	receive into service
envy	malice
event	outcome
excrement	outgrowth (of hair)
fact	evil deed
fancy	(1) love (2) imagination
fell	cruel
fellow	(1) companion (2) low person (often an insulting term if addressed to someone of approximately equal rank)
fond	foolish
free	(1) innocent (2) generous
glass	mirror
hap, haply	chance, by chance
head	army
humor	(1) mood (2) bodily fluid thought to control one's psychology
imp	child
intelligence	news
kind	natural, acting according to nature
let	hinder
lewd	base
mere(ly)	utter(ly)
modern	commonplace
natural	a fool, an idiot
naughty	(1) wicked (2) worthless
next	nearest
nice	(1) trivial (2) fussy
noise	music
policy	(1) prudence (2) stratagem
presently	immediately
prevent	anticipate
proper	handsome
prove	test

quick	alive
sad	serious
saw	proverb
secure	without care, incautious
silly	innocent
sensible	capable of being perceived by the senses
shrewd	sharp
so	provided that
starve	die
still	always
success	that which follows
tall	brave
tell	count
tonight	last night
wanton	playful, careless
watch	keep awake
will	lust
wink	close both eyes
wit	mind, intelligence

All glosses, of course, are mere approximations; sometimes one of Shakespeare's words may hover between an older meaning and a modern one, and as we have seen, his words often have multiple meanings.

3. Grammar. A few matters of grammar may be surveyed, though it should be noted at the outset that Shakespeare sometimes made up his own grammar. As E. A. Abbott says in *A Shakespearian Grammar,* "Almost any part of speech can be used as any other part of speech": a noun as a verb ("he childed as I fathered"); a verb as a noun ("She hath made compare"); or an adverb as an adjective ("a seldom pleasure"). There are hundreds, perhaps thousands, of such instances in the plays, many of which at first glance would not seem at all irregular and would trouble only a pedant. Here are a few broad matters.

Nouns: The Elizabethans thought the *-s* genitive ending for nouns (as in *man's*) derived from *his*; thus the line " 'gainst the count his galleys I did some service," for "the count's galleys."

Adjectives: By Shakespeare's time adjectives had lost the endings that once indicated gender, number, and case. About the only difference between Shakespeare's adjectives and ours is the use of the now redundant *more* or *most* with the comparative ("some more fitter place") or superlative ("This was the most unkindest cut of all"). Like double comparatives and double superlatives, double negatives were acceptable; Mercutio "will not budge for no man's pleasure."

Pronouns: The greatest change was in pronouns. In Middle English *thou, thy,* and *thee* were used among familiars and in speaking to children and inferiors; *ye, your,* and *you* were used in speaking to superiors (servants to masters, nobles to the king) or to equals with whom the speaker was not familiar. Increasingly the "polite" forms were used in all direct address, regardless of rank, and the accusative *you* displaced the nominative *ye*. Shakespeare sometimes uses *ye* instead of *you,* but even in Shakespeare's day *ye* was archaic, and it occurs mostly in rhetorical appeals.

Thou, thy, and *thee* were not completely displaced, however, and Shakespeare occasionally makes significant use of them, sometimes to connote familiarity or intimacy and sometimes to connote contempt. In *Twelfth Night* Sir Toby advises Sir Andrew to insult Cesario by addressing him as *thou:* "If thou thou'st him some thrice, it shall not be amiss" (3.2.46–47). In *Othello* when Brabantio is addressing an unidentified voice in the dark he says, "What are you?" (1.1.91), but when the voice identifies itself as the foolish suitor Roderigo, Brabantio uses the contemptuous form, saying, "I have charged thee not to haunt about my doors" (93). He uses this form for a while, but later in the scene, when he comes to regard Roderigo as an ally, he shifts back to the polite *you,* beginning in line 163, "What said she to you?" and on to the end of the scene. For reasons not yet satisfactorily explained, Elizabethans used *thou* in addresses to God— "O God, thy arm was here," the king says in *Henry V* (4.8.108)—and to supernatural characters such as ghosts and witches. A subtle variation occurs in *Hamlet.* When Hamlet first talks with the Ghost in 1.5, he uses *thou,* but when he sees the Ghost in his mother's room, in 3.4, he uses *you,* presumably because he is now convinced that the Ghost is not a counterfeit but is his father.

Perhaps the most unusual use of pronouns, from our point of view, is the neuter singular. In place of our *its, his* was often used, as in "How far that little candle throws *his* beams." But the use of a masculine pronoun for a neuter noun came to seem unnatural, and so *it* was used for the possessive as well as the nominative: "The hedge-sparrow fed the cuckoo so long / That it had it head bit off by it young." In the late sixteenth century the possessive form *its* developed, apparently by analogy with the *-s* ending used to indicate a genitive noun, as in *book*'s, but *its* was not yet common usage in Shakespeare's day. He seems to have used *its* only ten times, mostly in his later plays. Other usages, such as "you have seen Cassio and she together" or the substitution of *who* for *whom,* cause little problem even when noticed.

Verbs, Adverbs, and Prepositions: Verbs cause almost no difficulty: The third person singular present form commonly ends in *-s,* as in modern English (e.g., "He blesses"), but sometimes in *-eth* (Portia explains to Shylock that mercy "blesseth him that gives and him that takes"). Broadly speaking, the *-eth* ending was old-fashioned or dignified or "literary" rather than colloquial, except for the words *doth, hath,* and *saith.* The *-eth* ending (regularly used in the King James Bible, 1611) is very rare in Shakespeare's dramatic prose, though not surprisingly it occurs twice in the rather formal prose summary of the narrative poem *Lucrece.* Sometimes a plural subject, especially if it has collective force, takes a verb ending in *-s,* as in "My old bones aches." Some of our strong or irregular preterites (such as *broke*) have a different form in Shakespeare (*brake*); some verbs that now have a weak or regular preterite (such as *helped*) in Shakespeare have a strong or irregular preterite (*holp*). Some adverbs that today end in *-ly* were not inflected: "grievous sick," "wondrous strange." Finally, prepositions often are not the ones we expect: "We are such stuff as dreams are made on," "I have a king here to my flatterer."

Again, none of the differences (except meanings that have substantially changed or been lost) will cause much difficulty. But it must be confessed that for some elliptical passages there is no widespread agreement on meaning. Wise editors resist saying more than they know, and when they are uncertain they add a question mark to their gloss.

Shakespeare's Theater

In Shakespeare's infancy, Elizabethan actors performed wherever they could—in great halls, at court, in the courtyards of inns. These venues implied not only different audiences but also different playing conditions. The innyards must have made rather unsatisfactory theaters: on some days they were unavailable because carters bringing goods to London used them as depots; when available, they had to be rented from the innkeeper. In 1567, presumably to avoid such difficulties, and also to avoid regulation by the Common Council of London, which was not well disposed toward theatricals, one John Brayne, brother-in-law of the carpenter turned actor James Burbage, built the Red Lion in an eastern suburb of London. We know nothing about its shape or its capacity; we can say only that it may have been the first building in Europe constructed for the purpose of giving plays since the end of antiquity, a thousand years earlier. Even after the building of the Red Lion theatrical activity continued in London in makeshift circumstances, in marketplaces and inns, and always uneasily. In 1574 the Common Council required that plays and playing places in London be licensed because

> sundry great disorders and inconveniences have been found to ensue to this city by the inordinate haunting of great multitudes of people, specially youth, to plays, interludes, and shows, namely occasion of frays and quarrels, evil practices of incontinency in great inns having chambers and secret places adjoining to their open stages and galleries.

The Common Council ordered that innkeepers who wished licenses to hold performance put up a bond and make contributions to the poor.

The requirement that plays and innyard theaters be licensed, along with the other drawbacks of playing at inns and presumably along with the success of the Red Lion, led James Burbage to rent a plot of land northeast of the city walls, on property outside the jurisdiction of the city. Here he built England's second playhouse, called simply the Theatre. About all that is known of its construction is that it was wood. It soon had imitators, the most famous being the Globe (1599), essentially an amphitheater built across the Thames (again outside the city's jurisdiction), constructed with timbers of the Theatre, which had been dismantled when Burbage's lease ran out.

Admission to the theater was one penny, which allowed spectators to stand at the sides and front of the stage that jutted into the yard. An additional penny bought a seat in a covered part of the theater, and a third penny bought a more comfortable seat and a better location. It is notoriously difficult to translate prices into today's money, since some things that are inexpensive today would have been expensive in the past and vice versa—a pipeful of tobacco (imported, of course) cost a lot of money, about three pennies, and an orange (also imported) cost two or three times what a chicken cost—but perhaps we can get some idea of the low cost of the penny admission when we realize that a penny could also buy a pot of ale. An unskilled laborer made about five or sixpence a day, an artisan about twelve pence a day, and the hired actors (as opposed to the sharers in the company, such as Shakespeare) made about ten pence a performance. A printed play cost five or sixpence. Of course a visit to the theater (like a visit to a baseball game today) usually cost more than the admission since the spectator probably would also buy food and drink. Still, the low entrance fee meant that the theater was available to all except the very poorest people, rather as movies and most athletic events are today. Evidence indicates that the audience ranged from apprentices who somehow managed to scrape together the minimum entrance fee and to escape from their masters for a few hours, to prosperous members of the middle class and aristocrats who paid the additional fee for admission to the galleries.

The exact proportion of men to women cannot be determined, but women of all classes certainly were present. Theaters were open every afternoon but Sundays for much of the year, except in times of plague, when they were closed because of fear of infection. By the way, no evidence suggests the presence of toilet facilities. Presumably the patrons re-

Johannes de Witt, a Continental visitor to London, made a drawing of the Swan theater in about the year 1596. The original drawing is lost; this is Aernout van Buchell's copy of it.

lieved themselves by making a quick trip to the fields surrounding the playhouses.

There are four important sources of information about the
structure of Elizabethan public playhouses—drawings, a contract, recent excavations, and stage directions in the plays. Of
drawings, only the so-called de Witt drawing (c. 1596) of the
Swan—really his friend Aernout van Buchell's copy of Johannes de Witt's drawing—is of much significance. The
drawing, the only extant representation of the interior of an
Elizabethan theater, shows an amphitheater of three tiers,
with a stage jutting from a wall into the yard or center of the
building. The tiers are roofed, and part of the stage is covered by a roof that projects from the rear and is supported at
its front on two posts, but the groundlings, who paid a penny
to stand in front of the stage or at its sides, were exposed to
the sky. (Performances in such a playhouse were held only
in the daytime; artificial illumination was not used.) At the
rear of the stage are two massive doors; above the stage is a
gallery.

The second major source of information, the contract for
the Fortune (built in 1600), specifies that although the Globe
(built in 1599) is to be the model, the Fortune is to be square,
eighty feet outside and fifty-five inside. The stage is to be
forty-three feet broad, and is to extend into the middle of the
yard, i.e., it is twenty-seven and a half feet deep.

The third source of information, the 1989 excavations of
the Rose (built in 1587), indicate that the Rose was fourteen-
sided, about seventy-two feet in diameter with an inner yard
almost fifty feet in diameter. The stage at the Rose was about
sixteen feet deep, thirty-seven feet wide at the rear, and
twenty-seven feet wide downstage. The relatively small di-
mensions and the tapering stage, in contrast to the rectangu-
lar stage in the Swan drawing, surprised theater historians
and have made them more cautious in generalizing about the
Elizabethan theater. Excavations at the Globe have not
yielded much information, though some historians believe
that the fragmentary evidence suggests a larger theater, perhaps one hundred feet in diameter.

From the fourth chief source, stage directions in the plays,
one learns that entrance to the stage was by the doors at the

rear (*"Enter one citizen at one door, and another at the other"*). A curtain hanging across the doorway—or a curtain hanging between the two doorways—could provide a place where a character could conceal himself, as Polonius does, when he wishes to overhear the conversation between Hamlet and Gertrude. Similarly, withdrawing a curtain from the doorway could "discover" (reveal) a character or two. Such discovery scenes are very rare in Elizabethan drama, but a good example occurs in *The Tempest* (5.1.171), where a stage direction tells us, *"Here Prospero discovers Ferdinand and Miranda playing at chess."* There was also some sort of playing space "aloft" or "above" to represent, for instance, the top of a city's walls or a room above the street. Doubtless each theater had its own peculiarities, but perhaps we can talk about a "typical" Elizabethan theater if we realize that no theater need exactly fit the description, just as no mother is the average mother with 2.7 children.

This hypothetical theater is wooden, round, or polygonal (in *Henry V* Shakespeare calls it a "wooden *O*") capable of holding some eight hundred spectators who stood in the yard around the projecting elevated stage—these spectators were the "groundlings"—and some fifteen hundred additional spectators who sat in the three roofed galleries. The stage, protected by a "shadow" or "heavens" or roof, is entered from two doors; behind the doors is the "tiring house" (attiring house, i.e., dressing room), and above the stage is some sort of gallery that may sometimes hold spectators but can be used (for example) as the bedroom from which Romeo— according to a stage direction in one text—"goeth down." Some evidence suggests that a throne can be lowered onto the platform stage, perhaps from the "shadow"; certainly characters can descend from the stage through a trap or traps into the cellar or "hell." Sometimes this space beneath the stage accommodates a sound-effects man or musician (in *Antony and Cleopatra* "music of the hautboys [oboes] *is under the stage"*) or an actor (in *Hamlet* the *"Ghost cries under the stage"*). Most characters simply walk on and off through the doors, but because there is no curtain in front of the platform, corpses will have to be carried off (Hamlet obligingly clears the stage of Polonius's corpse, when he says, "I'll lug the guts into the neighbor room"). Other characters may have fallen at the rear, where a curtain on a doorway could be drawn to conceal them.

Such may have been the "public theater," so called because its inexpensive admission made it available to a wide range of the populace. Another kind of theater has been called the "private theater" because its much greater admission charge (sixpence versus the penny for general admission at the public theater) limited its audience to the wealthy or the prodigal. The private theater was basically a large room, entirely roofed and therefore artificially illuminated, with a stage at one end. The theaters thus were distinct in two ways: One was essentially an amphitheater that catered to the general public; the other was a hall that catered to the wealthy. In 1576 a hall theater was established in Blackfriars, a Dominican priory in London that had been suppressed in 1538 and confiscated by the Crown and thus was not under the city's jurisdiction. All the actors in this Blackfriars theater were boys about eight to thirteen years old (in the public theaters similar boys played female parts; a boy Lady Macbeth played to a man Macbeth). Near the end of this section on Shakespeare's theater we will talk at some length about possible implications in this convention of using boys to play female roles, but for the moment we should say that it doubtless accounts for the relative lack of female roles in Elizabethan drama. Thus, in *A Midsummer Night's Dream*, out of twenty-one named roles, only four are female; in *Hamlet*, out of twenty-four, only two (Gertrude and Ophelia) are female. Many of Shakespeare's characters have fathers but no mothers—for instance, King Lear's daughters. We need not bring in Freud to explain the disparity; a dramatic company had only a few boys in it.

To return to the private theaters, in some of which all of the performers were children—the "eyrie of . . . little eyases" (nest of unfledged hawks—2.2.347–48) which Rosencrantz mentions when he and Guildenstern talk with Hamlet. The theater in Blackfriars had a precarious existence, and ceased operations in 1584. In 1596 James Burbage, who had already made theatrical history by building the Theatre, began to construct a second Blackfriars theater. He died in 1597, and

for several years this second Blackfriars theater was used by
a troupe of boys, but in 1608 two of Burbage's sons and five
other actors (including Shakespeare) became joint operators
of the theater, using it in the winter when the open-air Globe
was unsuitable. Perhaps such a smaller theater, roofed, artificially illuminated, and with a tradition of a wealthy audience,
exerted an influence in Shakespeare's late plays.

Performances in the private theaters may well have had in-
termissions during which music was played, but in the public
theaters the action was probably uninterrupted, flowing from
scene to scene almost without a break. Actors would enter,
speak, exit, and others would immediately enter and establish
(if necessary) the new locale by a few properties and by
words and gestures. To indicate that the scene took place at
night, a player or two would carry a torch. Here are some
samples of Shakespeare establishing the scene:

This is Illyria, lady.   (*Twelfth Night*, 1.2.2)

Well, this is the Forest of Arden.   (*As You Like It*, 2.4.14)

This castle has a pleasant seat; the air
Nimbly and sweetly recommends itself
Unto our gentle senses.   (*Macbeth*, 1.6.1–3)

The west yet glimmers with some streaks of day.
                                          (*Macbeth*, 3.3.5)

Sometimes a speech will go far beyond evoking the minimal
setting of place and time, and will, so to speak, evoke the social world in which the characters move. For instance, early
in the first scene of *The Merchant of Venice* Salerio suggests
an explanation for Antonio's melancholy. (In the following
passage, *pageants* are decorated wagons, floats, and *cursy* is
the verb "to curtsy," or "to bow.")

Your mind is tossing on the ocean,
There where your argosies with portly sail—
Like signiors and rich burghers on the flood,

Or as it were the pageants of the sea—
Do overpeer the petty traffickers
That cursy to them, do them reverence,
As they fly by them with their woven wings.   (1.1.8–14)

Late in the nineteenth century, when Henry Irving produced
the play with elaborate illusionistic sets, the first scene
showed a ship moored in the harbor, with fruit vendors and
dock laborers, in an effort to evoke the bustling and exotic life
of Venice. But Shakespeare's words give us this exotic, rich
world of commerce in his highly descriptive language when
Salerio speaks of "argosies with portly sail" that fly with
"woven wings"; equally important, through Salerio Shakespeare conveys a sense of the orderly, hierarchical society in
which the lesser ships, "the petty traffickers," curtsy and
thereby "do ... reverence" to their superiors, the merchant
prince's ships, which are "Like signiors and rich burghers."

On the other hand, it is a mistake to think that except for
verbal pictures the Elizabethan stage was bare. Although
Shakespeare's Chorus in *Henry V* calls the stage an "unwor-
thy scaffold" (Prologue 1.10) and urges the spectators to
"eke out our performance with your mind" (Prologue 3.35),
there was considerable spectacle. The last act of *Macbeth*,
for instance, has five stage directions calling for *"drum and
colors,"* and another sort of appeal to the eye is indicated by
the stage direction *"Enter Macduff, with Macbeth's head."*
Some scenery and properties may have been substantial;
doubtless a throne was used, but the pillars supporting the
roof would have served for the trees on which Orlando pins
his poems in *As You Like It*.

Having talked about the public theater—"this wooden
O"—at some length, we should mention again that Shakespeare's plays were performed also in other locales. Alvin
Kernan, in *Shakespeare, the King's Playwright: Theater in
the Stuart Court 1603–1613* (1995) points out that "several
of [Shakespeare's] plays contain brief theatrical performances, set always in a court or some noble house. When
Shakespeare portrayed a theater, he did not, except for the
choruses in *Henry V*, imagine a public theater" (p. 195). (Ex-

amples include episodes in *The Taming of the Shrew, A Midsummer Night's Dream, Hamlet,* and *The Tempest.*)

A Note on the Use of Boy Actors in Female Roles

Until fairly recently, scholars were content to mention that the convention existed; they sometimes also mentioned that it continued the medieval practice of using males in female roles, and that other theaters, notably in ancient Greece and in China and Japan, also used males in female roles. (In classical Noh drama in Japan, males still play the female roles.) Prudery may have been at the root of the academic failure to talk much about the use of boy actors, or maybe there really is not much more to say than that it was a convention of a male-centered culture (Stephen Greenblatt's view, in *Shakespearean Negotiations* [1988]). Further, the very nature of a convention is that it is not thought about: Hamlet is a Dane and Julius Caesar is a Roman, but in Shakespeare's plays they speak English, and we in the audience never give this odd fact a thought. Similarly, a character may speak in the presence of others and we understand, again without thinking about it, that he or she is not heard by the figures on the stage (the aside); a character alone on the stage may speak (the soliloquy), and we do not take the character to be unhinged; in a realistic (box) set, the fourth wall, which allows us to see what is going on, is miraculously missing. The no-nonsense view, then, is that the boy actor was an accepted convention, accepted unthinkingly—just as today we know that Kenneth Branagh is not Hamlet, Al Pacino is not Richard III, and Denzel Washington is not the Prince of Aragon. In this view, the audience takes the performer for the role, and that is that; such is the argument we now make for race-free casting, in which African-Americans and Asians can play roles of persons who lived in medieval Denmark and ancient Rome. But gender perhaps is different, at least today. It is a matter of abundant academic study: The Elizabethan theater is now sometimes called a transvestite theater, and we hear much about cross-dressing.

Shakespeare himself in a very few passages calls attention to the use of boys in female roles. At the end of *As You Like*

It the boy who played Rosalind addresses the audience, and says, "O men, . . . if I were a woman, I would kiss as many of you as had beards that pleased me." But this is in the Epilogue; the plot is over, and the actor is stepping out of the play and into the audience's everyday world. A second reference to the practice of boys playing female roles occurs in *Antony and Cleopatra*, when Cleopatra imagines that she and Antony will be the subject of crude plays, her role being performed by a boy:

> The quick comedians
> Extemporally will stage us, and present
> Our Alexandrian revels: Antony
> Shall be brought drunken forth, and I shall see
> Some squeaking Cleopatra boy my greatness.   (5.2.216–20)

In a few other passages, Shakespeare is more indirect. For instance, in *Twelfth Night* Viola, played of course by a boy, disguises herself as a young man and seeks service in the house of a lord. She enlists the help of a Captain, and (by way of explaining away her voice and her beardlessness) says,

> I'll serve this duke
> Thou shalt present me as an eunuch to him.   (1.2.55–56)

In *Hamlet*, when the players arrive in 2.2, Hamlet jokes with the boy who plays a female role. The boy has grown since Hamlet last saw him: "By'r Lady, your ladyship is nearer to heaven than when I saw you last by the altitude of a chopine" (a lady's thick-soled shoe). He goes on: "Pray God your voice . . . be not cracked" (434–38).

Exactly how sexual, how erotic, this material was and is, is now much disputed. Again, the use of boys may have been unnoticed, or rather not thought about—an unexamined convention—by most or all spectators most of the time, perhaps *all* of the time, except when Shakespeare calls the convention to the attention of the audience, as in the passages just quoted. Still, an occasional bit seems to invite erotic thoughts. The clearest example is the name that Rosalind takes in *As You Like It*, Ganymede—the beautiful youth whom Zeus abducted. Did boys dressed to play female roles carry homoerotic appeal for straight men (Lisa Jardine's view, in *Still Harping on Daughters* [1983]), or for gay men, or for some or all women in the audience? Further, when the boy actor played a woman who (for the purposes of the plot) disguised herself as a male, as Rosalind, Viola, and Portia do—so we get a boy playing a woman playing a man—what sort of appeal was generated, and for what sort of spectator?

Some scholars have argued that the convention empowered women by letting female characters display a freedom unavailable in Renaissance patriarchal society; the convention, it is said, undermined rigid gender distinctions. In this view, the convention (along with plots in which female characters for a while disguised themselves as young men) allowed Shakespeare to say what some modern gender critics say: Gender is a constructed role rather than a biological given, something we make, rather than a fixed binary opposition of male and female (see Juliet Dusinberre, in *Shakespeare and the Nature of Women* [1975]). On the other hand, some scholars have maintained that the male disguise assumed by some female characters serves only to reaffirm traditional social distinctions since female characters who don male garb (notably Portia in *The Merchant of Venice* and Rosalind in *As You Like It*) return to their female garb and at least implicitly (these critics say) reaffirm the status quo. (For this last view, see Clara Claiborne Park, in an essay in *The Woman's Part*, ed. Carolyn Ruth Swift Lenz et al. [1980].) Perhaps no one answer is right for all plays; in *As You Like It* cross-dressing empowers Rosalind, but in *Twelfth Night* cross-dressing comically traps Viola.

Shakespeare's Dramatic Language: Costumes, Gestures and Silences; Prose and Poetry

Because Shakespeare was a dramatist, not merely a poet, he worked not only with language but also with costume, sound effects, gestures, and even silences. We have already discussed some kinds of spectacle in the preceding section, and now we will begin with other aspects of visual language; a theater, after all, is literally a "place for seeing." Consider the opening stage direction in *The Tempest*, the first play in the first published collection of Shakespeare's plays: *"A tempestuous noise of thunder and Lightning heard: Enter a Shipmaster, and a Boteswain."*

Costumes: What did that shipmaster and that boatswain wear? Doubtless they wore something that identified them as men of the sea. Not much is known about the costumes that Elizabethan actors wore, but at least three points are clear: (1) many of the costumes were splendid versions of contemporary Elizabethan dress; (2) some attempts were made to approximate the dress of certain occupations and of antique or exotic characters such as Romans, Turks, and Jews; (3) some costumes indicated that the wearer was supernatural. Evidence for elaborate Elizabethan clothing can be found in the plays themselves and in contemporary comments about the "sumptuous" players who wore the discarded clothing of noblemen, as well as in account books that itemize such things as "a scarlet cloak with two broad gold laces, with gold buttons down the sides."

The attempts at approximation of the dress of certain occupations and nationalities also can be documented from the plays themselves, and it derives additional confirmation from a drawing of the first scene of Shakespeare's *Titus Andronicus*—the only extant Elizabethan picture of an identifiable episode in a play. (See pp. xxxviii–xxxix.) The drawing, probably done in 1594 or 1595, shows Queen Tamora pleading for mercy. She wears a somewhat medieval-looking robe and a crown; Titus wears a toga and a wreath, but two soldiers behind him wear costumes fairly close to Elizabethan dress. We do not know, however, if the drawing represents an actual stage production in the public theater, or perhaps a private production, or maybe only a reader's visualization of an episode. Further, there is some conflicting evidence: In *Julius Caesar* a reference is made to Caesar's doublet (a close-fitting jacket), which, if taken literally, suggests that even the protagonist did not wear Roman clothing;

and certainly the lesser characters, who are said to wear hats, did not wear Roman garb.

It should be mentioned, too, that even ordinary clothing can be symbolic: Hamlet's "inky cloak," for example, sets him apart from the brightly dressed members of Claudius's court and symbolizes his mourning; the fresh clothes that are put on King Lear partly symbolize his return to sanity. Consider, too, the removal of disguises near the end of some plays. For instance, Rosalind in *As You Like It* and Portia and Nerissa in *The Merchant of Venice* remove their male attire, thus again becoming fully themselves.

Gestures and Silences: Gestures are an important part of a dramatist's language. King Lear kneels before his daughter Cordelia for a benediction (4.7.57–59), an act of humility that contrasts with his earlier speeches banishing her and that contrasts also with a comparable gesture, his ironic kneeling before Regan (2.4.153–55). Northumberland's failure to kneel before King Richard II (3.3.71–72) speaks volumes. As

for silences, consider a moment in *Coriolanus*: Before the protagonist yields to his mother's entreaties (5.3.182), there is this stage direction: *"Holds her by the hand, silent."* Another example of "speech in dumbness" occurs in *Macbeth*, when Macduff learns that his wife and children have been murdered. He is silent at first, as Malcolm's speech indicates: "What, man! Ne'er pull your hat upon your brows. Give sorrow words" (4.3.208–09). (For a discussion of such moments, see Philip C. McGuire's *Speechless Dialect: Shakespeare's Open Silences* [1985].)

Of course when we think of Shakespeare's work, we think primarily of his language, both the poetry and the prose.

Prose: Although two of his plays (*Richard II* and *King John*) have no prose at all, about half the others have at least one quarter of the dialogue in prose, and some have notably more: *1 Henry IV* and *2 Henry IV*, about half; *As You Like It* and *Twelfth Night*, a little more than half; *Much Ado About Nothing*, more than three quarters; and *The Merry Wives of Windsor*, a little more than five sixths. We should remember that despite Molière's joke about M. Jourdain, who was amazed to learn that he spoke prose, most of us do not speak prose. Rather, we normally utter repetitive, shapeless, and often ungrammatical torrents; prose is something very different—a sort of literary imitation of speech at its most coherent.

Today we may think of prose as "natural" for drama; or even if we think that poetry is appropriate for high tragedy we may still think that prose is the right medium for comedy. Greek, Roman, and early English comedies, however, were written in verse. In fact, prose was not generally considered a literary medium in England until the late fifteenth century; Chaucer tells even his bawdy stories in verse. By the end of the 1580s, however, prose had established itself on the English comic stage. In tragedy, Marlowe made some use of prose, not simply in the speeches of clownish servants but even in the speech of a tragic hero, Doctor Faustus. Still, before Shakespeare, prose normally was used in the theater only for special circumstances: (1) letters and proclamations, to set them off from the poetic dialogue; (2) mad characters, to indicate that normal thinking has become disordered; and (3) low comedy, or speeches uttered by clowns even when they are not being comic. Shakespeare made use of these conventions, but he also went far beyond them. Sometimes he begins a scene in prose and then shifts into verse as the emotion is heightened; or conversely, he may shift from verse to prose when a speaker is lowering the emotional level, as when Brutus speaks in the Forum.

Shakespeare's prose usually is not prosaic. Hamlet's prose includes not only small talk with Rosencrantz and Guildenstern but also princely reflections on "What a piece of work is a man" (2.2.312). In conversation with Ophelia, he shifts from light talk in verse to a passionate prose denunciation of women (3.1.103), though the shift to prose here is perhaps also intended to suggest the possibility of madness. (Consult Brian Vickers, *The Artistry of Shakespeare's Prose* [1968].)

Poetry: Drama in rhyme in England goes back to the Middle Ages, but by Shakespeare's day rhyme no longer dominated poetic drama; a finer medium, blank verse (strictly speaking, unrhymed lines of ten syllables, with the stress on every second syllable) had been adopted. But before looking at unrhymed poetry, a few things should be said about the chief uses of rhyme in Shakespeare's plays. (1) A couplet (a pair of rhyming lines) is sometimes used to convey emotional heightening at the end of a blank verse speech; (2) characters sometimes speak a couplet as they leave the stage, suggesting closure; (3) except in the latest plays, scenes fairly often conclude with a couplet, and sometimes, as in *Richard II*, 2.1.145–46, the entrance of a new character within a scene is preceded by a couplet, which wraps up the earlier portion of that scene; (4) speeches of two characters occasionally are linked by rhyme, most notably in *Romeo and Juliet*, 1.5.95–108, where the lovers speak a sonnet between them; elsewhere a taunting reply occasionally rhymes with the previous speaker's last line; (5) speeches with sententious or gnomic remarks are sometimes in rhyme, as in the duke's speech in *Othello* (1.3.199–206); (6) speeches of sardonic mockery are sometimes in rhyme—for example, Iago's speech on women in *Othello* (2.1.146–58)—and they sometimes conclude with an emphatic couplet, as in Bolingbroke's speech on comforting words in *Richard II* (1.3.301–2); (7) some characters are associated with rhyme, such as the fairies in *A Midsummer Night's Dream*; (8) in the early plays, especially *The Comedy of Errors* and *The Taming of the Shrew*, comic scenes that in later plays would be in prose are in jingling rhymes; (9) prologues, choruses, plays-within-the-play, inscriptions, vows, epilogues, and so on are often in rhyme, and the songs in the plays are rhymed.

Neither prose nor rhyme immediately comes to mind when we first think of Shakespeare's medium: It is blank verse, unrhymed iambic pentameter. (In a mechanically exact line there are five iambic feet. An iambic foot consists of two syllables, the second accented, as in *away*; five feet make a pentameter line. Thus, a strict line of iambic pentameter contains ten syllables, the even syllables being stressed more heavily than the odd syllables. Fortunately, Shakespeare usually varies the line somewhat.) The first speech in *A Midsummer*

Night's Dream, spoken by Duke Theseus to his betrothed, is an example of blank verse:

> Now, fair Hippolyta, our nuptial hour
> Draws on apace. Four happy days bring in
> Another moon; but, O, methinks, how slow
> This old moon wanes! She lingers my desires,
> Like to a stepdame, or a dowager,
> Long withering out a young man's revenue.   (1.1.1–6)

As this passage shows, Shakespeare's blank verse is not mechanically unvarying. Though the predominant foot is the iamb (as in *apace* or *desires*), there are numerous variations. In the first line the stress can be placed on "fair," as the regular metrical pattern suggests, but it is likely that "Now" gets almost as much emphasis; probably in the second line "Draws" is more heavily emphasized than "on," giving us a trochee (a stressed syllable followed by an unstressed one); and in the fourth line each word in the phrase "This old moon wanes" is probably stressed fairly heavily, conveying by two spondees (two feet, each of two stresses) the oppressive tedium that Theseus feels.

In Shakespeare's early plays much of the blank verse is end-stopped (that is, it has a heavy pause at the end of each line), but he later developed the ability to write iambic pentameter verse paragraphs (rather than lines) that give the illusion of speech. His chief techniques are (1) enjambing, i.e., running the thought beyond the single line, as in the first three lines of the speech just quoted; (2) occasionally replacing an iamb with another foot; (3) varying the position of the chief pause (the caesura) within a line; (4) adding an occasional unstressed syllable at the end of a line, traditionally called a feminine ending; (5) and beginning or ending a speech with a half line.

Shakespeare's mature blank verse has much of the rhythmic flexibility of his prose; both the language, though richly figurative and sometimes dense, and the syntax seem natural. It is also often highly appropriate to a particular character. Consider, for instance, this speech from *Hamlet*, in which Claudius, King of Denmark ("the Dane"), speaks to Laertes:

> And now, Laertes, what's the news with you?
> You told us of some suit. What is't, Laertes?
> You cannot speak of reason to the Dane
> And lose your voice. What wouldst thou beg, Laertes,
> That shall not be my offer, not thy asking?   (1.2.42–46)

Notice the short sentences and the repetition of the name "Laertes," to whom the speech is addressed. Notice, too, the shift from the royal "us" in the second line to the more intimate "my" in the last line, and from "you" in the first three lines to the more intimate "thou" and "thy" in the last two lines. Claudius knows how to ingratiate himself with Laertes.

For a second example of the flexibility of Shakespeare's blank verse, consider a passage from *Macbeth*. Distressed by the doctor's inability to cure Lady Macbeth and by the imminent battle, Macbeth addresses some of his remarks to the doctor and others to the servant who is arming him. The entire speech, with its pauses, interruptions, and irresolution (in "Pull't off, I say," Macbeth orders the servant to remove the armor that the servant has been putting on him), catches Macbeth's disintegration. (In the first line, *physic* means "medicine," and in the fourth and fifth lines, *cast the water* means "analyze the urine.")

> Throw physic to the dogs, I'll none of it.
> Come, put mine armor on. Give me my staff.
> Seyton, send out.—Doctor, the thanes fly from me.—
> Come, sir, dispatch. If thou couldst, doctor, cast
> The water of my land, find her disease
> And purge it to a sound and pristine health,
> I would applaud thee to the very echo,
> That should applaud again.—Pull't off, I say.—
> What rhubarb, senna, or what purgative drug,
> Would scour these English hence? Hear'st thou of them?
>   (5.3.47–56)

Blank verse, then, can be much more than unrhymed iambic pentameter, and even within a single play Shakespeare's blank verse often consists of several styles, depending on the speaker and on the speaker's emotion at the moment.

The Play Text as a Collaboration

Shakespeare's fellow dramatist Ben Jonson reported that the actors said of Shakespeare, "In his writing, whatsoever he penned, he never blotted out line," i.e., never crossed out material and revised his work while composing. None of Shakespeare's plays survives in manuscript (with the possible exception of a scene in *Sir Thomas More*), so we cannot fully evaluate the comment, but in a few instances the published work clearly shows that he revised his manuscript. Consider the following passage (shown here in facsimile) from the best early text of *Romeo and Juliet*, the Second Quarto (1599):

Ro. Would I were ſleepe and peace ſo ſweet to reſt
The grey eyde morne ſmiles on the frowning night,
Checking the Eaſterne Clouds with ſtreaks of light,
And darkneſſe fleckted like a drunkard reeles,
From forth daies pathway, made by *Tytans* wheeles.
Hence will I to my ghoſtly Friers cloſe cell,
His helpe to craue, and my deare hap to tell.

                                                      Exit.

Enter Frier alone with a basket.   (night,
Fri. The grey-eyed morne ſmiles on the frowning
Checking the Eaſterne clowdes with ſtreaks of light:
And fleckeld darkneſſe like a drunkard reeles,
From forth daies path, and *Titans* burning wheeles:
Now ere the ſun aduance his burning eie,

Romeo rather elaborately tells us that the sun at dawn is dispelling the night (morning is smiling, the eastern clouds are checked with light, and the sun's chariot—Titan's wheels—advances), and he will seek out his spiritual father, the Friar. He exits and, oddly, the Friar enters and says pretty much the same thing about the sun. Both speakers say that "the gray-eyed morn smiles on the frowning night," but there are small differences, perhaps having more to do with the business of printing the book than with the author's composition: For Romeo's "checkring," "fleckted," and "pathway," we get the Friar's "checking," "fleckeld," and "path." (Notice, by the way, the inconsistency in Elizabethan spelling: Romeo's "clouds" become the Friar's "clowdes.")

Both versions must have been in the printer's copy, and it seems safe to assume that both were in Shakespeare's manuscript. He must have written one version—let's say he first wrote Romeo's closing lines for this scene—and then he decided, no, it's better to give this lyrical passage to the Friar, as the opening of a new scene, but he neglected to delete the first version. Editors must make a choice, and they may feel that the reasonable thing to do is to print the text as Shakespeare intended it. But how can we know what he intended? Almost all modern editors delete the lines from Romeo's speech, and retain the Friar's lines. They don't do this because they know Shakespeare's intention, however. They give the lines to the Friar because the first published version (1597) of *Romeo and Juliet* gives only the Friar's version, and this text (though in many ways inferior to the 1599 text) is thought to derive from the memory of some actors, that is, it is thought to represent a performance, not just a script. Maybe during the course of rehearsals Shakespeare—an actor as well as an author—unilaterally decided that the Friar should speak the lines; if so (remember that we don't know this to be a fact) his final intention was to give the speech to the Friar. Maybe, however, the actors talked it over and settled on the Friar, with or without Shakespeare's approval. On the other hand, despite the 1597 version, one might argue (if only weakly) on behalf of giving the lines to Romeo rather than to the Friar, thus: (1) Romeo's comment on the coming of the daylight emphasizes his separation from Juliet, and (2) the figurative language seems more appropriate to Romeo than to the Friar. Having said this, in the Signet edition we have decided in this instance to draw on the evidence provided by earlier text and to give the lines to the Friar, on the grounds that since Q1 reflects a production, in the theater (at least on one occasion) the lines were spoken by the Friar.

A playwright sold a script to a theatrical company. The script thus belonged to the company, not the author, and au-

thor and company alike must have regarded this script not as
a literary work but as the basis for a play that the actors
would create on the stage. We speak of Shakespeare as the
author of the plays, but readers should bear in mind that the
texts they read, even when derived from a single text, such
as the First Folio (1623), are inevitably the collaborative
work not simply of Shakespeare with his company—
doubtless during rehearsals the actors would suggest
alterations—but also with other forces of the age. One force
was governmental censorship. In 1606 parliament passed "an
Act to restrain abuses of players," prohibiting the utterance
of oaths and the name of God. So where the earliest text of
Othello gives us "By heaven" (3.3.106), the first Folio gives
"Alas," presumably reflecting the compliance of stage practice with the law. Similarly, the 1623 version of *King Lear*
omits the oath "Fut"(probably from "By God's foot") at
1.2.142, again presumably reflecting the line as it was spoken
on the stage. Editors who seek to give the reader the play
that Shakespeare initially conceived—the "authentic" play
conceived by the solitary Shakespeare—probably will restore
the missing oaths and references to God. Other editors, who
see the play as a collaborative work, a construction made not
only by Shakespeare but also by actors and compositors and
even government censors, may claim that what counts is the
play as it was actually performed. Such editors regard the
censored text as legitimate, since it is the play that was (presumably) finally put on. A performed text, they argue, has
more historical reality than a text produced by an editor who
has sought to get at what Shakespeare initially wrote. In this
view, the text of a play is rather like the script of a film; the
script is not the film, and the play text is not the performed
play. Even if we want to talk about the play that Shakespeare
"intended," we will find ourselves talking about a script that
he handed over to a company with the intention that it be
implemented by actors. The "intended" play is the one that
the actors—we might almost say "society"—would help to
construct.

Further, it is now widely held that a play is also the work
of readers and spectators, who do not simply receive meaning, but who create it when they respond to the play. This

idea is fully in accord with contemporary post-structuralist critical thinking, notably Roland Barthes's "The Death of the Author," in *Image-Music-Text* (1977) and Michel Foucault's "What Is an Author?," in *The Foucault Reader* (1984). The gist of the idea is that an author is not an isolated genius; rather, authors are subject to the politics and other social structures of their age. A dramatist especially is a worker in a collaborative project, working most obviously with actors—parts may be written for particular actors—but working also with the audience. Consider the words of Samuel Johnson, written to be spoken by the actor David Garrick at the opening of a theater in 1747:

> The stage but echoes back the public voice;
> The drama's laws, the drama's patrons give,
> For we that live to please, must please to live.

The audience—the public taste as understood by the playwright—helps to determine what the play is. Moreover, even members of the public who are not part of the playwright's immediate audience may exert an influence through censorship. We have already glanced at governmental censorship, but there are also other kinds. Take one of Shakespeare's most beloved characters, Falstaff, who appears in three of Shakespeare's plays, the two parts of *Henry IV* and *The Merry Wives of Windsor*. He appears with this name in the earliest printed version of the first of these plays, *1 Henry IV*, but we know that Shakespeare originally called him (after an historical figure) Sir John Oldcastle. Oldcastle appears in Shakespeare's source (partly reprinted in the Signet edition of *1 Henry IV*), and a trace of the name survives in Shakespeare's play, 1.2.43–44, where Prince Hal punningly addresses Falstaff as "my old lad of the castle." But for some reason—perhaps because the family of the historical Oldcastle complained—Shakespeare had to change the name. In short, the play as we have it was (at least in this detail) subject to some sort of censorship. If we think that a text should present what we take to be the author's intention, we probably will want to replace *Falstaff* with *Oldcastle*. But if we recognize that a play is a collaboration, we may welcome the change, even if it was forced on Shakespeare. Somehow *Falstaff*, with its hint of *false-staff*, i.e., inadequate prop, seems just right for this fat knight who, to our delight, entertains the young prince with untruths. We can go as far as saying that, at least so far as a play is concerned, an insistence on the author's original intention (even if we could know it) can sometimes impoverish the text.

The tiny example of Falstaff's name illustrates the point that the text we read is inevitably only a version—something in effect produced by the collaboration of the playwright with his actors, audiences, compositors, and editors—of a fluid text that Shakespeare once wrote, just as the *Hamlet* that we see on the screen starring Kenneth Branagh is not the *Hamlet* that Shakespeare saw in an open-air playhouse starring Richard Burbage. *Hamlet* itself, as we shall note in a moment, also exists in several versions. It is not surprising that there is now much talk about the *instability* of Shakespeare's texts.

Because he was not only a playwright but was also an actor and a shareholder in a theatrical company, Shakespeare probably was much involved with the translation of the play from a manuscript to a stage production. He may or may not have done some rewriting during rehearsals, and he may or may not have been happy with cuts that were made. Some plays, notably *Hamlet* and *King Lear*, are so long that it is most unlikely that the texts we read were acted in their entirety. Further, for both of these plays we have more than one early text that demands consideration. In *Hamlet*, the Second Quarto (1604) includes some two hundred lines not found in the Folio (1623). Among the passages missing from the Folio are two of Hamlet's reflective speeches, the "dram of evil" speech (1.4.13–38) and "How all occasions do inform against me" (4.4.32–66). Since the Folio has more numerous and often fuller stage directions, it certainly looks as though in the Folio we get a theatrical version of the play, a text whose cuts were probably made—this is only a hunch, of course—not because Shakespeare was changing his conception of Hamlet but because the playhouse demanded a modified play. (The problem is complicated, since the Folio not only cuts some of the Quarto but adds some material. Various explanations have been offered.)

Or take an example from *King Lear*. In the First and Second Quarto (1608, 1619), the final speech of the play is given to Albany, Lear's surviving son-in-law, but in the First Folio version (1623), the speech is given to Edgar. The Quarto version is in accord with tradition—usually the highest-ranking character in a tragedy speaks the final words. Why does the Folio give the speech to Edgar? One possible answer is this: The Folio version omits some of Albany's speeches in earlier scenes, so perhaps it was decided (by Shakespeare? by the players?) not to give the final lines to so pale a character. In fact, the discrepancies are so many between the two texts, that some scholars argue we do not simply have texts showing different theatrical productions. Rather, these scholars say, Shakespeare substantially revised the play, and we really have two versions of *King Lear* (and of *Othello* also, say some)—two different plays—not simply two texts, each of which is in some ways imperfect.

In this view, the 1608 version of *Lear* may derive from Shakespeare's manuscript, and the 1623 version may derive from his later revision. The Quartos have almost three hundred lines not in the Folio, and the Folio has about a hundred lines not in the Quartos. It used to be held that all the texts were imperfect in various ways and from various causes—some passages in the Quartos were thought to have been set from a manuscript that was not entirely legible, other passages were thought to have been set by a compositor who was new to setting plays, and still other passages were thought to have been provided by an actor who misremembered some of the lines. This traditional view held that an editor must draw on the Quartos and the Folio in order to get Shakespeare's "real" play. The new argument holds (although not without considerable strain) that we have two authentic plays, Shakespeare's early version (in the Quarto) and Shakespeare's—or his theatrical company's—revised version (in the Folio). Not only theatrical demands but also Shakespeare's own artistic sense, it is argued, called for extensive revisions. Even the titles vary: Q1 is called *True Chronicle Historie of the life and death of King Lear and his three*

Daughters, whereas the Folio text is called *The Tragedie of King Lear*. To combine the two texts in order to produce what the editor thinks is the play that Shakespeare intended to write is, according to this view, to produce a text that is false to the history of the play. If the new view is correct, and we do have texts of two distinct versions of *Lear* rather than two imperfect versions of one play, it supports in a textual way the poststructuralist view that we cannot possibly have an unmediated vision of (in this case) a play by Shakespeare; we can only recognize a plurality of visions.

Editing Texts

Though eighteen of his plays were published during his lifetime, Shakespeare seems never to have supervised their publication. There is nothing unusual here; when a playwright sold a play to a theatrical company he surrendered his ownership to it. Normally a company would not publish the play, because to publish it meant to allow competitors to acquire the piece. Some plays did get published: Apparently hard-up actors sometimes pieced together a play for a publisher; sometimes a company in need of money sold a play; and sometimes a company allowed publication of a play that no longer drew audiences. That Shakespeare did not concern himself with publication is not remarkable; of his contemporaries, only Ben Jonson carefully supervised the publication of his own plays.

In 1623, seven years after Shakespeare's death, John Heminges and Henry Condell (two senior members of Shakespeare's company, who had worked with him for about twenty years) collected his plays—published and unpublished—into a large volume, of a kind called a folio. (A folio is a volume consisting of large sheets that have been folded once, each sheet thus making two leaves, or four pages. The size of the page of course depends on the size of the sheet—a folio can range in height from twelve to sixteen inches, and in width from eight to eleven; the pages in the 1623 edition of Shakespeare, commonly called the First Folio, are approximately thirteen inches tall and eight inches wide.) The eighteen plays published during Shakespeare's lifetime had been issued one play per volume in small formats called quartos. (Each sheet in a quarto has been folded twice, making four leaves, or eight pages, each page being about nine inches tall and seven inches wide, roughly the size of a large paperback.)

Heminges and Condell suggest in an address "To the great variety of readers" that the republished plays are presented in better form than in the quartos:

> Before you were abused with diverse stolen and surreptitious copies, maimed and deformed by the frauds and stealths of injurious impostors that exposed them; even those, are now offered to your view cured and perfect of their limbs, and all the rest absolute in their numbers, as he [i.e., Shakespeare] conceived them.

There is a good deal of truth to this statement, but some of the quarto versions are better than others; some are in fact preferable to the Folio text.

Whoever was assigned to prepare the texts for publication in the first Folio seems to have taken the job seriously and yet not to have performed it with uniform care. The sources of the texts seem to have been, in general, good unpublished copies or the best published copies. The first play in the collection, *The Tempest*, is divided into acts and scenes, has unusually full stage directions and descriptions of spectacle, and concludes with a list of the characters, but the editor was not able (or willing) to present all of the succeeding texts so fully dressed. Later texts occasionally show signs of carelessness: in one scene of *Much Ado About Nothing* the names of actors, instead of characters, appear as speech prefixes, as they had in the Quarto, which the Folio reprints; proofreading throughout the Folio is spotty and apparently was done without reference to the printer's copy; the pagination of *Hamlet* jumps from 156 to 257. Further, the proofreading was done while the presses continued to print, so that each play in each volume contains a mix of corrected and uncorrected pages.

Modern editors of Shakespeare must first select their copy; no problem if the play exists only in the Folio, but a considerable problem if the relationship between a Quarto and the Folio—or an early Quarto and a later one—is unclear. In the case of *Romeo and Juliet*, the First Quarto (Q1), published in 1597, is vastly inferior to the Second (Q2), published in 1599. The basis of Q1 apparently is a version put together from memory by some actors. Not surprisingly, it garbles many passages and is much shorter than Q2. On the other hand, occasionally Q1 makes better sense than Q2. For instance, near the end of the play, when the parents have assembled and learned of the deaths of Romeo and Juliet, in Q2 the Prince says (5.3.208–9),

> Come, *Montague;* for thou art early vp
> To see thy sonne and heire, now earling downe.

The last three words of this speech surely do not make sense, and many editors turn to Q1, which instead of "now earling downe" has "more early downe." Some modern editors take only "early" from Q1, and print "now early down"; others take "more early," and print "more early down." Further, Q1 (though, again, quite clearly a garbled and abbreviated text) includes some stage directions that are not found in Q2, and today many editors who base their text on Q2 are glad to add these stage directions, because the directions help to give us a sense of what the play looked like on Shakespeare's stage. Thus, in 4.3.58, after Juliet drinks the potion, Q1 gives us this stage direction, not in Q2: *"She falls upon her bed within the curtains."*

In short, an editor's decisions do not end with the choice of a single copy text. First of all, editors must reckon with Elizabethan spelling. If they are not producing a facsimile, they probably modernize the spelling, but ought they to preserve the old forms of words that apparently were pronounced quite unlike their modern forms—*lanthorn, alablaster*? If they preserve these forms are they really preserving Shakespeare's forms or perhaps those of a compositor in the printing house? What is one to do when one finds *lanthorn* and *lantern* in adjacent lines? (The editors of this series in general, but not invariably, assume that words should be spelled in their modern form, unless, for instance, a rhyme is involved.) Elizabethan punctuation, too, presents problems. For example, in the First Folio, the only text for the play, Macbeth rejects his wife's idea that he can wash the blood from his hand (2.2.60–62):

> No: this my Hand will rather
> The multitudinous Seas incarnardine,
> Making the Greene one, Red.

Obviously an editor will remove the superfluous capitals, and will probably alter the spelling to "incarnadine," but what about the comma before "Red"? If we retain the comma, Macbeth is calling the sea "the green one." If we drop the comma, Macbeth is saying that his bloody hand will make the sea ("the Green") *uniformly* red.

An editor will sometimes have to change more than spelling and punctuation. Macbeth says to his wife (1.7.46–47):

> I dare do all that may become a man,
> Who dares no more, is none.

For two centuries editors have agreed that the second line is unsatisfactory, and have emended "no" to "do": "Who dares do more is none." But when in the same play (4.2.21–22) Ross says that fearful persons

> Floate vpon a wilde and violent Sea
> Each way, and moue,

need we emend the passage? On the assumption that the compositor misread the manuscript, some editors emend "each way, and move" to "and move each way"; others emend "move" to "none" (i.e., "Each way and none"). Other editors, however, let the passage stand as in the original. The editors of the Signet Classic Shakespeare have restrained themselves from making abundant emendations. In their minds they hear Samuel Johnson on the dangers of emendation: "I have adopted the Roman sentiment, that it is more honorable to save a citizen than to kill an enemy." Some departures (in addition to spelling, punctuation, and lineation) from the copy text have of course been made, but the original readings are listed in a note following the play, so that readers can evaluate the changes for themselves.

Following tradition, the editors of the Signet Classic Shakespeare have prefaced each play with a list of characters, and throughout the play have regularized the names of the speakers. Thus, in our text of *Romeo and Juliet*, all speeches by Juliet's mother are prefixed "Lady Capulet," although the 1599 Quarto of the play, which provides our copy text, uses at various points seven speech tags for this one character: *Capu. Wi.* (i.e., Capulet's wife), *Ca. Wi., Wi., Wife, Old La.* (i.e., Old Lady), *La.,* and *Mo.* (i.e., Mother). Similarly, in *All's Well That Ends Well*, the character whom we regularly call "Countess" is in the Folio (the copy text) variously identified as *Mother, Countess, Old Countess, Lady,* and *Old Lady*. Admittedly there is some loss in regularizing, since the various prefixes may give us a hint of the way Shakespeare (or a scribe who copied Shakespeare's manuscript) was thinking of the character in a particular scene—for instance, as a mother, or as an old lady. But too much can be made of these differing prefixes, since the social relationships implied are *not* always relevant to the given scene.

We have also added line numbers and in many cases act and scene divisions as well as indications of locale at the beginning of scenes. The Folio divided most of the plays into acts and some into scenes. Early eighteenth-century editors increased the divisions. These divisions, which provide a convenient way of referring to passages in the plays, have been retained, but when not in the text chosen as the basis for the Signet Classic text they are enclosed within square brackets, [ ], to indicate that they are editorial additions. Similarly, though no play of Shakespeare's was equipped with indications of the locale at the heads of scene divisions, locales have here been added in square brackets for the convenience of readers, who lack the information that costumes, properties, gestures, and scenery afford to spectators. Spectators can tell at a glance they are in the throne room, but without an editorial indication the reader may be puzzled for a while. It should be mentioned, incidentally, that there are a few authentic stage directions—perhaps Shakespeare's, perhaps a prompter's—that suggest locales, such as *"Enter Brutus in his orchard,"* and *"They go up into the Senate house."* It is hoped that the bracketed additions in the Signet text will provide readers with the sort of help provided by these two authentic directions, but it is equally hoped that the reader will remember that the stage was not loaded with scenery.

Shakespeare on the Stage

Each volume in the Signet Classic Shakespeare includes a brief stage (and sometimes film) history of the play. When we read about earlier productions, we are likely to find them eccentric, obviously wrongheaded—for instance, Nahum Tate's version of *King Lear*, with a happy ending, which held the stage for about a century and a half, from the late seventeenth century until the end of the first quarter of the nineteenth. We see engravings of David Garrick, the greatest actor of the eighteenth century, in eighteenth-century garb as King Lear, and we smile, thinking how absurd the production must have been. If we are more thoughtful, we say, with the English novelist L. P. Hartley, "The past is a foreign country: they do things differently there." But if the eighteenth-century staging is a foreign country, what of the plays of the late sixteenth and seventeenth centuries? A foreign language, a foreign theater, a foreign audience.

Probably all viewers of Shakespeare's plays, beginning with Shakespeare himself, at times have been unhappy with the plays on the stage. Consider three comments about production that we find in the plays themselves, which suggest Shakespeare's concerns. The Chorus in *Henry V* complains that the heroic story cannot possibly be adequately staged:

> But pardon, gentles all,
> The flat unraisèd spirits that hath dared
> On this unworthy scaffold to bring forth
> So great an object. Can this cockpit hold
> The vasty fields of France? Or may we cram
> Within this wooden *O* the very casques

That did affright the air at Agincourt?

. . . .

Piece out our imperfections with your thoughts.

(Prologue 1.8–14,23)

Second, here are a few sentences (which may or may not represent Shakespeare's own views) from Hamlet's longish lecture to the players:

Speak the speech, I pray you, as I pronounced it to you, trippingly on the tongue. But if you mouth it, as many of our players do, I had as lief the town crier spoke my lines. . . . O, it offends me to the soul to hear a robustious periwig-pated fellow tear a passion to tatters, to very rags, to split the ears of the groundlings. . . . And let those that play your clowns speak no more than is set down for them, for there be of them that will themselves laugh, to set on some quantity of barren spectators to laugh too, though in the meantime some necessary question of the play be then to be considered. That's villainous and shows a most pitiful ambition in the fool that uses it. (3.2.1–47)

Finally, we can quote again from the passage cited earlier in this introduction, concerning the boy actors who played the female roles. Cleopatra imagines with horror a theatrical version of her activities with Antony:

> The quick comedians
> Extemporally will stage us, and present
> Our Alexandrian revels: Antony
> Shall be brought drunken forth, and I shall see
> Some squeaking Cleopatra boy my greatness
> I' th' posture of a whore.   (5.2.216–21)

It is impossible to know how much weight to put on such passages—perhaps Shakespeare was just being modest about his theater's abilities—but it is easy enough to think that he was unhappy with some aspects of Elizabethan production. Probably no production can fully satisfy a playwright, and for that matter, few productions can fully satisfy *us;* we regret this or that cut, this or that way of costuming the play, this or that bit of business.

One's first thought may be this: Why don't they just do "authentic" Shakespeare, "straight" Shakespeare, the play as Shakespeare wrote it? But as we read the plays—words written to be performed—it sometimes becomes clear that we do not know *how* to perform them. For instance, in *Antony and Cleopatra* Antony, the Roman general who has succumbed to Cleopatra and to Egyptian ways, says, "The nobleness of life / Is to do thus" (1.1.36–37). But what is "thus"? Does Antony at this point embrace Cleopatra? Does he embrace and kiss her? (There are, by the way, very few scenes of kissing on Shakespeare's stage, possibly because boys played the female roles.) Or does he make a sweeping gesture, indicating the Egyptian way of life?

This is not an isolated example; the plays are filled with lines that call for gestures, but we are not sure what the gestures should be. *Interpretation* is inevitable. Consider a passage in *Hamlet*. In 3.1, Polonius persuades his daughter, Ophelia, to talk to Hamlet while Polonius and Claudius eavesdrop. The two men conceal themselves, and Hamlet encounters Ophelia. At 3.1.131 Hamlet suddenly says to her, "Where's your father?" Why does Hamlet, apparently out of nowhere—they have not been talking about Polonius—ask this question? Is this an example of the "antic disposition" (fantastic behavior) that Hamlet earlier (1.5.172) had told Horatio and others—including us—he would display? That is, is the question about the whereabouts of her father a seemingly irrational one, like his earlier question (3.1.103) to Ophelia, "Ha, ha! Are you honest?" Or, on the other hand, has Hamlet (as in many productions) suddenly glimpsed Polonius's foot protruding from beneath a drapery at the rear? That is, does Hamlet ask the question because he has suddenly seen something suspicious and now is testing Ophelia? (By the way, in productions that do give Hamlet a physical cue, it is almost always Polonius rather than Claudius who provides the clue. This itself is an act of interpretation on the part of the director.) Or (a third possibility) does Hamlet get a clue from Ophelia, who inadvertently betrays the spies by nervously glancing at their place of hiding? This is the interpretation used in the BBC television version, where Ophelia glances in fear toward the hiding place just after Hamlet says "Why wouldst thou be a breeder of sinners?" (121–22). Hamlet, realizing that he is being observed, glances here and there *before* he asks "Where's your father?" The question thus is a climax to what he has been doing while speaking the preceding lines. Or (a fourth interpretation) does Hamlet suddenly, without the aid of any clue whatsoever, intuitively (insightfully, mysteriously, wonderfully) sense that someone is spying? Directors must decide, of course—and so must readers.

Recall, too, the preceding discussion of the texts of the plays, which argued that the texts—though they seem to be before us in permanent black on white—are unstable. The Signet text of *Hamlet*, which draws on the Second Quarto (1604) and the First Folio (1623) is considerably longer than any version staged in Shakespeare's time. Our version, even if spoken very briskly and played without any intermission, would take close to four hours, far beyond "the two hours' traffic of our stage" mentioned in the Prologue to *Romeo and Juliet*. (There are a few contemporary references to the duration of a play, but none mentions more than three hours.) Of Shakespeare's plays, only *The Comedy of Errors*, *Macbeth*, and *The Tempest* can be done in less than three hours without cutting. And even if we take a play that exists only in a short text, *Macbeth*, we cannot claim that we are experiencing the very play that Shakespeare conceived, partly because some of the Witches' songs almost surely are non-Shakespearean additions, and partly because we are not willing to watch the play performed without an intermission and with boys in the female roles.

Further, as the earlier discussion of costumes mentioned, the plays apparently were given chiefly in contemporary, that is, in Elizabethan dress. If today we give them in the costumes that Shakespeare probably saw, the plays seem not contemporary but curiously dated. Yet if we use our own dress, we find lines of dialogue that are at odds with what we see; we may feel that the language, so clearly not our own, is inappropriate coming out of people in today's dress. A common solution, incidentally, has been to set the plays in the nineteenth century, on the grounds that this attractively distances the plays (gives them a degree of foreignness, allowing for interesting costumes) and yet doesn't put them into a museum world of Elizabethan England.

Inevitably our productions are adaptations, *our* adaptations, and inevitably they will look dated, not in a century but in twenty years, or perhaps even in a decade. Still, we cannot escape from our own conceptions. As the director Peter Brook has said, in *The Empty Space* (1968):

> It is not only the hair-styles, costumes and make-ups that look dated. All the different elements of staging—the shorthands of behavior that stand for emotions; gestures, gesticulations and tones of voice—are all fluctuating on an invisible stock exchange all the time. . . . A living theatre that thinks it can stand aloof from anything as trivial as fashion will wilt. (p. 16)

As Brook indicates, it is through today's hairstyles, costumes, makeup, gestures, gesticulations, tones of voice—this includes our *conception* of earlier hairstyles, costumes, and so forth if we stage the play in a period other than our own—that we inevitably stage the plays.

It is a truism that every age invents its own Shakespeare, just as, for instance, every age has invented its own classical world. Our view of ancient Greece, a slave-holding society in which even free Athenian women were severely circumscribed, does not much resemble the Victorians' view of ancient Greece as a glorious democracy, just as, perhaps, our view of Victorianism itself does not much resemble theirs. We cannot claim that the Shakespeare on our stage is the true Shakespeare, but in our stage productions we find a Shakespeare that speaks to us, a Shakespeare that our ancestors doubtless did not know but one that seems to us to be the true Shakespeare—at least for a while.

Our age is remarkable for the wide variety of kinds of staging that it uses for Shakespeare, but one development deserves special mention. This is the now common practice of race-blind or color-blind or nontraditional casting, which allows persons who are not white to play in Shakespeare. Previously blacks performing in Shakespeare were limited to a

mere three roles, Othello, Aaron (in *Titus Andronicus*), and
the Prince of Morocco (in *The Merchant of Venice*), and
there were no roles at all for Asians. Indeed, African-
Americans rarely could play even one of these three roles,
since they were not welcome in white companies. Ira
Aldridge (c.1806–1867), a black actor of undoubted talent,
was forced to make his living by performing Shakespeare in
England and in Europe, where he could play not only
Othello but also—in whiteface—other tragic roles such as
King Lear. Paul Robeson (1898–1976) made theatrical history when he played Othello in London in 1930, and there
was some talk about bringing the production to the United
States, but there was more talk about whether American audiences would tolerate the sight of a black man—a real black
man, not a white man in blackface—kissing and then killing
a white woman. The idea was tried out in summer stock in
1942, the reviews were enthusiastic, and in the following
year Robeson opened on Broadway in a production that ran
an astounding 296 performances. An occasional all-black
company sometimes performed Shakespeare's plays, but
otherwise blacks (and other minority members) were in effect shut out from performing Shakespeare. Only since about
1970 has it been common for nonwhites to play major roles
along with whites. Thus, in a 1996–97 production of *Antony
and Cleopatra*, a white Cleopatra, Vanessa Redgrave, played
opposite a black Antony, David Harewood. Multiracial casting is now especially common at the New York Shakespeare
Festival, founded in 1954 by Joseph Papp, and in England,
where even siblings such as Claudio and Isabella in *Measure
for Measure* or Lear's three daughters may be of different
races. Probably most viewers today soon stop worrying about
the lack of realism, and move beyond the color of the performers' skin to the quality of the performance.

Nontraditional casting is not only a matter of color or race;
it includes sex. In the past, occasionally a distinguished
woman of the theater has taken on a male role—Sarah
Bernhardt (1844–1923) as Hamlet is perhaps the most famous example—but such performances were widely regarded as eccentric. Although today there have been some
performances involving cross-dressing (a drag *As You Like It*

staged by the National Theatre in England in 1966 and in the United States in 1974 has achieved considerable fame in the annals of stage history), what is more interesting is the casting of women in roles that traditionally are male but that need not be. Thus, a 1993–94 English production of *Henry V* used a woman—*not* cross-dressed—in the role of the governor of Harfleur. According to Peter Holland, who reviewed the production in *Shakespeare Survey* 48 (1995), "having a female Governor of Harfleur feminized the city and provided a direct response to the horrendous threat of rape and murder that Henry had offered, his language and her body in direct connection and opposition" (p. 210). Ten years from now the device may not play so effectively, but today it speaks to us. Shakespeare, born in the Elizabethan Age, has been dead nearly four hundred years, yet he is, as Ben Jonson said, "not of an age but for all time." We must understand, however, that he is "for all time" precisely because each age finds in his abundance something for itself and something of itself.

And here we come back to two issues discussed earlier in this introduction—the instability of the text and, curiously, the Bacon/Oxford heresy concerning the authorship of the plays. *Of course* Shakespeare wrote the plays, and we should daily fall on our knees to thank him for them—and yet there is something to the idea that he is not their only author. Every editor, every director and actor, and every reader to some degree shapes them, too, for when we edit, direct, act, or read, we inevitably become Shakespeare's collaborator and re-create the plays. The plays, one might say, are so cunningly contrived that they guide our responses, tell us how we ought to feel, and make a mark on us, but (for better or for worse) we also make a mark on them.

—SYLVAN BARNET
Tufts University

Introduction

The Tempest is probably the last play wholly written by Shakespeare. Generations of readers have for this reason been tempted to see it as a culmination of Shakespeare's vision, to identify Prospero with Shakespeare, and to read the famous speech in which Prospero breaks his magic wand as Shakespeare's farewell to his art. Although critics nowadays hesitate to identify Prospero with Shakespeare, those of us who love *The Tempest* cannot help feeling that it represents a culmination—that Shakespeare could not have written it without the wisdom and technique he had accumulated through writing all his other plays.

We get this impression because the characterizations, for example, are so simple—Prospero is wise, Miranda is pure, Caliban is base, Antonio is wicked. Yet these are not the simple characters of a playwright who cannot do any better. They are the simple characters of the playwright who has already created Hamlet and Macbeth and Lear. And we feel this; we feel we are in touch, through the characters of *The Tempest*, with very real and very powerful forces. Caliban, who speaks one of the most beautiful passages of poetry in the play, is enigmatic enough. But where will you come to an end of understanding Ariel? Ariel's complexity certainly does not lie in his characterization. It lies, you may say, in the poetry he speaks. But that is to beg the question.

It is the deliberate return to naïveté, after the tragic complexity, that makes us feel there is something special about the four plays of Shakespeare's final period. The special effect is most apparent in *The Tempest*, because it is the lightest in surface of the four. It is presented to us as a gorgeous bubble, which is blown up for our entertainment like the masque Prospero conjures for Ferdinand and Miranda, and which is just as easily dispelled in the end. Yet *The Tempest* contains the subject matter of tragedy, and it gives us throughout the sense of omniscience, of surveying all life, that we get only at the highest points of illumination in the tragedies. No wonder then that *The Tempest* seems the appropriate statement of age, of the man who having seen it all can teach us that the profoundest statement is the lightest and that life, when we see through it, is gay, is tragicomically gay—that the evil, the violence, the tragedy are all part of a providential design.

The Tempest was probably written during the fall and winter of 1610–1611. It was produced at court in the fall of 1611, and again during the winter of 1612–1613 as part of the festivities that preceded the marriage of the King's daughter Elizabeth to the Elector Palatine. The First Folio probably gives us the play as it was acted at court during the winter. But there is insufficient evidence to support the contention of some scholars that the play was radically revised for the wedding festivities and that the wedding masque in Act 4 was inserted in honor of the betrothed couple. Some scholars have even, in their disappointment with the verse of the wedding masque, supposed that the masque was not written by Shakespeare. But Shakespeare always uses a deliberately stilted style for a play within a play; and the masque depends for its effectiveness on spectacle rather than language. Unless new external evidence turns up, there is no reason to look outside the play itself for an explanation of the wedding masque, since the masque fits in subject matter and form into the very texture of *The Tempest*.

The masque brings to a climax the theme of nature versus art that is central to *The Tempest*. For Heaven and Earth, Juno and Ceres, unite in the masque to pronounce a blessing on the union of Ferdinand and Miranda, and to connect sexual union with nature's fruitfulness as seen in its ideal aspect. Venus and her son Cupid are, however, as representatives of lawless passion, specifically excluded from the natural force celebrated in the masque. This fits in with Prospero's severe warning to Ferdinand not to "break" Miranda's "virgin knot" before marriage. Nature is celebrated in the masque as a principle of order. And it is shown to be, as a principle of order, inextricably intertwined with art, civilization, idea.

There is good reason to believe that Shakespeare had in mind, when he wrote *The Tempest*, the reports that first reached England in September 1610 of the miraculous deliverance of the crew and passengers of a ship that had been lost the year before in a terrible tempest off the Bermudas—those stormy islands that Shakespeare refers to in *The Tempest* as "the still-vexed Bermoothes." The written accounts of the survivors (extracts from which appear under The Sources of *The Tempest*) emphasize the providential quality of their deliverance, for the castaways were saved by the magically beneficent nature of the island on which they found themselves. These so-called Bermuda pamphlets go on to see the very storm and shipwreck as providential, since they enabled the castaways to discover for the benefit of mankind that the islands that mariners had shunned as inhabited by devils were actually an island paradise.

In exclaiming over the ways of providence, the Bermuda pamphlets offer those paradoxes that are at the heart of the tragicomic vision—the sort of paradoxes Shakespeare uses in *The Tempest*. "Though the seas threaten, they are merciful," says Ferdinand in the end. And Gonzalo sums up the meaning of the play through a series of paradoxes. "Was Milan thrust from Milan, that his issue / Should become kings of Naples?" he asks,

> In one voyage
> Did Claribel her husband find at Tunis,
> And Ferdinand her brother found a wife
> Where he himself was lost; Prospero his dukedom
> In a poor isle; and all of us ourselves
> When no man was his own.

(5.1.205–6, 208–13)

This is the essential message of tragicomedy—that we lose in order to recover something greater, that we die in order to be reborn to a better life. One of the Bermuda pamphlets speaks paradoxically of "these infortunate (yet fortunate) islands," and even calls the shipwreck and deliverance "this tragical comedy."

The Bermuda episode must have raised again for Shakespeare the perennial question that became particularly pertinent after the discovery of the New World—the question of whether nature is not superior to art, and whether man is not nobler in a state of nature than in a state of civilization. It is not surprising that Shakespeare had also in mind, when he wrote *The Tempest*, the essay "Of the Cannibals" (also extracted under Sources) in which Montaigne praises the American Indians in terms that helped establish the ideal of the Noble Savage. Gonzalo's description of his ideal commonwealth is a close paraphrase of Montaigne's essay.

The island of *The Tempest* is in the Mediterranean, somewhere between Tunis and Naples; yet it seems more magically remote and unlocated than if it had been given a specific location, even one so far as the Bermudas. By setting his island in the Mediterranean, Shakespeare is able to bring the European tradition to bear on the question of nature versus art. He can assimilate the latest ideas about the New World to traditional ideas of the Golden Age and the Garden of Eden. He can remind us of Aeneas, who lost Troy that he might found Rome. Aeneas was driven by a storm to Carthage (specifically associated here with Tunis), from whence he sailed to Italy. In fulfilling his destiny, he underwent wanderings and ordeals analogous to those of the court party in *The Tempest*, including a banquet involving harpies. It is worth mentioning, in connection with Gonzalo's enigmatic references to "widow Dido" and "widower Aeneas," that two of the Bermuda pamphlets compare Dido and Aeneas, as colonizers of new territories, to the colonists of the New World.

Shakespeare addresses himself to the question of nature versus art by ringing all possible changes on the meaning of "nature." Caliban is natural in that he is earthy and earthbound, low, material. But Ariel is just as natural in that he represents the fluid elements of water and air and also those bodiless energies of nature that strike us as "spiritual." Caliban, whose name may derive from "cannibal," is the natural man seen in one aspect. But Miranda is also natural, and the two are contrasted throughout. Both were brought up in a state of nature; and if Miranda never saw a man other than her father, Caliban never saw a woman other than his mother. Caliban is natural in the sense that nature is rudimentary and mindless; he cannot be educated. Miranda is natural in the sense that we take the Golden Age or the Garden of Eden to be our natural condition. She has been superbly educated by Prospero, but education has with her been absorbed in the natural; knowledge has not lost her the Garden.

The case of Caliban is complex, because we cannot be certain that he is human. He was begotten by a devil on the witch Sycorax, and he is spoken of either as something between an animal and a man, or as something between a sea and a land animal. All the ironic changes on the meaning of "nature" can be heard in Trinculo's remark about Caliban: "That a monster should be such a natural!"—in which "natural" means "idiot." If we take nature to be a principle of order, then the primitive Caliban is a monster, a piece of disorder or deformity.

Trinculo's remark contrasts with Miranda's, when she thinks Ferdinand must be a god, "for nothing natural / I ever saw so noble" (1.2.419–20). Ferdinand, too, and in the end Alonso think for the same reason that Miranda must be a goddess. Shakespeare would seem to be telling us that your view of the natural depends on your view of the supernatural—on whether you see behind natural phenomena the evil machinations of the witch Sycorax and her devil-god Setebos, or whether you see at work a rational and benevolent providence. He seems to be telling us that every creature can be judged by its potential metamorphoses, by what it is capable of becoming. Miranda sees all the human beings in the play as godlike. But Caliban, who constantly shifts before our eyes between human and animal, fears that he and his drunken co-conspirators will turn into apes or into barnacles, geese believed to be the product of metamorphosis from shellfish.

There is no question as to which view of nature Shakespeare adheres to. He presents here, as in the history plays and the tragedies, a grand vision of order in nature and society; only the emphasis here, far more than in his other plays, is on nature. The fact that Caliban takes the drunken butler, Stephano, for a god is a sign of how high man ranks on the scale of life. It is because we recognize the differences of degree within the human scale that we laugh at Caliban's illusion, but give our poetic faith to the illusion of Ferdinand and Miranda when they take each other for divine. Caliban's crime in conspiring against Prospero is a sin against degree—like the plot of Antonio and Sebastian against Alonso, and Antonio's usurpation of Prospero's throne. Prospero erred in attempting to educate Caliban, just as he erred in allowing Antonio to play the duke in Milan. In both cases, he blurred distinctions of degree and helped create the disorder that followed.

This Renaissance idea of degree is ignored in recent colonialist interpretations of *The Tempest*, which see Caliban as the exploited native who is deprived of his rightful possession of the island by the intruding colonialist Prospero. Although Caliban claims the island by inheritance from his mother, the witch Sycorax, she was not indigenous. When pregnant with him, Sycorax was exiled to the island and found there Ariel, whom she imprisoned, so was herself a usurper. Shakespeare seems to anticipate twentieth-century charges of colonialism with Prospero's answer to Caliban's assertion: "This island's mine" (1.2.331). "I have used thee," says Prospero,

> (Filth as thou art) with humane care, and lodged thee
> In mine own cell till thou didst seek to violate
> The honor of my child.   (345–48)

Is this rejection of Caliban as a mate for Miranda a sign of racism? Caliban—who is described in the Names of the Actors as "a savage and deformed slave" and is later repeatedly addressed as "monster" (3.2)—hardly seems a suitable match for the beautiful, innocent Miranda, daughter of the Duke of Milan. Even though Prospero never disputes Caliban's claim to the island, he cannot be considered a colonialist since he does not want to remain on the island but uses the island as a means for returning home. In the end he leaves the island to Caliban, who has been improved by his confrontation with Prospero.

The other important new reinterpretation of *The Tempest* derives from New Historicism. As explained by Stephen Greenblatt, whose book *Shakespearean Negotiations* (1988) illustrates the principles of the movement, the New Historicist does not look for the meaning of a literary work in an autonomous text or even in the individual genius of the author, but from "the circulation of social energy" (p. 13) from society to the work and from the work back to society. Greenblatt is interested in "what can only be glimpsed at the margins of the text . . . insight into the half-hidden cultural transactions through which great works of art are empowered." He takes seriously "the collective production of literary pleasure" and the way in which "collective beliefs and experiences were shaped, moved from one medium to another, concentrated in manageable aesthetic form." The "Shakespearean theater [was] manifestly the product of collective intentions" (pp. 4–5). The New Historicist method can be fruitful, as we see in Greenblatt's excerpted discussion of *The Tempest*, printed below on pages 156–79.

To return to Caliban and the idea of degree, he is only evil when judged by human standards, or when he himself aspires to get above his place. In attempting to be "free," he only exchanges masters; for a slave he is and should be, as he himself recognizes in the end. Ariel, on the other hand, is by nature a free spirit (he seems free enough even in the bondage of which he complains), and he is therefore appropriately freed in the end. There is a connection in Shakespeare's worldview between biological and social rank and moral obligation. Thus, Antonio's crime against his brother and sovereign is also spoken of as "unnatural." But Antonio is much worse than Caliban, because much higher up on the scale. For the same reason, Stephano and Trinculo seem even baser than Caliban and even more ridiculous in their aspiration to get above themselves.

With the exception of Antonio, all the characters in the play are saved in the end according to their degree. They undergo a ritual temptation and punishment. Caliban, Stephano, and Trinculo are befouled in a horsepond for their temptation to murder Prospero; and when Stephano and Trinculo are tempted to steal the clothes left out for them as bait, all three conspirators are chased away by spirits in the shape of dogs. These punishments are appropriate to the level of their moral life.

The court party are ritualistically tempted and punished by the banquet that disappears when they start to eat of it. Antonio and Sebastian have also been tempted to murder Alonso; and Alonso has been ritualistically punished by the supposed loss of his son and by his brother's temptation to do to him what he helped Antonio do to Prospero. When Ariel, who is invisible to everyone except Prospero, accuses Alonso, Antonio, and Sebastian of being "three men of sin," his voice comes to them as an inner voice. Alonso's attack of conscience comes as a total illumination. He now understands the union of the natural and moral order:

> Methought the billows spoke and told me of it;
> The winds did sing it to me; and the thunder,
>
> . . . .
>
>   did bass my trespass.
> Therefore my son i' th' ooze is bedded.   (3.3.96–100)

Since Ferdinand and Miranda start without guilt, their development is mystical rather than moral. Ferdinand's ordeal prepares him to share with Miranda the vision of heaven on earth that Prospero sets before them in the wedding masque. They themselves appear in a masque-like vision of perfection, when Prospero draws a curtain to reveal them to the court party. Note that Ferdinand repeats in his ordeal the bondage of Caliban. But bondage at the lovers' high level of existence is transformed into freedom and happiness.

Prospero himself is, I think, tempted, when he remembers Caliban's conspiracy against him, to take revenge against the court party; for Caliban's conspiracy reminds him of the conspiracy of Antonio and Alonso. It is inconsistent with Prospero's role of a providence in the play to suppose that he did not from the start plan for events to work out as they do, and that he is actually converted from some original purpose of revenge by Ariel's remark that he would pity the court party were he human. Since Prospero obviously planned the marriage of Ferdinand and Miranda, it is likely that he also planned to be reconciled with Alonso and the others and that Ariel recalls him to his purpose. The point where, at the thought of Caliban, Prospero interrupts the masque, and is shaken by emotion, is the one point where he seems fallible like the other human beings in the play. We seem to be getting, in his lapse from and return to his purpose, the repetition of a moral conversion from thoughts of revenge that took place before the play begins. All the tragic events of Prospero's earlier life are portrayed for us through such repetitions; so that the tragic events appear to us in a comic perspective, since we now see how well everything turned out.

Almost all the characters pair off. As sovereign and father, Prospero pairs off with Alonso; and as magician, he pairs off with Caliban's mother, the witch Sycorax, who practiced black magic on the island as against Prospero's white magic. Ferdinand pairs off with Miranda; Antonio with Sebastian; Stephano with Trinculo; Caliban with Ariel. In his role of providence, Prospero stands alone at the top of the design. Such symmetries are at the heart of comic technique, perhaps because they make us feel we are seeing events from above, as part of a pattern, and can therefore restrain sympathy in the confidence that all is well. The design also explains the sense in which Shakespeare is not realistic in *The Tempest*. He is dealing in simplifications like those of the mathematician. He is giving us a diagram of the order of things.

The play begins with a scene of disorder—a tempest at sea that renders meaningless the usual social order. The sailors are disrespectful to the aristocrats, who in trying to assert authority get in the way of the ship's organization. The good-humored courage of Gonzalo stands out against the irrationality of Antonio and Sebastian, who scream abuse at the sailors—though they are later in the play to think themselves very rational in plotting social disorder. The storm gives the boatswain a chance to display a natural superiority that has nothing to do with rank.

In the next scene, we learn that the tempest is an illusion

created to regenerate the social order—to restore a reformed Prospero to the throne of Milan, and to lead Ferdinand and Miranda to the throne of Naples. Ariel turns the noise and confusion of the tempest into music, the music that leads Ferdinand to Miranda. The play is pervaded, as G. Wilson Knight has shown in *The Shakespearean Tempest,* by the imagery of tempest, sea, natural noise, and music. This imagery sets the play in a world where disorder is seen to be not merely at the service of order, but inextricably inter-twined, indeed identical, with it. It requires only a trans-formation of perception to recognize order in disorder.

It is, I think, because Ariel makes music out of the natural noises of the island that there is an undersong of animal noises behind one of his songs, and the sound of the sea be-hind another. When Caliban says, "Be not afeard; the isle is full of noises,/ Sounds and sweet airs that give delight and hurt not," he catches the world of nature between metamor-phoses, between noise and music, sleep and waking. We say he renders the magical atmosphere of the island. We mean by this that, like Ariel in his songs, Caliban in this lovely speech shows the appearance of things as fluid and ever-changing aspects of a single force—a force that is beneficent, though it may seem in certain aspects evil.

This force is represented by the sea that washes through every nook and cranny of the play, moving the characters to their destiny both by carrying them there and by washing right up into their consciousness. When Prospero tells Miranda of the "sea sorrow" that brought them to the island, he describes the sea as both threatening and loving. We were cast adrift, he says,

> To cry to th' sea that roared to us; to sigh
> To th' winds, whose pity, sighing back again,
> Did us but loving wrong.   (1.2.149–51)

The supposed drownings of Ferdinand and Alonso are spo-ken of in attractive images. And when one of Alonso's cour-tiers suggests that Ferdinand may have made it to land, he makes us see that, by struggling against the waves,

Ferdinand actually rode them to shore as you ride a fiery steed.

> I saw him beat the surges under him
> And ride upon their backs. He trod the water,
> Whose enmity he flung aside, and breasted
> The surge most swol'n that met him. His bold head
> 'Bove the contentious waves he kept, and oared
> Himself with his good arms in lusty stroke
> To th' shore ...
>
> (2.1.119–25)

The passage—which is, in its complexity of implication and its metrical suppleness, a good example of Shakespeare's late style—turns violence into harmony. It is but a step away from the song in which Ariel makes drowning seem so desirable, because it is, like all aspects of existence in this play, "a sea change/ Into something rich and strange"(1.2.401–02)—into the one force that moves all things. Prospero's magic is a portion of nature's; his providential design is a portion of God's.

Antonio, when he tempts Sebastian to murder the King, uses sea imagery, connecting it with the imagery of sleep and dream to signify the force of Sebastian's real desire. Antonio speaks, through his imagery, truer than he knows; for even his plot is necessary to the providential design of the play. Antonio is an effective villain, because he manipulates real, which is to say magical, forces. Prospero uses the imagery of metamorphosis when he tells Miranda how Antonio so transformed the Milanese court as to make real Antonio's appearance of being duke. The wild sounds of sea and tempest turn for Alonso into rational music that tells him of his crime. And Prospero brings the sea imagery to a climax when he says in the end of the court party,

> Their understanding
> Begins to swell, and the approaching tide
> Will shortly fill the reasonable shore,
> That now lies foul and muddy.
>
> (5.1.79–82)

The sea is now identified with rationality.

The most admirable characters are those who can perceive order in disorder, because they have the capacity for wonder. When Ferdinand says "Admired Miranda," he is playing on the meaning of her name; he is saying, "O wonderful woman, who is to be wondered at." And when, during the masque, he calls Prospero "So rare a wond'red father" (a father possessed of wonders and therefore to be wondered at), it is a sign that he now sees Prospero right. There is an irony in Miranda's famous remark at the end, when she first beholds the court party:

> O, wonder!
> How many goodly creatures are there here!
> How beauteous mankind is! O brave new world
> That has such people in't!

(181–84)

Nevertheless, it is the whole point of the play to make us feel that Miranda is right—that she, in her innocence, sees all these people as they really are, as through all their metamorphoses they are tending to be.

It is to Caliban's credit that he exhibits a capacity for wonder lacking in Stephano and Trinculo and in Antonio and Sebastian. That is because Caliban is natural. His faults do not stem from a perversion of reason, as do those of the four witty characters who do not exhibit a capacity for wonder. Only Gonzalo combines both wit and wonder. In the first appearance of the court party, we see how differently the same phenomena may strike different people. For only Gonzalo sees that their deliverance was miraculous and that the island is a paradise. To be in the Garden of Eden is, we are to understand, a matter of perception. Antonio and Sebastian are with their witty quibbling—their quibble, for example, over the few miles that separate modern Tunis from ancient Carthage—merely destructive.

The effect of wonder is created in *The Tempest* through a combination of several genres—tragicomedy, pastoral, romance, and masque. Antonio's temptation of Sebastian has been compared to the temptation of Macbeth by Lady Macbeth; it is the stuff of tragedy. Our view of it, however, is comic, because we know that Ariel is watching over the scene and has brought it about as part of Prospero's design. The whole action is comic in this sense. The abbreviation of time (*The Tempest* and *The Comedy of Errors* are the only plays in which Shakespeare observes the classical unity of time) enables us to see even Prospero's tragedy in Milan as, in retrospect, for the best. The comic perspective does not, however, make us laugh. It makes us marvel.

Not only the tragedy, but the comedy, too, is dissolved in wonder. Bernard Knox has, in the essay reprinted in this volume, connected *The Tempest* with Roman comedies about slaves. Nevertheless, Caliban and Ariel are too marvelous to be laughed at as we laugh at the slaves in Roman comedies. Stephano and Trinculo seem a kind of comic relief, just because we do so little laughing at the main action of *The Tempest*. Through Prospero's eyes, *The Tempest* shows us life as God must see it. God could not view life tragically, because He knows that all is for the best. God also knows, as Prospero knows of Ferdinand, that the ordeals He sets for us are for our own good and are not so hard or serious as we think them. Neither, however, could God laugh at us as we laugh at the characters in comedies; for He would not ridicule us, or be dazzled by our wit.

Prospero's view of life is set forth in the famous speech in which he says, after dispelling the wedding masque, "We are such stuff/ As dreams are made on." He is, I think, recovering his perspective in this speech after the relapse into thoughts of revenge. The speech is, like Miranda's exclamations, an expression of the marvelous quality of life. Prospero implies, in consoling Ferdinand for the disappearance of the masque, that if life is as illusory as the masque, it is also as gorgeously illusory. He implies also that there is a reality behind life just as there is Prospero behind the masque.

In his detachment from the appearances of life, Prospero regains an innocence of vision analogous to Miranda's. It is the vision of pastoral, the genre that deals with man and nature in their unfallen state. By swiftly recapitulating all the facts of life, tragicomedy leads us to see through life with the eyes of Miranda who never left the Garden. Tragicomedy uses to this end the devices of romance. For romance deals in marvelous events and solves its problems through metamorphoses and recognition scenes—through, in other words, transformations of perception. When Alonso recognizes Prospero and Ferdinand, both of whom he had thought dead, he recognizes their magical preciousness and thus really *sees* them for the first time. The same is true of the crew's response to the ship, when it is magically restored to them. The recognized objects are transformed through the transformed eyes of the beholders; so that more is restored than has been lost.

The masque, with its emphasis on spectacle and surprise, subordinates all other effects to the effect of wonder. "The fringed curtains of thine eye advance," says Prospero to Miranda when the spectacle of Ferdinand is about to break upon her. It is as though a theater curtain were to be raised; as, indeed, it is raised or drawn when the spectacle of the lovers breaks upon the court party. All the scenes that offer the characters illumination are masquelike and illusory. Yet it is through these illusions that the characters come to understand reality. We all found ourselves, says Gonzalo in the end, "when no man was his own."

Art is just such an experience of enchantment. The speech in which Prospero breaks his magic wand is not so much Shakespeare's farewell to his art as it is his comment on the relation between art and life. For in breaking his wand and taking himself and the others back to Italy, Prospero seems to be saying that the enchanted island is no abiding place, but rather a place through which we pass in order to renew and strengthen our sense of reality.

In spite of its fantastic elements, *The Tempest*, as F. R. Leavis has pointed out, never confuses but rather clarifies our sense of reality. That is no small part of its achievement—though it is characteristic of our time that Leavis prefers *The Winter's Tale* just because it is less realistic than *The Tempest*. With its bias against realism, and its interest in a symbolic art, our time is better equipped than any time since Shakespeare's to appreciate the last plays. The seventeenth and eighteenth centuries liked best of all Shakespeare's early comedies. The nineteenth century liked the tragedies best, and on the whole we still do. But it may be that the last plays—and especially *The Tempest*, which is as I see it the best of them—will in future have most to say to us. Certainly, the interest in them has in the last generation risen steadily.

—ROBERT LANGBAUM
University of Virginia

The Tempest

The Scene: An uninhabited island.

Names of the Actors

Alonso, King of Naples
Sebastian, his brother
Prospero, the right Duke of Milan
Antonio, his brother, the usurping Duke of Milan
Ferdinand, son to the King of Naples
Gonzalo, an honest old councilor
Adrian and Francisco, lords
Caliban, a savage and deformed slave
Trinculo, a jester
Stephano, a drunken butler
Master of a ship
Boatswain
Mariners
Miranda, daughter to Prospero
Ariel, an airy spirit
Iris ⎫
Ceres ⎪
Juno ⎬ [presented by] spirits
Nymphs ⎪
Reapers ⎭
[Other Spirits attending on Prospero]

The Tempest

ACT 1

Scene 1. [*On a ship at sea.*]

A tempestuous noise of thunder and lightning heard. Enter a Shipmaster and a Boatswain.

Master. Boatswain!

Boatswain. Here, master. What cheer?

Master. Good,°¹ speak to th' mariners! Fall to't yarely,° or we run ourselves aground. Bestir, bestir!
Exit.

Enter Mariners.

Boatswain. Heigh, my hearts! Cheerly, cheerly, my   5
hearts! Yare, yare! Take in the topsail! Tend to th'
master's whistle! Blow till thou burst thy wind, if
room enough!°

Enter Alonso, Sebastian, Antonio, Ferdinand, Gonzalo, and others.

Alonso. Good boatswain, have care. Where's the master? Play the men.°   10

Boatswain. I pray now, keep below.

¹ The degree sign (°) indicates a footnote, which is keyed to the text by line number. Text references are printed in **boldface** type; the annotation follows in roman type.
1.1.3. **Good** good fellow   4 **yarely** briskly   7–8 **Blow till . . . room enough** the storm can blow and split itself as long as there is open sea without rocks to maneuver in   10 **Play the men** act like men

Antonio. Where is the master, bos'n?

Boatswain. Do you not hear him? You mar our labor.
Keep your cabins; you do assist the storm.

15 *Gonzalo.* Nay, good, be patient.

Boatswain. When the sea is. Hence! What cares these
roarers for the name of king? To cabin! Silence!
Trouble us not!

Gonzalo. Good, yet remember whom thou hast
20 aboard.

Boatswain. None that I more love than myself. You
are a councilor; if you can command these elements
to silence and work the peace of the present,° we
will not hand° a rope more. Use your authority. If
25 you cannot, give thanks you have lived so long, and
make yourself ready in your cabin for the mischance of the hour, if it so hap. Cheerly, good
hearts! Out of our way, I say.   *Exit.*

Gonzalo. I have great comfort from this fellow. Me-
30 thinks he hath no drowning mark upon him; his
complexion is perfect gallows.° Stand fast, good
Fate, to his hanging! Make the rope of his destiny
our cable, for our own doth little advantage.° If he
be not born to be hanged, our case is miserable.
                                   Exit [with the rest.]

Enter Boatswain.

35 *Boatswain.* Down with the topmast! Yare! Lower,
lower! Bring her to try with main course!° *(A cry
within.)* A plague upon this howling! They are
louder than the weather or our office.°

23 **work the peace of the present** restore the present to peace (since as a
councilor his job is to quell disorder)   24 **hand** handle   30–31 **no
drowning mark . . . gallows** (alluding to the proverb, "He that's born to
be hanged need fear no drowning")   33 **doth little advantage** gives us
little advantage   36 **Bring her to try with main course** heave to, under
the mainsail   37–38 **They are louder . . . office** these passengers make
more noise than the tempest or than we do at our work

Enter Sebastian, Antonio, and Gonzalo.

Yet again? What do you here? Shall we give o'er° 40
and drown? Have you a mind to sink?

Sebastian. A pox o' your throat, you bawling, blas-
phemous, incharitable dog!

Boatswain. Work you, then.

Antonio. Hang, cur! Hang, you whoreson, insolent
noisemaker! We are less afraid to be drowned than 45
thou art.

Gonzalo. I'll warrant him for° drowning, though the
ship were no stronger than a nutshell and as leaky
as an unstanched° wench.

Boatswain. Lay her ahold, ahold! Set her two 50
courses!° Off to sea again! Lay her off!°

Enter Mariners wet.

Mariners. All lost! To prayers, to prayers! All lost!
[*Exeunt.*]

Boatswain. What, must our mouths be cold?

Gonzalo. The King and Prince at prayers! Let's assist
them,
For our case is as theirs.

Sebastian.   I am out of patience. 55

Antonio. We are merely° cheated of our lives by
drunkards.
This wide-chopped° rascal—would thou mightst lie
drowning
The washing of ten tides!°

39 **give o'er** give up trying to run the ship   47 **warrant him for** guarantee him against   49 **unstanched** wide-open   50–51 **Lay her ahold. . . .
courses** (the ship is still being blown dangerously to shore, so the boatswain orders that the foresail be set in addition to the mainsail; but the
ship still moves toward shore)   51 **Lay her off** i.e., away from the
shore   56 **merely** completely   57 **wide-chopped** big-mouthed   58
ten tides (pirates were hanged on the shore and left there until three tides
had washed over them)

Gonzalo.   He'll be hanged yet,
  Though every drop of water swear against it
  And gape at wid'st to glut him.

60 *A confused noise within:* "Mercy on us!"
  "We split, we split!" "Farewell, my wife and chil-
    dren!"
  "Farewell, brother!" "We split, we split, we split!"
                                    [*Exit Boatswain.*]

Antonio. Let's all sink wi' th' King.

Sebastian.   Let's take leave of him.
                                    Exit [*with Antonio*].

Gonzalo. Now would I give a thousand furlongs of
65 sea for an acre of barren ground—long heath,°
  brown furze, anything. The wills above be done, but
  I would fain die a dry death.   *Exit.*

Scene 2. [*The island. In front of Prospero's cell.*]

Enter Prospero and Miranda.

Miranda. If by your art, my dearest father, you have
  Put the wild waters in this roar, allay them.
  The sky, it seems, would pour down stinking pitch
  But that the sea, mounting to th' welkin's cheek,°
5 Dashes the fire out. O, I have suffered
  With those that I saw suffer! A brave° vessel
  (Who had no doubt some noble creature in her)
  Dashed all to pieces! O, the cry did knock

65 **heath** heather   1.2.4 **welkin's cheek** face of the sky   6 **brave** fine,
gallant (the word often has this meaning in the play)

Against my very heart! Poor souls, they perished!
Had I been any god of power, I would   *10*
Have sunk the sea within the earth or ere
It should the good ship so have swallowed and
The fraughting° souls within her.

Prospero.   Be collected.
No more amazement.° Tell your piteous heart
There's no harm done.

Miranda.   O, woe the day!

Prospero.   No harm.   *15*
I have done nothing but in care of thee,
Of thee my dear one, thee my daughter, who
Art ignorant of what thou art, naught knowing
Of whence I am, nor that I am more better
Than Prospero, master of a full poor cell,   *20*
And thy no greater father.°

Miranda.   More to know
Did never meddle° with my thoughts.

Prospero.   'Tis time
I should inform thee farther. Lend thy hand
And pluck my magic garment from me. So.
                              [*Lays down his robe.*]
Lie there, my art. Wipe thou thine eyes; have
     comfort.   *25*
The direful spectacle of the wrack, which touched
The very virtue° of compassion in thee,
I have with such provision° in mine art
So safely ordered that there is no soul—
No, not so much perdition° as an hair   *30*
Betid° to any creature in the vessel
Which thou heard'st cry, which thou saw'st sink.
     Sit down;
For thou must now know farther.

13 **fraughting** forming her freight   14 **amazement** consternation   21 **thy no greater father** i.e., thy father, no greater than the Prospero just described   22 **meddle** mingle   27 **virtue** essence   28 **provision** foresight   30 **perdition** loss   31 **Betid** happened

Miranda.   You have often
  Begun to tell me what I am; but stopped
35 And left me to a bootless inquisition,
  Concluding, "Stay; not yet."

Prospero.   The hour's now come;
  The very minute bids thee ope thine ear.
  Obey, and be attentive. Canst thou remember
  A time before we came unto this cell?
40 I do not think thou canst, for then thou wast not
  Out° three years old.

Miranda.   Certainly, sir, I can.

Prospero. By what? By any other house or person?
  Of anything the image tell me that
  Hath kept with thy remembrance.

Miranda.   'Tis far off,
45 And rather like a dream than an assurance
  That my remembrance warrants.° Had I not
  Four or five women once that tended me?

Prospero. Thou hadst, and more, Miranda. But how
    is it
  That this lives in thy mind? What seest thou else
50 In the dark backward and abysm of time?
  If thou rememb'rest aught ere thou cam'st here,
  How thou cam'st here thou mayst.

Miranda.   But that I do not.

Prospero. Twelve year since, Miranda, twelve year
    since,
  Thy father was the Duke of Milan° and
  A prince of power.

55 *Miranda.*   Sir, are not you my father?

Prospero. Thy mother was a piece° of virtue, and
  She said thou wast my daughter; and thy father
  Was Duke of Milan; and his only heir

41 **Out** fully   46 **remembrance warrants** memory guarantees   54
Milan (pronounced "Mílan")   56 **piece** masterpiece

And princess, no worse issued.°

Miranda.   O the heavens!
What foul play had we that we came from thence?   60
Or blessèd was't we did?

Prospero.   Both, both, my girl!
By foul play, as thou say'st, were we heaved thence,
But blessedly holp° hither.

Miranda.   O, my heart bleeds
To think o' th' teen that I have turned you to,°
Which is from° my remembrance! Please you,
    farther.   65

Prospero. My brother and thy uncle, called
        Antonio—
I pray thee mark me—that a brother should
Be so perfidious!—he whom next thyself
Of all the world I loved, and to him put
The manage of my state,° as at that time   70
Through all the signories° it was the first,
And Prospero the prime duke, being so reputed
In dignity, and for the liberal arts
Without a parallel. Those being all my study,
The government I cast upon my brother   75
And to my state grew stranger, being transported
And rapt in secret studies. Thy false uncle—
Dost thou attend me?

Miranda.   Sir, most heedfully.

Prospero. Being once perfected° how to grant suits,
How to deny them, who t' advance, and who   80
To trash for overtopping,° new-created
The creatures that were mine, I say—or changed
    'em,

59 **no worse issued** of no meaner lineage than he   63 **holp** helped
64 **teen that I have turned you to** sorrow I have caused you to
remember   65 **from** out of   70 **manage of my state** management of
my domain   71 **signories** lordships (of Italy)   79 **perfected** grown
skillful   81 **trash for overtopping** (1) check the speed of (as of hounds)
(2) cut down to size (as of overtall trees) the aspirants for political favor
who are growing too bold

Or else new-formed 'em°—having both the key°
Of officer and office, set all hearts i' th' state
85   To what tune pleased his ear, that now he was
The ivy which had hid my princely trunk
And sucked my verdure out on't. Thou attend'st
      not?

Miranda. O, good sir, I do.

Prospero.   I pray thee mark me.
I thus neglecting worldly ends, all dedicated
90   To closeness° and the bettering of my mind—
With that which, but by being so retired,
O'erprized all popular rate, in my false brother
Awaked an evil nature,° and my trust,
Like a good parent,° did beget of him
95   A falsehood in its contrary as great
As my trust was, which had indeed no limit,
A confidence sans bound. He being thus lorded—
Not only with what my revenue° yielded
But what my power might else exact, like one
100 Who having into truth—by telling of it,°
Made such a sinner of his memory
To° credit his own lie, he did believe
He was indeed the Duke, out o' th' substitution
And executing th' outward face of royalty
With all prerogative.° Hence his ambition
105   growing—
Dost thou hear?

81–83 **new-created/The creatures . . . new-formed 'em** i.e., he recre-
ated my following—either exchanging my adherents for his own, or else
transforming my adherents into different people   83 **key** (a pun leading to the musical metaphor)   90 **closeness** seclusion   91–93 **With
that . . . evil nature** i.e., with that dedication to the mind which, were it
not that it kept me from exercising the duties of my office would surpass
in value all ordinary estimate, I awakened evil in my brother's nature
94 **good parent** (alluding to the proverb cited by Miranda in line
120)   98 **revenue** (pronounced "rèvènue")   99–100 **like one/Who
having . . . of it** i.e., like one who really had these things—by repeatedly
saying he had them (*into* = unto)   102 **To** as to   103–05 **out o' th' substitution . . . all prerogative** i.e., as a result of his acting as my substitute
and performing the outward functions of royalty with all its prerogatives

Miranda.   Your tale, sir, would cure deafness.

Prospero. To have no screen between this part he
    played
  And him he played it for, he needs will be
  Absolute Milan.° Me (poor man) my library
  Was dukedom large enough. Of temporal royalties   *110*
  He thinks me now incapable; confederates
  (So dry° he was for sway) wi' th' King of Naples
  To give him annual tribute, do him homage,
  Subject his coronet to his crown, and bend
  The dukedom, yet unbowed (alas, poor Milan!),   *115*
  To most ignoble stooping.

Miranda.   O the heavens!

Prospero. Mark his condition,° and th' event;° then
    tell me
  If this might be a brother.

Miranda.   I should sin
  To think but nobly of my grandmother.
  Good wombs have borne bad sons.

Prospero.   Now the condition. *120*
  This King of Naples, being an enemy
  To me inveterate, hearkens my brother's suit;
  Which was, that he, in lieu o' th' premises°
  Of homage and I know not how much tribute,
  Should presently extirpate me and mine   *125*
  Out of the dukedom and confer fair Milan,
  With all the honors, on my brother. Whereon,
  A treacherous army levied, one midnight
  Fated to th' purpose, did Antonio open
  The gates of Milan; and, i' th' dead of darkness,   *130*
  The ministers° for th' purpose hurried thence
  Me and thy crying self.

Miranda.   Alack, for pity!

109 **Absolute Milan** Duke of Milan in fact 112 **dry** thirsty
117 **condition** terms of his pact with Naples 117 **event** outcome
123 **in lieu o' th' premises** in return for the guarantees 131 **ministers**
agents

I, not rememb'ring how I cried out then,
Will cry it o'er again; it is a hint°
That wrings mine eyes to't.

135 *Prospero.*   Hear a little further,
And then I'll bring thee to the present business
Which now's upon's; without the which this story
Were most impertinent.°

Miranda.   Wherefore did they not
That hour destroy us?

Prospero.   Well demanded, wench.
My tale provokes that question. Dear, they durst
140 not,
So dear the love my people bore me; nor set
A mark so bloody on the business; but,
With colors fairer, painted their foul ends.
In few,° they hurried us aboard a bark;
145 Bore us some leagues to sea, where they prepared
A rotten carcass of a butt,° not rigged,
Nor tackle, sail, nor mast; the very rats
Instinctively have quit it. There they hoist us,
To cry to th' sea that roared to us; to sigh
150 To th' winds, whose pity, sighing back again,
Did us but loving wrong.

Miranda.   Alack, what trouble
Was I then to you!

Prospero.   O, a cherubin
Thou wast that did preserve me! Thou didst smile,
Infusèd with a fortitude from heaven,
155 When I have decked° the sea with drops full salt,
Under my burden groaned; which° raised in me
An undergoing stomach,° to bear up
Against what should ensue.

Miranda.   How came we ashore?

---

134 **hint** occasion   138 **impertinent** inappropriate   144 **few** few words
146 **butt** tub   155 **decked** covered (wept salt tears into the sea)
156 **which** i.e., Miranda's smile   157 **undergoing stomach** spirit of en-
durance

Prospero. By providence divine.
  Some food we had, and some fresh water, that   160
  A noble Neapolitan, Gonzalo,
  Out of his charity, who being then appointed
  Master of this design, did give us, with
  Rich garments, linens, stuffs, and necessaries
  Which since have steaded° much. So, of his gentle-
    ness,   165
  Knowing I loved my books, he furnished me
  From mine own library with volumes that
  I prize above my dukedom.

Miranda.   Would I might
  But ever see that man!

Prospero.   Now I arise.
  Sit still, and hear the last of our sea sorrow.   170
  Here in this island we arrived; and here
  Have I, thy schoolmaster, made thee more profit
  Than other princess' can,° that have more time
  For vainer hours, and tutors not so careful.

Miranda. Heavens thank you for't! And now I pray
    you, sir—   175
  For still 'tis beating in my mind—your reason
  For raising this sea storm?

Prospero.   Know thus far forth.
  By accident most strange, bountiful Fortune
  (Now my dear lady)° hath mine enemies
  Brought to this shore; and by my prescience   180
  I find my zenith° doth depend upon
  A most auspicious star, whose influence
  If now I court not, but omit,° my fortunes
  Will ever after droop. Here cease more questions.
  Thou art inclined to sleep. 'Tis a good dullness,   185
  And give it way. I know thou canst not choose.
                            [*Miranda sleeps.*]

---

165 **steaded** been of use   173 **princess' can** princesses can have
179 **Now my dear lady** i.e., formerly my foe, now my patroness
181 **zenith** apex of fortune   183 **omit** neglect

Come away,° servant, come! I am ready now.
Approach, my Ariel! Come!

Enter Ariel.

Ariel. All hail, great master! Grave sir, hail! I come
190 To answer thy best pleasure; be't to fly,
To swim, to dive into the fire, to ride
On the curled clouds. To thy strong bidding task°
Ariel and all his quality.°

Prospero.   Hath thou, spirit,
Performed, to point,° the tempest that I bade thee?

195 *Ariel.* To every article.
I boarded the King's ship. Now on the beak,°
Now in the waist,° the deck,° in every cabin,
I flamed amazement.° Sometime I'd divide
And burn in many places; on the topmast,
200 The yards, and boresprit° would I flame distinctly,°
Then meet and join. Jove's lightnings, the precursors
O' th' dreadful thunderclaps, more momentary
And sight-outrunning were not. The fire and cracks
Of sulfurous roaring the most mighty Neptune
205 Seem to besiege, and make his bold waves tremble;
Yea, his dread trident shake.

Prospero.   My brave spirit!
Who was so firm, so constant, that this coil°
Would not infect his reason?

Ariel.   Not a soul
But felt a fever of the mad and played
210 Some tricks of desperation. All but mariners
Plunged in the foaming brine and quit the vessel,
Then all afire with me. The King's son Ferdinand,

187 **Come away** i.e., come from where you are; come here   192 **task** tax
to the utmost   193 **quality** cohorts (Ariel is leader of a band of spirits)
194 **to point** in every detail   196 **beak** prow   197 **waist** amidships
197 **deck** poop   198 **flamed amazement** struck terror by appearing as
(St. Elmo's) fire   200 **boresprit** bowsprit   200 **distinctly** in different
places   207 **coil** uproar

With hair up-staring° (then like reeds, not hair),
Was the first man that leapt; cried "Hell is empty,
And all the devils are here!"

Prospero.   Why, that's my spirit! 215
But was not this nigh shore?

Ariel.   Close by, my master.

Prospero. But are they, Ariel, safe?

Ariel.   Not a hair perished.
On their sustaining° garments not a blemish,
But fresher than before; and as thou bad'st me,
In troops I have dispersed them 'bout the isle.   220
The King's son have I landed by himself,
Whom I left cooling of the air with sighs
In an odd angle of the isle, and sitting,
His arms in this sad knot.

                [Illustrates with a gesture.]

Prospero.   Of the King's ship,
The mariners, say how thou hast disposed,   225
And all the rest o' th' fleet.

Ariel.   Safely in harbor
Is the King's ship; in the deep nook where once
Thou call'dst me up at midnight to fetch dew
From the still-vexed Bermoothes,° there she's hid;
The mariners all under hatches stowed,   230
Who, with a charm joined to their suff'red° labor,
I have left asleep. And for the rest o' th' fleet,
Which I dispersed, they all have met again,
And are upon the Mediterranean flote°
Bound sadly home for Naples,   235
Supposing that they saw the King's ship wracked
And his great person perish.

Prospero.   Ariel, thy charge
Exactly is performed; but there's more work.

---

213 **up-staring** standing on end 218 **sustaining** buoying them up
229 **Bermoothes** Bermudas 231 **suff'red** undergone 234 **flote** sea

What is the time o' th' day?

Ariel.   Past the mid season.°

Prospero. At least two glasses.° The time 'twixt six
240   and now
Must by us both be spent most preciously.

Ariel. Is there more toil? Since thou dost give me
        pains,°
Let me remember° thee what thou hast promised,
Which is not yet performed me.

Prospero.   How now? Moody?
What is't thou canst demand?

245 *Ariel.*   My liberty.

Prospero. Before the time be out? No more!

Ariel.   I prithee,
Remember I have done thee worthy service,
Told thee no lies, made thee no mistakings, served
Without or grudge or grumblings. Thou did
        promise
To bate me° a full year.

250 *Prospero.*   Dost thou forget
From what a torment I did free thee?

Ariel.   No.

Prospero. Thou dost; and think'st it much to tread
        the ooze
Of the salt deep,
To run upon the sharp wind of the North,
255   To do me business in the veins° o' th' earth
When it is baked° with frost.

Ariel.   I do not, sir.

Prospero. Thou liest, malignant thing! Hast thou
        forgot

---

239 mid season noon **240 two glasses** two o'clock **242 pains** hard
tasks **243 remember** remind **250 bate me** reduce my term of
service **255 veins** streams **256 baked** caked

The foul witch Sycorax,° who with age and envy°
Was grown into a hoop? Hast thou forgot her?

Ariel. No, sir.

Prospero.   Thou hast. Where was she born? Speak!
    Tell me!   260

Ariel. Sir, in Argier.°

Prospero.   O, was she so? I must
    Once in a month recount what thou hast been,
    Which thou forget'st. This damned witch Sycorax,
    For mischiefs manifold, and sorceries terrible
    To enter human hearing, from Argier,   265
    Thou know'st, was banished. For one thing she did
    They would not take her life. Is not this true?

Ariel. Ay, sir.

Prospero. This blue-eyed° hag was hither brought
    with child
    And here was left by th' sailors. Thou, my slave,   270
    As thou report'st thyself, wast then her servant.
    And, for thou wast a spirit too delicate
    To act her earthy and abhorred commands,
    Refusing her grand hests,° she did confine thee,
    By help of her more potent ministers,°   275
    And in her most unmitigable rage,
    Into a cloven pine; within which rift
    Imprisoned thou didst painfully remain
    A dozen years; within which space she died
    And left thee there, where thou didst vent thy
    groans   280
    As fast as millwheels strike. Then was this island
    (Save for the son that she did litter here,
    A freckled whelp, hagborn) not honored with
    A human shape.

---

258 **Sycorax** (name not found elsewhere; probably derived from Greek
sys, "sow," and *korax*, which means both "raven"—see line 322—and
"hook"—hence perhaps "hoop")   258 **envy** malice   261 **Argier** Algiers   269 **blue-eyed** (referring to the livid color of the eyelid, a sign of
pregnancy)   274 **hests** commands   275 **her more potent ministers**
her agents, spirits more powerful than thou

Ariel.   Yes, Caliban her son.

285 *Prospero.* Dull thing, I say so! He, that Caliban
      Whom now I keep in service. Thou best know'st
      What torment I did find thee in; thy groans
      Did make wolves howl and penetrate the breasts
      Of ever-angry bears. It was a torment
290 To lay upon the damned, which Sycorax
      Could not again undo. It was mine art,
      When I arrived and heard thee, that made gape
      The pine, and let thee out.

Ariel.   I thank thee, master.

Prospero. If thou more murmur'st, I will rend an oak
295 And peg thee in his° knotty entrails till
      Thou hast howled away twelve winters.

Ariel.   Pardon, master.
      I will be correspondent° to command
      And do my spriting gently.°

Prospero.   Do so; and after two days
      I will discharge thee.

Ariel.   That's my noble master!
300 What shall I do? Say what? What shall I do?

Prospero. Go make thyself like a nymph o' th' sea. Be
      subject
      To no sight but thine and mine, invisible
      To every eyeball else.° Go take this shape
      And hither come in't. Go! Hence with diligence!
                                        Exit [Ariel].
305 Awake, dear heart, awake! Thou hast slept well.
      Awake!

Miranda. The strangeness of your story put
      Heaviness in me.

295 **his** its   297 **correspondent** obedient   298 **do my spriting gently**
render graciously my services as a spirit   302–03 **invisible/ To every
eyeball else** (Ariel is invisible to everyone in the play except Prospero;
Henslowe's *Diary,* an Elizabethan stage account, lists "a robe for to go
invisible")

Prospero.   Shake it off. Come on.
  We'll visit Caliban, my slave, who never
  Yields us kind answer.

Miranda.   'Tis a villain, sir,
  I do not love to look on.

Prospero.   But as 'tis,   *310*
  We cannot miss° him. He does make our fire,
  Fetch in our wood, and serves in offices
  That profit us. What, ho! Slave! Caliban!
  Thou earth, thou! Speak!

Caliban. (Within)   There's wood enough within.

Prospero. Come forth, I say! There's other business *315*
    for thee.
  Come, thou tortoise! When?°

            Enter Ariel like a water nymph.

  Fine apparition! My quaint° Ariel,
  Hark in thine ear.   *[Whispers.]*

Ariel.   My lord, it shall be done. *Exit.*

Prospero. Thou poisonous slave, got by the devil
    himself
  Upon thy wicked dam, come forth!   *320*

                Enter Caliban.

Caliban. As wicked dew as e'er my mother brushed
  With raven's feather from unwholesome fen
  Drop on you both! A southwest blow on ye
  And blister you all o'er!

Prospero. For this, be sure, tonight thou shalt have
    cramps,   *325*
  Side-stitches that shall pen thy breath up. Urchins°
  Shall, for that vast of night that they may work,°

---

311 **miss** do without   316 **When** (expression of impatience) 317 **quaint**
ingenious   326 **Urchins** goblins in the shape of hedgehogs   327 **vast
of night . . . work** (the long, empty stretch of night during which malignant spirits are allowed to be active)

All exercise on thee; thou shalt be pinched
As thick as honeycomb, each pinch more stinging
Than bees that made 'em.

330 *Caliban.*   I must eat my dinner.
This island's mine by Sycorax my mother,
Which thou tak'st from me. When thou cam'st first,
Thou strok'st me and made much of me; wouldst give me
Water with berries in't; and teach me how
335 To name the bigger light, and how the less,
That burn by day and night. And then I loved thee
And showed thee all the qualities o' th' isle,
The fresh springs, brine pits, barren place and fertile.
Cursed be I that did so! All the charms
340 Of Sycorax—toads, beetles, bats, light on you!
For I am all the subjects that you have,
Which first was mine own king; and here you sty me
In this hard rock, whiles you do keep from me
The rest o' th' island.

Prospero.   Thou most lying slave,
Whom stripes° may move, not kindness! I have
345   used thee
(Filth as thou art) with humane care, and lodged thee
In mine own cell till thou didst seek to violate
The honor of my child.

Caliban. O ho, O ho! Would't had been done!
350 Thou didst prevent me; I had peopled else
This isle with Calibans.

Miranda.°   Abhorrèd slave,
Which any print of goodness wilt not take,
Being capable of all ill!° I pitied thee,

---

345 **stripes** lashes   351 (many editors transfer this speech to Prospero
as inappropriate to Miranda)   353 **capable of all ill** susceptible only to
evil impressions

Took pains to make thee speak, taught thee each
  hour
One thing or other. When thou didst not, savage,   *355*
Know thine own meaning, but wouldst gabble like
A thing most brutish, I endowed thy purposes
With words that made them known. But thy vile
  race,
Though thou didst learn, had that in't which good
  natures
Could not abide to be with. Therefore wast thou   *360*
Deservedly confined into this rock, who hadst
Deserved more than a prison.

Caliban. You taught me language, and my profit on't
Is, I know how to curse. The red plague rid° you
For learning me your language!

Prospero.   Hagseed, hence!   *365*
Fetch us in fuel. And be quick, thou'rt best,°
To answer other business. Shrug'st thou, malice?
If thou neglect'st or dost unwillingly
What I command, I'll rack thee with old° cramps,
Fill all thy bones with aches,° make thee roar   *370*
That beasts shall tremble at thy din.

Caliban.   No, pray thee.
[*Aside*] I must obey. His art is of such pow'r
It would control my dam's god, Setebos,
And make a vassal of him.

Prospero.   So, slave; hence!   *Exit Caliban.*

*Enter Ferdinand; and Ariel (invisible), playing
  and singing.*

Ariel's song.

Come unto these yellow sands,   *375*

---

364 **rid** destroy   366 **thou'rt best** you'd better   369 **old** plenty of
(with an additional suggestion, "such as old people have")   370 **aches**
(pronounced "aitches")

And then take hands.
                Curtsied when you have and kissed
                    The wild waves whist,°
                Foot it featly° here and there;
380   And, sweet sprites, the burden bear.
                Hark, hark!
                    Burden, dispersedly.° Bow, wow!
                The watchdogs bark.
                    [*Burden, dispersedly.*] Bow, wow!
385   Hark, hark! I hear
                The strain of strutting chanticleer
                    Cry cock-a-diddle-dow.

Ferdinand. Where should this music be? I' th' air or
            th' earth?
            It sounds no more; and sure it waits upon
390   Some god o' th' island. Sitting on a bank,
            Weeping again the King my father's wrack,
            This music crept by me upon the waters,
            Allaying both their fury and my passion°
            With its sweet air. Thence I have followed it,
395   Or it hath drawn me rather; but 'tis gone.
            No, it begins again.

Ariel's song.

            Full fathom five thy father lies;
                Of his bones are coral made;
            Those are pearls that were his eyes;
400   Nothing of him that doth fade
            But doth suffer a sea change
            Into something rich and strange.
            Sea nymphs hourly ring his knell:
                            Burden. Ding-dong.
405   Hark! Now I hear them—ding-dong bell.

377–78 **kissed/The wild waves whist** i.e., when you have, through the
harmony of kissing in the dance, kissed the wild waves into silence (?);
when you have kissed in the dance, the wild waves being silenced (?)
379 **featly** nimbly   382 **Burden, dispersedly** (an undersong, coming
from all parts of the stage; it imitates the barking of dogs and perhaps in
the end the crowing of a cock)   393 **passion** grief

Ferdinand. The ditty does remember my drowned
    father.
  This is no mortal business, nor no sound
  That the earth owes.° I hear it now above me.

Prospero. The fringèd curtains of thine eye advance°
  And say what thou seest yond.

Miranda.   What is't? A spirit? *410*
  Lord, how it looks about! Believe me, sir,
  It carries a brave form. But 'tis a spirit.

Prospero. No, wench; it eats, and sleeps, and hath
    such senses
  As we have, such. This gallant which thou seest
  Was in the wrack; and, but he's something stained *415*
  With grief (that's beauty's canker), thou mightst
    call him
  A goodly person. He hath lost his fellows
  And strays about to find 'em.

Miranda.   I might call him
  A thing divine; for nothing natural
  I ever saw so noble.

Prospero.   [*Aside*] It goes on, I see,   *420*
  As my soul prompts it. Spirit, fine spirit, I'll free
    thee
  Within two days for this.

Ferdinand.   Most sure, the goddess
  On whom these airs attend! Vouchsafe my prayer
  May know if you remain° upon this island,
  And that you will some good instruction give   *425*
  How I may bear me° here. My prime request,
  Which I do last pronounce, is (O you wonder!)
  If you be maid or no?

Miranda.   No wonder, sir,
  But certainly a maid.

408 **owes** owns   409 **advance** raise   423–24 **Vouchsafe my prayer . . .
remain** may my prayer induce you to inform me whether you dwell
426 **bear me** conduct myself

Ferdinand.   My language? Heavens!
430   I am the best of them that speak this speech,
        Were I but where 'tis spoken.

Prospero.   How? The best?
        What wert thou if the King of Naples heard thee?

Ferdinand. A single° thing, as I am now, that won-
        ders
        To hear thee speak of Naples. He does hear me;
435   And that he does I weep. Myself am Naples,
        Who with mine eyes, never since at ebb, beheld
        The King my father wracked.

Miranda.   Alack, for mercy!

Ferdinand. Yes, faith, and all his lords, the Duke of
        Milan
        And his brave son° being twain.°

Prospero.   [*Aside*] The Duke of Milan
440   And his more braver daughter could control° thee,
        If now 'twere fit to do't. At the first sight
        They have changed eyes.° Delicate Ariel,
        I'll set thee free for this. [*To Ferdinand*] A word,
        good sir.
        I fear you have done yourself some wrong.° A
        word!

445 *Miranda.* Why speaks my father so ungently? This
        Is the third man that e'er I saw; the first
        That e'er I sighed for. Pity move my father
        To be inclined my way!

Ferdinand.   O, if a virgin,
        And your affection not gone forth, I'll make you
        The Queen of Naples.

450 *Prospero.*   Soft, sir! One word more.
        [*Aside*] They are both in either's pow'rs. But this
            swift business

433 **single** (1) solitary (2) helpless   439 **son** (the only time Antonio's
son is mentioned)   439 **twain** two (of these lords)   440 **control** refute
442 **changed eyes** i.e., fallen in love   444 **done yourself some wrong**
said what is not so

I must uneasy make, lest too light winning
Make the prize light. [*To Ferdinand*] One word
    more! I charge thee
That thou attend me. Thou dost here usurp
The name thou ow'st° not, and hast put thyself   455
Upon this island as a spy, to win it
From me, the lord on't.

Ferdinand.   No, as I am a man!

Miranda. There's nothing ill can dwell in such a
    temple.
If the ill spirit have so fair a house,
Good things will strive to dwell with't.

Prospero.   Follow me.   460
[*To Miranda*] Speak not you for him; he's a traitor.
    [*To Ferdinand*] Come!
I'll manacle thy neck and feet together;
Sea water shalt thou drink; thy food shall be
The fresh-brook mussels, withered roots, and husks
Wherein the acorn cradled. Follow!

Ferdinand.   No.   465
I will resist such entertainment till
Mine enemy has more pow'r.
            He draws, and is charmed from moving.

Miranda.   O dear father,
Make not too rash a trial of him, for
He's gentle and not fearful.°

Prospero.   What, I say,
My foot my tutor?° [*To Ferdinand*] Put thy sword
    up, traitor—   470
Who mak'st a show but dar'st not strike, thy con-
    science
Is so possessed with guilt! Come, from thy ward!°
For I can here disarm thee with this stick°
And make thy weapon drop.

---

455 **ow'st** ownest   469 **gentle and not fearful** of noble birth and no
coward   470 **My foot my tutor** am I to be instructed by my inferior
472 **ward** fighting posture   473 **stick** i.e., his wand

Miranda.   Beseech you, father!

Prospero. Hence! Hang not on my garments.

475 *Miranda.*   Sir, have pity.
  I'll be his surety.

Prospero.   Silence! One word more
  Shall make me chide thee, if not hate thee. What,
  An advocate for an impostor? Hush!
  Thou think'st there is no more such shapes as he,
480 Having seen but him and Caliban. Foolish wench!
  To th' most of men this is a Caliban,
  And they to him are angels.

Miranda.   My affections
  Are then most humble. I have no ambition
  To see a goodlier man.

Prospero. [*To Ferdinand*] Come on, obey!
485 Thy nerves° are in their infancy again
  And have no vigor in them.

Ferdinand.   So they are.
  My spirits, as in a dream, are all bound up.
  My father's loss, the weakness which I feel,
  The wrack of all my friends, nor this man's threats
490 To whom I am subdued, are but light to me,
  Might I but through my prison once a day
  Behold this maid. All corners else o' th' earth
  Let liberty make use of. Space enough
  Have I in such a prison.

Prospero. [*Aside*] It works. [*To Ferdinand*] Come on.
  [*To Ariel*] Thou hast done well, fine Ariel! [*To*
495   *Ferdinand*] Follow me.
  [*To Ariel*] Hark what thou else shalt do me.

Miranda.   Be of comfort.
  My father's of a better nature, sir,
  Than he appears by speech. This is unwonted
  Which now came from him.

485 **nerves** sinews

Prospero.   Thou shalt be as free
  As mountain winds; but then° exactly do   *500*
  All points of my command.

Ariel.   To th' syllable.

Prospero. [*To Ferdinand*] Come, follow. [*To Miranda*] Speak not for him.   *Exeunt.*

ACT 2

Scene 1. [*Another part of the island.*]

*Enter Alonso, Sebastian, Antonio, Gonzalo,
  Adrian, Francisco, and others.*

Gonzalo. Beseech you, sir, be merry. You have cause
  (So have we all) of joy; for our escape
  Is much beyond our loss. Our hint of° woe
  Is common; every day some sailor's wife,
  The master of some merchant,° and the merchant,   *5*
  Have just our theme of woe. But for the miracle,
  I mean our preservation, few in millions
  Can speak like us. Then wisely, good sir, weigh
  Our sorrow with° our comfort.

Alonso.   Prithee, peace.

Sebastian. [*Aside to Antonio*] He receives comfort   *10*
  like cold porridge.°

Antonio. [*Aside to Sebastian*] The visitor° will not
  give him o'er so.°

Sebastian. Look, he's winding up the watch of his
  wit; by and by it will strike.   *15*

---

500 **then** till then   2.1.3 **hint of** occasion for   5 **master of some merchant** captain of some merchant ship   9 **with** against   10–11 **He receives comfort like cold porridge** ("He" is Alonso; pun on "peace,"
since porridge contained peas)   12 **visitor** spiritual comforter   13 **give
him o'er so** release him so easily

Gonzalo. Sir—

Sebastian. [*Aside to Antonio*] One. Tell.°

Gonzalo. When every grief is entertained, that's°
   offered
   Comes to th' entertainer—

20 *Sebastian.* A dollar.

Gonzalo. Dolor comes to him, indeed. You have
   spoken truer than you purposed.

Sebastian. You have taken it wiselier° than I meant
   you should.

25 *Gonzalo.* Therefore, my lord—

Antonio. Fie, what a spendthrift is he of his tongue!

Alonso. I prithee, spare.°

Gonzalo. Well, I have done. But yet—

Sebastian. He will be talking.

30 *Antonio.* Which, of he or Adrian, for a good wager,
   first° begins to crow?

Sebastian. The old cock.°

Antonio. The cock'rel.°

Sebastian. Done! The wager?

35 *Antonio.* A laughter.°

Sebastian. A match!

Adrian. Though this island seem to be desert—

Antonio. Ha, ha, ha!

Sebastian. So, you're paid.

17 **One. Tell** he has struck one; keep count 18 **that's** that which
is 23 **wiselier** i.e., understood my pun 27 **spare** spare your words
30–31 **Which, of he or Adrian . . . first** let's wager which of the two,
Gonzalo or Adrian, will first 32 **old cock** i.e., Gonzalo 33 **cock'rel**
young cock; i.e., Adrian 35 **laughter** the winner will have the laugh on
the loser

Adrian. Uninhabitable and almost inaccessible—   40

Sebastian. Yet—

Adrian. Yet—

Antonio. He could not miss't.

Adrian. It must needs be of subtle, tender, and delicate temperance.°   45

Antonio. Temperance was a delicate wench.

Sebastian. Ay, and a subtle, as he most learnedly
delivered.

Adrian. The air breathes upon us here most sweetly.

Sebastian. As if it had lungs, and rotten ones.   50

Antonio. Or as 'twere perfumed by a fen.

Gonzalo. Here is everything advantageous to life.

Antonio. True; save means to live.

Sebastian. Of that there's none, or little.

Gonzalo. How lush and lusty the grass looks! How   55
green!

Antonio. The ground indeed is tawny.

Sebastian. With an eye° of green in't.

Antonio. He misses not much.

Sebastian. No; he doth but mistake the truth totally.   60

Gonzalo. But the rarity of it is—which is indeed almost beyond credit—

Sebastian. As many vouched rarities are.

Gonzalo. That our garments, being, as they were,
drenched in the sea, hold, notwithstanding, their   65
freshness and glosses, being rather new-dyed than
stained with salt water.

---

45 **temperance** climate (in the next line, a girl's name)   58 **eye** spot
(also perhaps Gonzalo's eye)

   Antonio. If but one of his pockets could speak,
      would it not say he lies?°

70 *Sebastian*. Ay, or very falsely pocket up his report.°

   Gonzalo. Methinks our garments are now as fresh as
      when we put them on first in Afric, at the marriage
      of the King's fair daughter Claribel to the King of
      Tunis.

75 *Sebastian*. 'Twas a sweet marriage, and we prosper
      well in our return.

   Adrian. Tunis was never graced before with such a
      paragon to° their queen.

   Gonzalo. Not since widow Dido's time.

80 *Antonio*. Widow? A pox o' that! How came that
      "widow" in? Widow Dido!

   Sebastian. What if he had said "widower Aeneas"°
      too? Good Lord, how you take it!

   Adrian. "Widow Dido," said you? You make me
85   study of that. She was of Carthage, not of Tunis.

   Gonzalo. This Tunis, sir, was Carthage.

   Adrian. Carthage?

   Gonzalo. I assure you, Carthage.

   Antonio. His word is more than the miraculous
90   harp.°

   Sebastian. He hath raised the wall and houses too.

   Antonio. What impossible matter will he make easy
      next?

68–69 **If but ... he lies** i.e., the inside of Gonzalo's pockets are
stained   70 **Ay, or ... his report** unless the pocket were, like a false
knave, to receive without resentment the imputation that it is unstained
78 **to** for   81–82 **Widow Dido ... "widower Aeneas"** (the point of the
joke is that Dido was a widow, but one doesn't ordinarily think of her that
way; and the same with Aeneas)   89–90 **miraculous harp** (of Amphion,
which only raised the *walls* of Thebes; whereas Gonzalo has rebuilt the
whole ancient city of Carthage by identifying it mistakenly with modern
Tunis)

Sebastian. I think he will carry this island home in his
pocket and give it his son for an apple.   95

Antonio. And, sowing the kernels of it in the sea,
bring forth more islands.

Gonzalo. Ay!

Antonio. Why, in good time.°

Gonzalo. [*To Alonso*] Sir, we were talking that our   100
garments seem now as fresh as when we were at
Tunis at the marriage of your daughter, who is now
Queen.

Antonio. And the rarest that e'er came there.

Sebastian. Bate,° I beseech you, widow Dido.   105

Antonio. O, widow Dido? Ay, widow Dido!

Gonzalo. Is not, sir, my doublet as fresh as the first
day I wore it? I mean, in a sort.°

Antonio. That "sort" was well fished for.

Gonzalo. When I wore it at your daughter's marriage.   110

Alonso. You cram these words into mine ears against
The stomach of my sense.° Would I had never
Married my daughter there! For, coming thence,
My son is lost; and, in my rate,° she too,
Who is so far from Italy removed   115
I ne'er again shall see her. O thou mine heir
Of Naples and of Milan, what strange fish
Hath made his meal on thee?

Francisco.   Sir, he may live.
I saw him beat the surges under him
And ride upon their backs. He trod the water,   120
Whose enmity he flung aside, and breasted

99 **Why, in good time** (hearing Gonzalo reaffirm his false statement
about Tunis and Carthage, Antonio suggests that Gonzalo will indeed, at
the first opportunity, carry this island home in his pocket)   105 **Bate**
except   108 **in a sort** so to speak   111–12 **against/ The stomach of
my sense** i.e., though my mind (or feelings) have no appetite for them
114 **rate** opinion

The surge most swol'n that met him. His bold head
'Bove the contentious waves he kept, and oared
Himself with his good arms in lusty stroke
To th' shore, that o'er his° wave-worn basis
125   bowed,°
As stooping to relieve him. I not doubt
He came alive to land.

Alonso.   No, no, he's gone.

Sebastian. [*To Alonso*] Sir, you may thank yourself for
    this great loss,
That would not bless our Europe with your
    daughter,
130 But rather loose her to an African,
Where she, at least, is banished from your eye
Who hath cause to wet the grief on't.

Alonso.   Prithee, peace.

Sebastian. You were kneeled to and importuned
    otherwise
By all of us; and the fair soul herself
135 Weighed, between loathness and obedience, at
Which end o' th' beam should bow.° We have lost
    your son,
I fear, forever. Milan and Naples have
Moe° widows in them of this business' making
Than we bring men to comfort them.
The fault's your own.

140 Alonso.   So is the dear'st° o' th' loss.

Gonzalo. My Lord Sebastian,
The truth you speak doth lack some gentleness,
And time to speak it in. You rub the sore
When you should bring the plaster.

Sebastian.   Very well.

125 **his** its   125 **wave-worn basis bowed** (the image is of a guardian
cliff on the shore)   135–36 **Weighed, between . . . should bow** (Claribel's unwillingness to marry was outweighed by her obedience to her
father)   138 **Moe** more   140 **dear'st** (intensifies the meaning of the
noun)

Antonio. And most chirurgeonly.°   *145*

Gonzalo. [*To Alonso*] It is foul weather in us all, good sir,
When you are cloudy.

Sebastian. [*Aside to Antonio*] Foul weather?

Antonio. [*Aside to Sebastian*]   Very foul.

Gonzalo. Had I plantation° of this isle, my lord—

Antonio. He'd sow't with nettle seed.

Sebastian.   Or docks, or mallows.

Gonzalo. And were the king on't, what would I do?   *150*

Sebastian. Scape being drunk for want of wine.

Gonzalo. I' th' commonwealth I would by contraries°
Execute all things. For no kind of traffic°
Would I admit; no name of magistrate;
Letters° should not be known; riches, poverty,   *155*
And use of service,° none; contract, succession,°
Bourn,° bound of land, tilth,° vineyard, none;
No use of metal, corn, or wine, or oil;
No occupation; all men idle, all;
And women too, but innocent and pure;   *160*
No sovereignty.

Sebastian.   Yet he would be king on't.

Antonio. The latter end of his commonwealth forgets
the beginning.

Gonzalo. All things in common nature should produce
Without sweat or endeavor. Treason, felony,   *165*
Sword, pike, knife, gun, or need of any engine°
Would I not have; but nature should bring forth,
Of it° own kind, all foison,° all abundance,

---

145 **chirurgeonly** like a surgeon   148 **plantation** colonization (Antonio then puns by taking the word in its other sense)   152 **contraries** in contrast to the usual customs   153 **traffic** trade   155 **Letters** learning 156 **service** servants   156 **succession** inheritance 157 **Bourn** boundary 157 **tilth** agriculture   166 **engine** weapon   168 **it** its   168 **foison** abundance

To feed my innocent people.

170 *Sebastian.* No marrying 'mong his subjects?

Antonio. None, man, all idle—whores and knaves.

Gonzalo. I would with such perfection govern, sir,
T' excel the Golden Age.

Sebastian. [*Loudly*]   Save his Majesty!

Antonio. [*Loudly*] Long live Gonzalo!

Gonzalo.   And—do you mark me, sir?

Alonso. Prithee, no more. Thou dost talk nothing to
175 me.

Gonzalo. I do well believe your Highness; and did
it to minister occasion° to these gentlemen, who
are of such sensible° and nimble lungs that they
always use to laugh at nothing.

180 *Antonio.* 'Twas you we laughed at.

Gonzalo. Who in this kind of merry fooling am nothing to you; so you may continue, and laugh at
nothing still.

Antonio. What a blow was there given!

185 *Sebastian.* And° it had not fall'n flatlong.°

Gonzalo. You are gentlemen of brave mettle; you
would lift the moon out of her sphere if she would
continue in it five weeks without changing.

Enter Ariel [*invisible*] *playing solemn music.*

Sebastian. We would so, and then go a-batfowling.°

190 *Antonio.* Nay, good my lord, be not angry.

---

177 **minister occasion** afford opportunity   178 **sensible** sensitive
185 **And** if   185 **flatlong** with the flat of the sword   189 **We would so,
and then go a-batfowling** we would use the moon for a lantern in order
to hunt birds at night by attracting them with a light and beating them
down with bats; i.e., in order to gull simpletons like you (?)

Gonzalo. No, I warrant you; I will not adventure my
   discretion so weakly.° Will you laugh me asleep?
   For I am very heavy.

Antonio. Go sleep, and hear us.
   [*All sleep except Alonso, Sebastian, and Antonio.*]

Alonso. What, all so soon asleep? I wish mine eyes   *195*
   Would, with themselves, shut up my thoughts. I
      find
   They are inclined to do so.

Sebastian.   Please you, sir,
   Do not omit° the heavy offer of it.
   It seldom visits sorrow; when it doth,
   It is a comforter.

Antonio.   We two, my lord,   *200*
   Will guard your person while you take your rest,
   And watch your safety.

Alonso.   Thank you. Wondrous heavy.
                    [*Alonso sleeps. Exit Ariel.*]

Sebastian. What a strange drowsiness possesses them!

Antonio. It is the quality o' th' climate.

Sebastian.   Why
   Doth it not then our eyelids sink? I find not   *205*
   Myself disposed to sleep.

Antonio.   Nor I: my spirits are nimble.
   They fell together all, as by consent.
   They dropped as by a thunderstroke. What might,
   Worthy Sebastian—O, what might?—No more!
   And yet methinks I see it in thy face,   *210*
   What thou shouldst be. Th' occasion speaks° thee,
      and
   My strong imagination sees a crown
   Dropping upon thy head.

191–92 **adventure my discretion so weakly** risk my reputation for good
sense because of your weak wit   198 **omit** neglect   211 **speaks** speaks
to

Sebastian.   What? Art thou waking?

Antonio. Do you not hear me speak?

Sebastian.   I do; and surely
215   It is a sleepy language, and thou speak'st
       Out of thy sleep. What is it thou didst say?
       This is a strange repose, to be asleep
       With eyes wide open; standing, speaking, moving,
       And yet so fast asleep.

Antonio.   Noble Sebastian,
220   Thou let'st thy fortune sleep—die, rather; wink'st°
       Whiles thou art waking.

Sebastian.   Thou dost snore distinctly;
       There's meaning in thy snores.

Antonio. I am more serious than my custom. You
       Must be so too, if heed° me; which to do
       Trebles thee o'er.°

225 *Sebastian.*   Well, I am standing water.

Antonio. I'll teach you how to flow.

Sebastian.   Do so. To ebb
       Hereditary sloth instructs me.

Antonio.   O,
       If you but knew how you the purpose cherish
       Whiles thus you mock it; how, in stripping it,
230   You more invest it!° Ebbing men, indeed,
       Most often do so near the bottom run
       By their own fear or sloth.

Sebastian.   Prithee, say on.
       The setting of thine eye and cheek proclaim
       A matter° from thee; and a birth, indeed,
       Which throes thee much° to yield.

235 *Antonio.*   Thus, sir:

220 **wink'st** dost shut thine eyes   224 **if heed** if you heed   225 **Trebles thee o'er** makes thee three times what thou now art   229–30 **in stripping . . . invest it** in stripping the purpose off you, you clothe yourself with it all the more   234 **matter** matter of importance   235 **throes thee much** costs thee much pain

Although this lord of weak remembrance,° this
Who shall be of as little memory°
When he is earthed,° hath here almost persuaded
(For he's a spirit of persuasion, only
Professes to persuade°) the King his son's alive,　　240
'Tis as impossible that he's undrowned
As he that sleeps here swims.

Sebastian.　　　　　　　　　　　　I have no hope
That he's undrowned.

Antonio.　　　　　　　　　　O, out of that no hope
What great hope have you! No hope that way is
Another way so high a hope that even　　　　　245
Ambition cannot pierce a wink beyond,
But doubt discovery there.° Will you grant with me
That Ferdinand is drowned?

Sebastian.　　　　　　　　　　He's gone.

Antonio.　　　　　　　　　　　Then tell me,
Who's the next heir of Naples?

Sebastian.　　　　　　　　　Claribel.

Antonio. She that is Queen of Tunis; she that dwells　250
Ten leagues beyond man's life;° she that from
　　Naples
Can have no note—unless the sun were post;°
The man i' th' moon's too slow—till newborn chins
Be rough and razorable;° she that from whom
We all were sea-swallowed,° though some cast°
　　again,　　　　　　　　　　　　　　　　　255

236 **remembrance** memory　237 **of as little memory** as little remembered　238 **earthed** buried　239–40 **only/Professes to persuade** his
only profession is to persuade　246–47 **Ambition cannot . . . discovery
there** the eye of ambition can reach no farther, but must even doubt the
reality of what it discerns thus far　251 **ten leagues beyond man's life** it
would take a lifetime to get within ten leagues of the place　252 **post**
messenger　253–54 **till newborn chins/Be rough and razorable** till
babies just born be ready to shave　254–55 **she that . . . were sea-
swallowed** she who is separated from Naples by so dangerous a sea that
we were ourselves swallowed up by it　255 **cast** cast upon the shore
(with a suggestion of its theatrical meaning that leads to the next metaphor)

And, by that destiny, to perform an act
Whereof what's past is prologue, what to come,
In yours and my discharge.

Sebastian.   What stuff is this? How say you?
    'Tis true my brother's daughter's Queen of Tunis;
260 So is she heir of Naples; 'twixt which regions
    There is some space.

Antonio.   A space whose ev'ry cubit
    Seems to cry out "How shall that Claribel
    Measure us back to Naples? Keep in Tunis,
    And let Sebastian wake!" Say this were death
265 That now hath seized them, why, they were no
    worse
    Than now they are. There be that can rule Naples
    As well as he that sleeps; lords that can prate
    As amply and unnecessarily
    As this Gonzalo; I myself could make
270 A chough° of as deep chat. O, that you bore
    The mind that I do! What a sleep were this
    For your advancement! Do you understand me?

Sebastian. Methinks I do.

Antonio.   And how does your content
    Tender° your own good fortune?

Sebastian.   I remember /
    You did supplant your brother Prospero.

275 *Antonio.*   True.
    And look how well my garments sit upon me,
    Much feater° than before. My brother's servants
    Were then my fellows; now they are my men.

Sebastian. But, for your conscience—

280 *Antonio.* Ay, sir, where lies that? If 'twere a kibe,°
    'Twould put me to my slipper; but I feel not
    This deity in my bosom. Twenty consciences

270 **chough** jackdaw (a bird that can be taught to speak a few words)
274 **Tender** regard (i.e., do you like your good fortune)   277 **feater**
more becomingly   280 **kibe** chilblain on the heel

That stand 'twixt me and Milan, candied be they
And melt, ere they molest! Here lies your brother,
No better than the earth he lies upon—   285
If he were that which now he's like, that's dead°—
Whom I with this obedient steel (three inches
    of it)
Can lay to bed forever; whiles you, doing thus,
To the perpetual wink° for aye might put
This ancient morsel, this Sir Prudence, who   290
Should not upbraid our course. For all the rest,
They'll take suggestion as a cat laps milk;
They'll tell the clock° to any business that
We say befits the hour.

Sebastian.   Thy case, dear friend,
Shall be my precedent. As thou got'st Milan,   295
I'll come by Naples. Draw thy sword. One stroke
Shall free thee from the tribute which thou payest,
And I the King shall love thee.

Antonio.   Draw together;
And when I rear my hand, do you the like,
To fall it on Gonzalo.   [*They draw.*]

Sebastian.   O, but one word!   300

        Enter Ariel [invisible] with music and song.

Ariel. My master through his art foresees the danger
That you, his friend, are in, and sends me forth
(For else his project dies) to keep them living.
                    Sings in Gonzalo's ear.

            While you here do snoring lie,
            Open-eyed conspiracy   305
                His time doth take.
            If of life you keep a care,
            Shake off slumber and beware.
                Awake, awake!

286 **that's dead** that is, if he were dead   289 **wink** eye-shut   293 **tell
the clock** say yes

Antonio. Then let us both be sudden.

310 *Gonzalo.* [*Wakes*]   Now good angels
    Preserve the King!   [*The others wake.*]

Alonso. Why, how now? Ho, awake! Why are you
    drawn?
    Wherefore this ghastly looking?

Gonzalo.   What's the matter?

Sebastian. Whiles we stood here securing your repose,
315   Even now, we heard a hollow burst of bellowing
    Like bulls, or rather lions. Did't not wake you?
    It struck mine ear most terribly.

Alonso.   I heard nothing.

Antonio. O, 'twas a din to fright a monster's ear,
    To make an earthquake! Sure it was the roar
    Of a whole herd of lions.

320 *Alonso.*   Heard you this, Gonzalo?

Gonzalo. Upon mine honor, sir, I heard a humming,
    And that a strange one too, which did awake me.
    I shaked you, sir, and cried. As mine eyes opened,
    I saw their weapons drawn. There was a noise,
325   That's verily.° 'Tis best we stand upon our guard,
    Or that we quit this place. Let's draw our weapons.

Alonso. Lead off this ground, and let's make further
    search
    For my poor son.

Gonzalo.   Heavens keep him from these beasts!
    For he is, sure, i' th' island.

Alonso.   Lead away.

330 *Ariel.* Prospero my lord shall know what I have done.
    So, King, go safely on to seek thy son.   *Exeunt.*

325 **verily** the truth

Scene 2. [*Another part of the island.*]

Enter Caliban with a burden of wood. A noise of thunder heard.

Caliban. All the infections that the sun sucks up
  From bogs, fens, flats, on Prosper fall, and make him
  By inchmeal° a disease! His spirits hear me,
  And yet I needs must curse. But they'll nor pinch,
  Fright me with urchin shows,° pitch me i' th' mire,   *5*
  Nor lead me, like a firebrand,° in the dark
  Out of my way, unless he bid 'em. But
  For every trifle are they set upon me;
  Sometime like apes that mow° and chatter at me,
  And after bite me; then like hedgehogs which   *10*
  Lie tumbling in my barefoot way and mount
  Their pricks at my footfall; sometime am I
  All wound with adders, who with cloven tongues
  Do hiss me into madness.

Enter Trinculo.

              Lo, now, lo!
  Here comes a spirit of his, and to torment me   *15*
  For bringing wood in slowly. I'll fall flat.
  Perchance he will not mind me.   [*Lies down.*]

Trinculo. Here's neither bush nor shrub to bear off°
  any weather at all, and another storm brewing; I
  hear it sing i' th' wind. Yond same black cloud,   *20*
  yond huge one, looks like a foul bombard° that
  would shed his liquor. If it should thunder as it

2.2.3 **By inchmeal** inch by inch   **5 urchin shows** impish apparitions   **6 like a firebrand** in the form of a will-o'-the-wisp   **9 mow** make faces   **18 bear off** ward off   **21 bombard** large leather jug

did before, I know not where to hide my head.
Yond same cloud cannot choose but fall by pail-
25 fuls. What have we here? A man or a fish? Dead
or alive? A fish! He smells like a fish; a very ancient and fishlike smell; a kind of not of the new-
est Poor John.° A strange fish! Were I in England
now, as once I was, and had but this fish painted,°
30 not a holiday fool there but would give a piece of
silver. There would this monster make a man;° any
strange beast there makes a man. When they will
not give a doit° to relieve a lame beggar, they will
lay out ten to see a dead Indian. Legged like a man!
35 And his fins like arms! Warm, o' my troth! I do
now let loose my opinion, hold it no longer. This
is no fish, but an islander, that hath lately suffered
by a thunderbolt. [*Thunder.*] Alas, the storm is
come again! My best way is to creep under his
40 gaberdine; there is no other shelter hereabout. Misery acquaints a man with strange bedfellows. I will
here shroud till the dregs of the storm be past.
                    [*Creeps under Caliban's garment.*]

Enter Stephano, singing, [*a bottle in his hand.*]

Stephano. I shall no more to sea, to sea;
          Here shall I die ashore.

45 This is a very scurvy tune to sing at a man's funeral. Well, here's my comfort.   *Drinks.*

          The master, the swabber, the boatswain, and I,
              The gunner, and his mate,
          Loved Mall, Meg, and Marian, and Margery,
50   But none of us cared for Kate.
              For she had a tongue with a tang,
              Would cry to a sailor "Go hang!"
          She loved not the savor of tar nor of pitch;

---

28 **Poor John** dried hake   29 **painted** i.e., as a sign hung outside a
booth at a fair   31 **make a man** (pun: make a man's fortune)   33 **doit**
smallest coin

Yet a tailor might scratch her where'er she did itch.
    Then to sea, boys, and let her go hang!   55

This is a scurvy tune too; but here's my comfort.
                                                    Drinks.

Caliban. Do not torment me! O!

Stephano. What's the matter? Have we devils here?
    Do you put tricks upon 's with savages and men
    of Inde, ha! I have not scaped drowning to be   60
    afeard now of your four legs. For it hath been
    said, "As proper a man as ever went on four legs
    cannot make him give ground"; and it shall be said
    so again, while Stephano breathes at' nostrils.°

Caliban. The spirit torments me. O!   65

Stephano. This is some monster of the isle, with four
    legs, who hath got, as I take it, an ague. Where the
    devil should he learn our language? I will give him
    some relief, if it be but for that. If I can recover°
    him, and keep him tame, and get to Naples with   70
    him, he's a present for any emperor that ever trod
    on neat's leather.°

Caliban. Do not torment me, prithee; I'll bring my
    wood home faster.

Stephano. He's in his fit now and does not talk after   75
    the wisest. He shall taste of my bottle; if he have
    never drunk wine afore, it will go near to remove
    his fit. If I can recover him and keep him tame, I
    will not take too much° for him. He shall pay for
    him that hath him, and that soundly.   80

Caliban. Thou dost me yet but little hurt. Thou wilt
    anon;° I know it by thy trembling.° Now Prosper
    works upon thee.

Stephano. Come on your ways, open your mouth;

64 **at' nostrils** at the nostrils   69 **recover** cure   72 **neat's leather** cow-
hide   79 **not take too much** too much will not be enough   82 **anon**
soon   82 **trembling** (Trinculo is shaking with fear)

85   here is that which will give language to you, cat.°
      Open your mouth. This will shake your shaking,
      I can tell you, and that soundly. [*Gives Caliban
      drink.*] You cannot tell who's your friend. Open
      your chaps° again.

90   *Trinculo.* I should know that voice. It should be—
      but he is drowned; and these are devils. O, defend
      me!

      Stephano. Four legs and two voices—a most delicate
      monster! His forward voice now is to speak well
95   of his friend; his backward voice is to utter foul
      speeches and to detract. If all the wine in my bottle
      will recover him, I will help his ague. Come! [*Gives
      drink.*] Amen! I will pour some in thy other
      mouth.

100   *Trinculo.* Stephano!

      Stephano. Doth thy other mouth call me? Mercy,
      mercy! This is a devil, and no monster. I will leave
      him; I have no long spoon.°

      Trinculo. Stephano! If thou beest Stephano, touch me
105   and speak to me; for I am Trinculo—be not afeard
      —thy good friend Trinculo.

      Stephano. If thou beest Trinculo, come forth. I'll pull
      thee by the lesser legs. If any be Trinculo's legs,
      these are they. [*Draws him out from under Cali-
110   ban's garment.*] Thou art very Trinculo indeed!
      How cam'st thou to be the siege° of this moon-
      calf?° Can he vent Trinculos?

      Trinculo. I took him to be killed with a thunder-
      stroke. But art thou not drowned, Stephano? I
115   hope now thou art not drowned. Is the storm over-
      blown? I hid me under the dead mooncalf's gaber-
      dine for fear of the storm. And art thou living,

85 **cat** (alluding to the proverb "Liquor will make a cat talk")   89 **chaps**
jaws   103 **long spoon** (alluding to the proverb "He who sups with [i.e.,
from the same dish as] the devil must have a long spoon")   111 **siege**
excrement   111–12 **mooncalf** monstrosity

Stephano? O Stephano, two Neapolitans scaped!

Stephano. Prithee do not turn me about; my stomach
is not constant.   *120*

Caliban. [*Aside*] These be fine things, and if° they be
not sprites.
That's a brave god and bears celestial liquor.
I will kneel to him.

Stephano. How didst thou scape? How cam'st thou
hither? Swear by this bottle how thou cam'st *125*
hither. I escaped upon a butt of sack which the
sailors heaved o'erboard—by this bottle which I
made of the bark of a tree with mine own hands
since I was cast ashore.

Caliban. I'll swear upon that bottle to be thy true *130*
subject, for the liquor is not earthly.

Stephano. Here! Swear then how thou escap'dst.

Trinculo. Swum ashore, man, like a duck. I can swim
like a duck, I'll be sworn.

Stephano. Here, kiss the book. [*Gives him drink.*] *135*
Though thou canst swim like a duck, thou art made
like a goose.

Trinculo. O Stephano, hast any more of this?

Stephano. The whole butt, man. My cellar is in a
rock by th' seaside, where my wine is hid. How *140*
now, mooncalf? How does thine ague?

Caliban. Hast thou not dropped from heaven?

Stephano. Out o' th' moon, I do assure thee. I was the
Man i' th' Moon when time was.°

Caliban. I have seen thee in her, and I do adore thee. *145*
My mistress showed me thee, and thy dog, and
thy bush.°

121 **and if** if   144 **when time was** once upon a time   146–47 **thee,
and thy dog, and thy bush** (the Man in the Moon was banished there,
according to legend, for gathering brushwood with his dog on Sunday)

Stephano. Come, swear to that; kiss the book. [*Gives him drink.*] I will furnish it anon with new con-
150   tents. Swear. [*Caliban drinks.*]

Trinculo. By this good light, this is a very shallow monster! I afeard of him? A very weak monster! The Man i' th' Moon? A most poor credulous monster! Well drawn,° monster, in good sooth!

155 *Caliban.* I'll show thee every fertile inch o' th' island; and I will kiss thy foot. I prithee, be my god.

Trinculo. By this light, a most perfidious and drunken monster! When's god's asleep, he'll rob his bottle.

Caliban. I'll kiss thy foot. I'll swear myself thy sub-
160   ject.

Stephano. Come on then. Down, and swear!

Trinculo. I shall laugh myself to death at this puppy-headed monster. A most scurvy monster! I could find in my heart to beat him—

165 *Stephano.* Come, kiss.

Trinculo. But that the poor monster's in drink. An abominable monster!

Caliban. I'll show thee the best springs; I'll pluck thee berries;
I'll fish for thee, and get thee wood enough.
170   A plague upon the tyrant that I serve!
I'll bear him no more sticks, but follow thee,
Thou wondrous man.

Trinculo. A most ridiculous monster, to make a wonder of a poor drunkard!

Caliban. I prithee let me bring thee where crabs°
175   grow;
And I with my long nails will dig thee pignuts,°
Show thee a jay's nest, and instruct thee how

154 **Well drawn** a good pull at the bottle   175 **crabs** crab apples
176 **pignuts** earthnuts

To snare the nimble marmoset. I'll bring thee
To clust'ring filberts, and sometimes I'll get thee
Young scamels° from the rock. Wilt thou go with
    me?   180

Stephano. I prithee now, lead the way without any
more talking. Trinculo, the King and all our company else being drowned, we will inherit here.
Here, bear my bottle. Fellow Trinculo, we'll fill
him by and by again.   185
                          Caliban sings drunkenly.

Caliban. Farewell, master; farewell, farewell!

Trinculo. A howling monster! A drunken monster!

Caliban. No more dams° I'll make for fish,
            Nor fetch in firing
          At requiring,
        Nor scrape trenchering,° nor wash dish.   190
          'Ban, 'Ban, Ca—Caliban
        Has a new master. Get a new man!
Freedom, high day! High day, freedom! Freedom,
high day, freedom!   195

Stephano. O brave monster! Lead the way.   *Exeunt.*

ACT 3

Scene 1. [*In front of Prospero's cell.*]

Enter Ferdinand, bearing a log.

Ferdinand. There be some sports are painful, and
    their labor
  Delight in them sets off;° some kinds of baseness

180 **scamels** (perhaps a misprint for "seamels" or "seamews," a kind of
sea bird)   188 **dams** (to catch fish and keep them)   191 **trenchering**
trenchers, wooden plates   3.1.2 **sets off** cancels

Are nobly undergone, and most poor matters
Point to rich ends. This my mean task
5   Would be as heavy to me as odious, but
The mistress which I serve quickens° what's dead
And makes my labors pleasures. O, she is
Ten times more gentle than her father's crabbed;
And he's composed of harshness. I must remove
10   Some thousands of these logs and pile them up,
Upon a sore injunction.° My sweet mistress
Weeps when she sees me work, and says such baseness
Had never like executor. I forget;°
But these sweet thoughts do even refresh my labors,
Most busiest when I do it.°

    Enter Miranda; and Prospero [behind, unseen].

15 *Miranda.*   Alas, now pray you,
Work not so hard! I would the lightning had
Burnt up those logs that you are enjoined to pile!
Pray set it down and rest you. When this burns,
'Twill weep° for having wearied you. My father
20   Is hard at study; pray now rest yourself;
He's safe for these three hours.

Ferdinand.   O most dear mistress,
The sun will set before I shall discharge
What I must strive to do.

Miranda.   If you'll sit down,
I'll bear your logs the while. Pray give me that;
I'll carry it to the pile.

25 *Ferdinand.*   No, precious creature,
I had rather crack my sinews, break my back,
Than you should such dishonor undergo
While I sit lazy by.

---

6 **quickens** brings to life   11 **sore injunction** severe command 13 **forget** i.e., my task   15 **Most busiest when I do it** i.e., my thoughts are busiest when I am (the Folio's *busie lest* has been variously emended; *it* may refer to "task," line 4, the understood object in line 13)   19 **weep** i.e., exude resin

Miranda.   It would become me
  As well as it does you; and I should do it
  With much more ease; for my good will is to it,   30
  And yours it is against.

Prospero. [*Aside*]   Poor worm, thou art infected!
  This visitation° shows it.

Miranda.   You look wearily.

Ferdinand. No, noble mistress, 'tis fresh morning with
    me
  When you are by at night.° I do beseech you,
  Chiefly that I might set it in my prayers,   35
  What is your name?

Miranda.   Miranda. O my father,
  I have broke your hest° to say so!

Ferdinand.   Admired Miranda!°
  Indeed the top of admiration, worth
  What's dearest to the world! Full many a lady
  I have eyed with best regard, and many a time   40
  Th' harmony of their tongues hath into bondage
  Brought my too diligent ear. For several virtues
  Have I liked several women; never any
  With so full soul but some defect in her
  Did quarrel with the noblest grace she owed,°   45
  And put it to the foil.° But you, O you,
  So perfect and so peerless, are created
  Of every creature's best.

Miranda.   I do not know
  One of my sex; no woman's face remember,
  Save, from my glass, mine own. Nor have I seen   50
  More that I may call men than you, good friend,
  And my dear father. How features are abroad
  I am skilless° of; but, by my modesty

32 **visitation** (1) visit (2) attack of plague (referring to metaphor of
"infected")   34 **at night** i.e., even at night when I am very tired
37 **hest** command   37 **Admired Miranda** ("admired" means "to be
wondered at"; the Latin "Miranda" means "wonderful")   45 **owed**
owned   46 **put it to the foil** defeated it   53 **skilless** ignorant

(The jewel in my dower), I would not wish
55   Any companion in the world but you;
Nor can imagination form a shape,
Besides yourself, to like of.° But I prattle
Something too wildly, and my father's precepts
I therein do forget.

Ferdinand.   I am, in my condition,
60   A prince, Miranda; I do think, a king
(I would not so), and would no more endure
This wooden slavery than to suffer
The fleshfly blow my mouth. Hear my soul speak!
The very instant that I saw you, did
65   My heart fly to your service; there resides,
To make me slave to it; and for your sake
Am I this patient log-man.

Miranda.   Do you love me?

Ferdinand. O heaven, O earth, bear witness to this
    sound,
And crown what I profess with kind event°
70   If I speak true! If hollowly, invert
What best is boded me° to mischief! I,
Beyond all limit of what else i' th' world,
Do love, prize, honor you.

Miranda.   I am a fool
To weep at what I am glad of.

Prospero.   *[Aside]* Fair encounter
75   Of two most rare affections! Heavens rain grace
On that which breeds between 'em!

Ferdinand.   Wherefore weep you?

Miranda. At mine unworthiness, that dare not offer
What I desire to give, and much less take
What I shall die to want.° But this is trifling;°
80   And all the more it seeks to hide itself,

---

57 **like of** like   69 **event** outcome   71 **What best is boded me** whatever good fortune fate has in store for me   79 **to want** if I lack   79 **trifling** i.e., to speak in riddles like this

The bigger bulk it shows. Hence, bashful cunning,
And prompt me, plain and holy innocence!
I am your wife, if you will marry me;
If not, I'll die your maid. To be your fellow°
You may deny me; but I'll be your servant,   85
Whether you will or no.

Ferdinand.   My mistress, dearest,
And I thus humble ever.

Miranda.   My husband then?

Ferdinand. Ay, with a heart as willing
As bondage e'er of freedom.° Here's my hand.

Miranda. And mine, with my heart in't; and now
    farewell   90
Till half an hour hence.

Ferdinand.   A thousand thousand!
                Exeunt [*Ferdinand and Miranda*
                        in different directions].

Prospero. So glad of this as they I cannot be,
Who are surprised withal;° but my rejoicing
At nothing can be more. I'll to my book;
For yet ere suppertime must I perform   95
Much business appertaining.°   *Exit.*

Scene 2. [*Another part of the island.*]

Enter Caliban, Stephano, and Trinculo.

Stephano. Tell not me! When the butt is out, we will
drink water; not a drop before. Therefore bear up
and board 'em!° Servant monster, drink to me.

Trinculo. Servant monster? The folly of this island!

---

84 **fellow** equal   89 **of freedom** i.e., to win freedom   93 **withal** by
it   96 **appertaining** i.e., to my plan   3.2.2–3 **bear up and board 'em**
i.e., drink up

5 They say there's but five upon this isle; we are
three of them. If th' other two be brained like us,
the state totters.

Stephano. Drink, servant monster, when I bid thee;
thy eyes are almost set in thy head.

10 *Trinculo.* Where should they be set else? He were a
brave monster indeed if they were set in his tail.

Stephano. My man-monster hath drowned his tongue
in sack. For my part, the sea cannot drown me. I
swam, ere I could recover the shore, five-and-thirty
15 leagues off and on, by this light. Thou shalt be my
lieutenant, monster, or my standard.°

Trinculo. Your lieutenant, if you list;° he's no standard.

Stephano. We'll not run,° Monsieur Monster.

20 *Trinculo.* Nor go° neither; but you'll lie° like dogs,
and yet say nothing neither.

Stephano. Mooncalf, speak once in thy life, if thou
beest a good mooncalf.

Caliban. How does thy honor? Let me lick thy shoe.
25 I'll not serve him; he is not valiant.

Trinculo. Thou liest, most ignorant monster; I am in
case° to justle° a constable. Why, thou deboshed°
fish thou, was there ever man a coward that hath
drunk so much sack as I today? Wilt thou tell a
30 monstrous lie, being but half a fish and half a
monster?

Caliban. Lo, how he mocks me! Wilt thou let him,
my lord?

16 **standard** standard-bearer, ensign (pun since Caliban is so drunk he
cannot stand) 17 **if you list** if it please you (with pun on "list" as per-
taining to a ship that leans over to one side) 19–20 **run, lie** (with puns
on secondary meanings: "make water," "excrete") 20 **go** walk 27
case fit condition 27 **justle** jostle 27 **deboshed** debauched

Trinculo. "Lord" quoth he? That a monster should
  be such a natural!°   35

Caliban. Lo, lo, again! Bite him to death, I prithee.

Stephano. Trinculo, keep a good tongue in your head.
  If you prove a mutineer—the next tree!° The poor
  monster's my subject, and he shall not suffer in-
  dignity.   40

Caliban. I thank my noble lord. Wilt thou be pleased
  to hearken once again to the suit I made to thee?

Stephano. Marry,° will I. Kneel and repeat it; I will
  stand, and so shall Trinculo.

Enter Ariel, invisible.

Caliban. As I told thee before, I am subject to a
    tyrant,   45
  A sorcerer, that by his cunning hath
  Cheated me of the island.

Ariel. Thou liest.

Caliban.   Thou liest, thou jesting monkey
    thou!
  I would my valiant master would destroy thee.
  I do not lie.   50

Stephano. Trinculo, if you trouble him any more in's
  tale, by this hand, I will supplant some of your
  teeth.

Trinculo. Why, I said nothing.

Stephano. Mum then, and no more. Proceed.   55

Caliban. I say by sorcery he got this isle;
  From me he got it. If thy greatness will
  Revenge it on him—for I know thou dar'st,
  But this thing° dare not—

---

35 **natural** idiot   38 **the next tree** i.e., you will be hanged   43 **Marry**
(an expletive, from "By the Virgin Mary")   59 **this thing** i.e., Trinculo

60   *Stephano.* That's most certain.

Caliban. Thou shalt be lord of it, and I'll serve thee.

Stephano. How now shall this be compassed?
  Canst thou bring me to the party?

Caliban. Yea, yea, my lord! I'll yield him thee asleep,
65   Where thou mayst knock a nail into his head.

Ariel. Thou liest; thou canst not.

Caliban. What a pied° ninny's this! Thou scurvy
  patch!°
  I do beseech thy greatness, give him blows
  And take his bottle from him. When that's gone,
  He shall drink naught but brine, for I'll not show
70   him
  Where the quick freshes° are.

Stephano. Trinculo, run into no further danger! Inter-
  rupt the monster one word further and, by this
  hand, I'll turn my mercy out o' doors and make a
75   stockfish° of thee.

Trinculo. Why, what did I? I did nothing. I'll go farther off.

Stephano. Didst thou not say he lied?

Ariel. Thou liest.

80   *Stephano.* Do I so? Take thou that! [*Strikes Trinculo.*] As you like this, give me the lie another time.

Trinculo. I did not give the lie. Out o' your wits, and
  hearing too? A pox o' your bottle! This can sack
  and drinking do. A murrain° on your monster, and
85   the devil take your fingers!

Caliban. Ha, ha, ha!

Stephano. Now forward with your tale. [*To Trinculo*]
  Prithee, stand further off.

---

67 **pied** (referring to Trinculo's parti-colored jester's costume)   67
patch clown   71 **quick freshes** living springs of fresh water   75 **stock-
fish** dried cod, softened by beating   84 **murrain** plague (that infects
cattle)

Caliban. Beat him enough. After a little time
  I'll beat him too.

Stephano.   Stand farther. Come, proceed.   90

Caliban. Why, as I told thee, 'tis a custom with him
  I' th' afternoon to sleep. There thou mayst brain
    him,
  Having first seized his books, or with a log
  Batter his skull, or paunch° him with a stake,
  Or cut his wezand° with thy knife. Remember   95
  First to possess his books; for without them
  He's but a sot,° as I am, nor hath not
  One spirit to command. They all do hate him
  As rootedly as I. Burn but his books.
  He has brave utensils° (for so he calls them)   100
  Which, when he has a house, he'll deck withal.
  And that most deeply to consider is
  The beauty of his daughter. He himself
  Calls her a nonpareil. I never saw a woman
  But only Sycorax my dam and she;   105
  But she as far surpasseth Sycorax
  As great'st does least.

Stephano.   Is it so brave a lass?

Caliban. Ay, lord. She will become thy bed, I
    warrant,
  And bring thee forth brave brood.

Stephano. Monster, I will kill this man. His daughter   110
  and I will be King and Queen—save our Graces!—
  and Trinculo and thyself shall be viceroys. Dost
  thou like the plot, Trinculo?

Trinculo. Excellent.

Stephano. Give me thy hand. I am sorry I beat thee;   115
  but while thou liv'st, keep a good tongue in thy
  head.

---

94 **paunch** stab in the belly   95 **wezand** windpipe   97 **sot** fool   100
brave utensils fine furnishings (pronounced "útensils")

Caliban. Within this half hour will he be asleep.
Wilt thou destroy him then?

Stephano.　　　　　　　　Ay, on mine honor.

120 *Ariel.* This will I tell my master.

Caliban. Thou mak'st me merry; I am full of pleasure.
Let us be jocund. Will you troll the catch°
You taught me but whilere?°

Stephano. At thy request, monster, I will do reason,
125　any reason.° Come on, Trinculo, let us sing. *Sings.*

　　　　　　Flout 'em and scout° 'em
　　　　　　And scout 'em and flout 'em!
　　　　　　Thought is free.

Caliban. That's not the tune.
　　　　　Ariel plays the tune on a tabor° and pipe.

130 *Stephano.* What is this same?

Trinculo. This is the tune of our catch, played by the
picture of Nobody.°

Stephano. If thou beest a man, show thyself in thy
likeness. If thou beest a devil, take't as thou list.

135 *Trinculo.* O, forgive me my sins!

Stephano. He that dies pays all debts. I defy thee.
Mercy upon us!

Caliban. Art thou afeard?

Stephano. No, monster, not I.

140 *Caliban.* Be not afeard; the isle is full of noises,
Sounds and sweet airs that give delight and hurt
not.

122 **troll the catch** sing the round　123 **but whilere** just now　124–
25 **reason, any reason** i.e., anything within reason　126 **scout** jeer
at　129 s.d. **tabor** small drum worn at the side　132 **Nobody** (alluding
to the picture of No-body—a man all head, legs, and arms, but without
trunk—on the title page of the anonymous comedy **No-body and Some-
body**)

Sometimes a thousand twangling instruments
Will hum about mine ears; and sometime voices
That, if I then had waked after long sleep,
Will make me sleep again; and then, in dreaming,   *145*
The clouds methought would open and show riches
Ready to drop upon me, that, when I waked,
I cried to dream again.

Stephano. This will prove a brave kingdom to me,
where I shall have my music for nothing.   *150*

Caliban. When Prospero is destroyed.

Stephano. That shall be by and by; I remember the
story.

Trinculo. The sound is going away; let's follow it, and
after do our work.   *155*

Stephano. Lead, monster; we'll follow. I would I
could see this taborer; he lays it on.

Trinculo. [*To Caliban*] Wilt come?° I'll follow Stephano.   *Exeunt.*

Scene 3. [*Another part of the island.*]

*Enter Alonso, Sebastian, Antonio, Gonzalo,
Adrian, Francisco, etc.*

Gonzalo. By'r Lakin,° I can go no further, sir;
My old bones aches. Here's a maze trod indeed
Through forthrights and meanders.° By your
patience,
I needs must rest me.

Alonso.   Old lord, I cannot blame thee,
Who am myself attached° with weariness   5

158 **Wilt come** (Caliban lingers because the other two are being
distracted from his purpose by the music) 3.3.1 **By'r Lakin** by
our Lady   3 **forthrights and meanders** straight and winding paths
5 **attached** seized

To th' dulling of my spirits. Sit down and rest.
Even here I will put off my hope, and keep it
No longer for my flatterer. He is drowned
Whom thus we stray to find; and the sea mocks
Our frustrate search on land. Well, let him go.

Antonio. [*Aside to Sebastian*] I am right glad that
    he's so out of hope.
Do not for one repulse forgo the purpose
That you resolved t' effect.

Sebastian. [*Aside to Antonio*] The next advantage
Will we take throughly.°

Antonio. [*Aside to Sebastian*] Let it be tonight;
For, now they are oppressed with travel, they
Will not nor cannot use such vigilance
As when they are fresh.

Sebastian. [*Aside to Antonio*] I say tonight. No more.

*Solemn and strange music; and Prospero on the top°
(invisible). Enter several strange Shapes, bringing in a banquet; and dance about it with gentle
actions of salutations; and, inviting the King etc.
to eat, they depart.*

Alonso. What harmony is this? My good friends,
    hark!

Gonzalo. Marvelous sweet music!

Alonso. Give us kind keepers,° heavens! What were
    these?

Sebastian. A living drollery.° Now I will believe
That there are unicorns; that in Arabia

14 **throughly** thoroughly   17 s.d. **the top** upper stage (or perhaps a
playing area above it)   20 **kind keepers** guardian angels   21 **drollery**
puppet show

There is one tree, the phoenix' throne; one phoenix
At this hour reigning there.

Antonio.   I'll believe both;
And what does else want credit,° come to me,   25
And I'll be sworn 'tis true. Travelers ne'er did lie,
Though fools at home condemn 'em.

Gonzalo.   If in Naples
I should report this now, would they believe me
If I should say I saw such islanders?
(For certes these are people of the island)   30
Who, though they are of monstrous shape, yet note,
Their manners are more gentle, kind, than of
Our human generation you shall find
Many—nay, almost any.

Prospero.   [*Aside*] Honest lord,
Thou hast said well; for some of you there present   35
Are worse than devils.

Alonso.   I cannot too much muse°
Such shapes, such gesture, and such sound, ex-
          pressing
(Although they want the use of tongue) a kind
Of excellent dumb discourse.

Prospero.   [*Aside*] Praise in departing.°

Francisco. They vanished strangely.

Sebastian.   No matter, since   40
They have left their viands behind; for we have
          stomachs.
Will't please you taste of what is here?

Alonso.   Not I.

Gonzalo. Faith, sir, you need not fear. When we were
          boys,
Who would believe that there were mountaineers

25 **credit** believing   36 **muse** wonder at   39 **Praise in departing** save
your praise for the end

Dewlapped° like bulls, whose throats had hanging
45   at 'em
Wallets of flesh? Or that there were such men
Whose heads stood in their breasts? Which now
          we find
Each putter-out of five for one° will bring us
Good warrant of.

Alonso.   I will stand to, and feed;
50   Although my last, no matter, since I feel
The best is past. Brother, my lord the Duke,
Stand to, and do as we.

*Thunder and lightning. Enter Ariel, like a harpy;
  claps his wings upon the table; and with a
  quaint device° the banquet vanishes.*

Ariel. You are three men of sin, whom destiny—
That hath to instrument° this lower world
55   And what is in't—the never-surfeited sea
Hath caused to belch up you and on this island,
Where man doth not inhabit, you 'mongst men
Being most unfit to live. I have made you mad;
And even with suchlike valor° men hang and
          drown
Their proper selves.
          [*Alonso, Sebastian, etc. draw their swords.*]
60   You fools! I and my fellows
Are ministers of Fate. The elements,
Of whom your swords are tempered,° may as well
Wound the loud winds, or with bemocked-at stabs
Kill the still-closing° waters, as diminish
One dowle° that's in my plume.° My fellow min-
65   isters

45 **Dewlapped** with skin hanging from the neck (like mountaineers with
goiter)   48 **putter-out of five for one** traveler who insures himself by
depositing a sum of money to be repaid fivefold if he returns safely (i.e.,
any ordinary traveler will confirm nowadays those reports we used to
think fanciful)   52 s.d. **quaint device** ingenious device (of stage
mechanism)   54 **to instrument** as its instrument   59 **suchlike valor** i.e.,
the courage that comes of madness   62 **tempered** composed   64 **still-
closing** ever closing again (as soon as wounded)   65 **dowle** bit of
down   65 **plume** plumage

Are like invulnerable. If you could hurt,°
Your swords are now too massy° for your strengths
And will not be uplifted. But remember
(For that's my business to you) that you three
From Milan did supplant good Prospero;   70
Exposed unto the sea, which hath requit it,°
Him and his innocent child; for which foul deed
The pow'rs, delaying, not forgetting, have
Incensed the seas and shores, yea, all the creatures,
Against your peace. Thee of thy son, Alonso,   75
They have bereft; and do pronounce by me
Ling'ring perdition (worse than any death
Can be at once) shall step by step attend
You and your ways; whose wraths to guard you
  from,
Which here, in this most desolate isle, else falls   80
Upon your heads, is nothing but heart's sorrow°
And a clear life ensuing.

*He vanishes in thunder; then, to soft music, enter
  the Shapes again, and dance with mocks and
  mows,° and carrying out the table.*

Prospero. Bravely the figure of this harpy hast thou
  Performed, my Ariel; a grace it had, devouring.°
  Of my instruction hast thou nothing bated°   85
  In what thou hadst to say. So, with good life°
  And observation strange,° my meaner ministers°
  Their several kinds have done.° My high charms
    work,
  And these, mine enemies, are all knit up
  In their distractions. They now are in my pow'r; 90
  And in these fits I leave them, while I visit

66 **If you could hurt** even if you could hurt us 67 **massy** heavy
71 **requit it** avenged that crime 81 **nothing but heart's sorrow** only
repentance (will protect you from the wrath of these powers) 82 s.d.
mocks and mows mocking gestures and grimaces 84 **devouring** i.e.,
in making the banquet disappear 85 **bated** omitted 86 **good life** good
lifelike acting 87 **observation strange** remarkable attention to my
wishes 87 **meaner ministers** i.e., inferior to Ariel 88 **Their several
kinds have done** have acted the parts their natures suited them for

Young Ferdinand, whom they suppose is drowned,
And his and mine loved darling.   [*Exit above.*]

Gonzalo. I' th' name of something holy, sir, why
      stand you
In this strange stare?

95 *Alonso.*   O, it is monstrous, monstrous!
Methought the billows spoke and told me of it;
The winds did sing it to me; and the thunder,
That deep and dreadful organ pipe, pronounced
The name of Prosper; it did bass my trespass.°
100 Therefore my son i' th' ooze is bedded; and
I'll seek him deeper than e'er plummet sounded
And with him there lie mudded.   *Exit.*

Sebastian.   But one fiend at a time,
I'll fight their legions o'er!°

Antonio.   I'll be thy second.
            Exeunt [*Sebastian and Antonio*].

Gonzalo. All three of them are desperate; their great
      guilt,
105 Like poison given to work a great time after,
Now 'gins to bite the spirits. I do beseech you,
That are of suppler joints, follow them swiftly
And hinder them from what this ecstasy°
May now provoke them to.

Adrian.   Follow, I pray you.
            Exeunt omnes.

99 **bass my trespass** i.e., made me understand my trespass by turning it
into music for which the thunder provided the bass part   103 **o'er** one
after another to the last   108 **ecstasy** madness

ACT 4

Scene 1. [*In front of Prospero's cell.*]

Enter Prospero, Ferdinand, and Miranda.

Prospero. If I have too austerely punished you,
　Your compensation makes amends; for I
　Have given you here a third of mine own life,
　Or that for which I live; who once again
　I tender to thy hand. All thy vexations　　　　　　*5*
　Were but my trials of thy love, and thou
　Hast strangely° stood the test. Here, afore heaven,
　I ratify this my rich gift. O Ferdinand,
　Do not smile at me that I boast her off,°
　For thou shalt find she will outstrip all praise　*10*
　And make it halt° behind her.

Ferdinand.　　　　　　　　　I do believe it
　Against an oracle.°

Prospero. Then, as my gift, and thine own acquisition
　Worthily purchased, take my daughter. But
　If thou dost break her virgin-knot before　　　*15*
　All sanctimonious° ceremonies may
　With full and holy rite be minist'red,

4.1.7 **strangely** wonderfully　9 **boast her off** (includes perhaps idea of
showing her off)　11 **halt** limp　12 **Against an oracle** though an oracle should declare otherwise　16 **sanctimonious** holy

No sweet aspersion° shall the heavens let fall
To make this contract grow;° but barren hate,
20 Sour-eyed disdain, and discord shall bestrew
The union of your bed with weeds so loathly
That you shall hate it both. Therefore take heed,
As Hymen's lamps shall light you.°

Ferdinand.   As I hope
For quiet days, fair issue, and long life,
25 With such love as 'tis now, the murkiest den,
The most opportune° place, the strong'st sug-
    gestion
Our worser genius can,° shall never melt
Mine honor into lust, to take away
The edge° of that day's celebration
When I shall think or Phoebus' steeds are foun-
30   dered°
Or Night kept chained below.°

Prospero.   Fairly spoke.
Sit then and talk with her; she is thine own.
What, Ariel!° My industrious servant, Ariel!

Enter Ariel.

Ariel. What would my potent master? Here I am.

Prospero. Thou and thy meaner fellows your last
35   service
Did worthily perform; and I must use you
In such another trick. Go bring the rabble,°
O'er whom I give thee pow'r, here to this place.
Incite them to quick motion; for I must

---

18 **aspersion** blessing (like rain on crops)   19 **grow** become fruitful
23 **As Hymen's lamps shall light you** i.e., as earnestly as you pray that
the torch of the god of marriage shall burn without smoke (a good omen for
wedded happiness)   26 **opportune** (pronounced "oppórtune")   27 **Our
worser genius can** our evil spirit can offer   29 **edge** keen enjoyment
30 **foundered** lamed   30–31 **or Phoebus' steeds . . . below** i.e., that either day will never end or night will never come   33 **What, Ariel** (sum-
moning Ariel)   37 **rabble** "thy meaner fellows"

Bestow upon the eyes of this young couple   40
Some vanity of° mine art. It is my promise,
And they expect it from me.

Ariel.   Presently?

Prospero. Ay, with a twink.

Ariel. Before you can say "Come" and "Go,"
And breathe twice and cry, "So, so,"   45
Each one, tripping on his toe,
Will be here with mop and mow.°
Do you love me, master? No?

Prospero. Dearly, my delicate Ariel. Do not approach
Till thou dost hear me call.

Ariel.   Well; I conceive.°   *Exit.*   50

Prospero. Look thou be true.° Do not give dalliance
Too much the rein; the strongest oaths are straw
To th' fire i' th' blood. Be more abstemious,
Or else good night your vow!

Ferdinand.   I warrant you, sir.
The white cold virgin snow upon my heart°   55
Abates the ardor of my liver.°

Prospero.   Well.
Now come, my Ariel; bring a corollary°
Rather than want a spirit. Appear, and pertly!
No tongue! All eyes! Be silent.   *Soft music.*

Enter Iris.°

Iris. Ceres, most bounteous lady, thy rich leas°   60
Of wheat, rye, barley, fetches,° oats, and peas;

41 **vanity of** illusion conjured up by   47 **mop and mow** gestures and
grimaces   50 **conceive** understand   51 **be true** (Prospero appears to
have caught the lovers in an embrace)   55 **The white cold . . . heart** her
pure white breast on mine (?)   56 **liver** (supposed seat of sexual
passion)   57 **corollary** surplus (of spirits)   59 s.d. **Iris** goddess of the
rainbow and Juno's messenger   60 **leas** meadows   61 **fetches** vetch (a
kind of forage)

Thy turfy mountains, where live nibbling sheep,
And flat meads thatched with stover,° them to
    keep;
Thy banks with pionèd and twillèd brims,°
65   Which spongy April at thy hest betrims
To make cold nymphs chaste crowns; and thy
    broom groves,
Whose shadow the dismissèd bachelor loves,
Being lasslorn; thy pole-clipt vineyard;°
And thy sea-marge, sterile and rocky-hard,
Where thou thyself dost air°—the queen o' th'
70   sky,°
Whose wat'ry arch and messenger am I,
Bids thee leave these, and with her sovereign grace,

Juno descends.°

Here on this grass plot, in this very place,
To come and sport; her peacocks fly amain.°
75   Approach, rich Ceres, her to entertain.

Enter Ceres.

Ceres. Hail, many-colored messenger, that ne'er
Dost disobey the wife of Jupiter,
Who, with thy saffron wings, upon my flow'rs
Diffusest honey drops, refreshing show'rs,
80   And with each end of thy blue bow dost crown
My bosky° acres and my unshrubbed down,
Rich scarf to my proud earth. Why hath thy queen
Summoned me hither to this short-grassed green?

Iris. A contract of true love to celebrate

63   **meads thatched with stover** (meadows covered with a kind of grass used for winter fodder)   64 **pionèd and twillèd brims** (obscure; may refer to the trenched and ridged edges of banks that have been repaired after the erosions of winter)   68 **pole-clipt vineyard** i.e., vineyard whose vines grow neatly around (embrace) poles (though possibly the word is "poll-clipped," i.e., pruned)   70 **air** take the air   70 **queen o' th' sky** Juno   72 s.d. (this direction seems to come too soon, but the machine may have lowered her very slowly)   74 **amain** swiftly (peacocks, sacred to Juno, drew her chariot)   81 **bosky** shrubbed

And some donation freely to estate°   85
On the blessed lovers.

Ceres.   Tell me, heavenly bow,
If Venus or her son, as thou dost know,
Do now attend the Queen? Since they did plot
The means that dusky Dis my daughter got,°
Her and her blind boy's scandaled° company   90
I have forsworn.

Iris.   Of her society
Be not afraid; I met her Deity
Cutting the clouds towards Paphos,° and her son
Dove-drawn with her. Here thought they to have
    done
Some wanton charm upon this man and maid,   95
Whose vows are, that no bed-right shall be paid
Till Hymen's torch be lighted. But in vain;
Mars's hot minion is returned again;°
Her waspish-headed son° has broke his arrows,
Swears he will shoot no more, but play with
    sparrows   100
And be a boy right out.°

[*Juno alights.*]

Ceres.   Highest queen of state,
Great Juno, comes; I know her by her gait.

Juno. How does my bounteous sister? Go with me
To bless this twain, that they may prosperous be
And honored in their issue.   105

They sing.

Juno.   Honor, riches, marriage blessing,

85 **estate** bestow   89 **dusky Dis my daughter got** (alluding to the abduction of Proserpine by Pluto [Dis], god of the underworld)   90 **scandaled** scandalous   93 **Paphos** (in Cyprus, center of Venus' cult)   98 **Mars's hot minion is returned again** i.e., Mars's lustful mistress (Venus) is on her way back to Paphos   99 **waspish-headed son** (Cupid is irritable and stings with his arrows)   101 **a boy right out** an ordinary boy

                    Long continuance, and increasing,
                    Hourly joys be still° upon you!
                    Juno sings her blessings on you.
110 [*Ceres.*]   Earth's increase, foison° plenty,
                    Barns and garners never empty,
                    Vines with clust'ring bunches growing,
                    Plants with goodly burden bowing;
                    Spring come to you at the farthest
115   In the very end of harvest.°
                    Scarcity and want shall shun you,
                    Ceres' blessing so is on you.

      Ferdinand. This is a most majestic vision, and
            Harmonious charmingly. May I be bold
            To think these spirits?

120 *Prospero.*   Spirits, which by mine art
            I have from their confines called to enact
            My present fancies.

      Ferdinand.   Let me live here ever!
            So rare a wond'red° father and a wise
            Makes this place Paradise.

            Juno and Ceres whisper, and send Iris on employment.

      Prospero.   Sweet now, silence!
125   Juno and Ceres whisper seriously.
            There's something else to do. Hush and be mute,
            Or else our spell is marred.

      Iris. You nymphs, called Naiades, of the windring°
                brooks,
            With your sedged crowns and ever-harmless looks,
130   Leave your crisp° channels, and on this green land
            Answer your summons; Juno does command.
            Come, temperate nymphs, and help to celebrate
            A contract of true love; be not too late.

---

108 **still** ever   110 **foison** abundance   114–115 **Spring come to you . . .
harvest** i.e., may there be no winter in your lives   123 **wond'red** possessed of wonders; i.e., both wonderful and wonder-working, and therefore to be wondered at   128 **windring** winding and wandering (?)
130 **crisp** rippling

Enter certain Nymphs.

You sunburned sicklemen, of August weary,
Come hither from the furrow and be merry.   *135*
Make holiday; your rye-straw hats put on,
And these fresh nymphs encounter everyone
In country footing.°

*Enter certain Reapers, properly habited. They
join with the Nymphs in a graceful dance; towards the end whereof Prospero starts suddenly and speaks;° after which, to a strange,
hollow, and confused noise, they heavily°
vanish.*

Prospero. [*Aside*] I had forgot that foul conspiracy
Of the beast Caliban and his confederates   *140*
Against my life. The minute of their plot
Is almost come. [*To the Spirits*] Well done!
    Avoid!° No more!

Ferdinand. This is strange. Your father's in some
    passion
That works him strongly.

Miranda.   Never till this day
Saw I him touched with anger so distempered.°   *145*

Prospero. You do look, my son, in a movèd sort,°
As if you were dismayed; be cheerful, sir.
Our revels now are ended. These our actors,
As I foretold you, were all spirits and
Are melted into air, into thin air;   *150*
And, like the baseless fabric of this vision,
The cloud-capped towers, the gorgeous palaces,
The solemn temples, the great globe itself,
Yea, all which it inherit,° shall dissolve,

138 **footing** dance   138 s.d. **speaks** (breaking the spell, which depends
on silence)   138 s.d. **heavily** reluctantly   142 **Avoid** begone   145 **distempered** violent   146 **movèd sort** troubled state   154 **it inherit** oc-
cupy it

155 And, like this insubstantial pageant faded,
Leave not a rack° behind. We are such stuff
As dreams are made on, and our little life
Is rounded with a sleep. Sir, I am vexed.
Bear with my weakness; my old brain is troubled.
160 Be not disturbed with my infirmity.
If you be pleased, retire into my cell
And there repose. A turn or two I'll walk
To still my beating mind.

Ferdinand, Miranda.   We wish your peace.
                              Exit [Ferdinand with Miranda].

Prospero. Come with a thought! I thank thee, Ariel.°
  Come.

                          Enter Ariel.

Ariel. Thy thoughts I cleave to. What's thy pleasure?

165 *Prospero.*   Spirit,
  We must prepare to meet with Caliban.

Ariel. Ay, my commander. When I presented° Ceres,
  I thought to have told thee of it, but I feared
  Lest I might anger thee.

Prospero. Say again, where didst thou leave these
170   varlets?°

Ariel. I told you, sir, they were red-hot with drinking;
  So full of valor that they smote the air
  For breathing in their faces, beat the ground
  For kissing of their feet; yet always bending°
175 Towards their project. Then I beat my tabor;
  At which like unbacked° colts they pricked their
    ears,
  Advanced° their eyelids, lifted up their noses
  As they smelt music. So I charmed their ears

156 **rack** wisp of cloud   164 **I thank thee, Ariel** (for the masque?)
167 **presented** acted the part of (?) introduced (?)   170 **varlets** ruffi-
ans   174 **bending** directing their steps   176 **unbacked** unbroken
177 **Advanced** lifted up

That calflike they my lowing followed through
Toothed briers, sharp furzes, pricking goss,° and   180
    thorns,
Which ent'red their frail shins. At last I left them
I' th' filthy mantled° pool beyond your cell,
There dancing up to th' chins, that the foul lake
O'erstunk their feet.

Prospero.   This was well done, my bird.
Thy shape invisible retain thou still.   185
The trumpery° in my house, go bring it hither
For stale° to catch these thieves.

Ariel.   I go, I go.   *Exit.*

Prospero. A devil, a born devil, on whose nature
Nurture can never stick; on whom my pains,
Humanely taken, all, all lost, quite lost!   190
And as with age his body uglier grows,
So his mind cankers. I will plague them all,
Even to roaring.

   Enter Ariel, loaden with glistering apparel, etc.

Come, hang them on this line.°

[*Prospero and Ariel remain, invisible.*] *Enter
    Caliban, Stephano, and Trinculo, all wet.*

Caliban. Pray you tread softly, that the blind mole
    may not
Hear a foot fall. We now are near his cell.   195

Stephano. Monster, your fairy, which you say is a
    harmless fairy, has done little better than played the
    Jack° with us.

Trinculo. Monster, I do smell all horse piss, at which
    my nose is in great indignation.   200

180 **goss** gorse   182 **filthy mantled** covered with filthy scum 186 **trum-
pery** (the "glistering apparel" mentioned in the next stage direction)
187 **stale** decoy   193 **line** lime tree (linden)   198 **Jack** (1) knave (2)
jack-o'-lantern, will-o'-the-wisp

Stephano. So is mine. Do you hear, monster? If I
should take a displeasure against you, look you—

Trinculo. Thou wert but a lost monster.

Caliban. Good my lord, give me thy favor still.
205 Be patient, for the prize I'll bring thee to
Shall hoodwink° this mischance. Therefore speak
softly.
All's hushed as midnight yet.

Trinculo. Ay, but to lose our bottles in the pool—

Stephano. There is not only disgrace and dishonor in
210 that, monster, but an infinite loss.

Trinculo. That's more to me than my wetting. Yet this
is your harmless fairy, monster.

Stephano. I will fetch off my bottle, though I be o'er
ears° for my labor.

215 *Caliban.* Prithee, my king, be quiet. Seest thou here?
This is the mouth o' th' cell. No noise, and enter.
Do that good mischief which may make this island
Thine own forever, and I, thy Caliban,
For aye thy footlicker.

220 *Stephano.* Give me thy hand. I do begin to have
bloody thoughts.

Trinculo. O King Stephano! O peer!° O worthy
Stephano, look what a wardrobe here is for thee!

Caliban. Let it alone, thou fool! It is but trash.

225 *Trinculo.* O, ho, monster! We know what belongs to
a frippery.° O King Stephano!

Stephano. Put off that gown, Trinculo! By this hand,
I'll have that gown!

---

206 **hoodwink** put out of sight   213–14 **o'er ears** i.e., over my ears in
water   222 **peer** (alluding to the song "King Stephen was and a worthy
peer;/His breeches cost him but a crown," quoted in **Othello** 2.
3)   226 **frippery** old-clothes shop; i.e., we are good judges of castoff
clothes

Trinculo. Thy Grace shall have it.

Caliban. The dropsy drown this fool! What do you
    mean 230
To dote thus on such luggage?° Let't alone,
And do the murder first. If he awake,
From toe to crown he'll fill our skins with pinches,
Make us strange stuff.

Stephano. Be you quiet, monster. Mistress line, is not 235
this my jerkin?° [*Takes it down.*] Now is the jerkin
under the line.° Now, jerkin, you are like to lose
your hair and prove a bald jerkin.°

Trinculo. Do, do!° We steal by line and level,° and't
like° your Grace. 240

Stephano. I thank thee for that jest. Here's a garment
for't. Wit shall not go unrewarded while I am king
of this country. "Steal by line and level" is an excellent pass of pate.° There's another garment for't.

Trinculo. Monster, come put some lime° upon your 245
fingers, and away with the rest.

Caliban. I will have none on't. We shall lose our time
And all be turned to barnacles,° or to apes
With foreheads villainous low.

Stephano. Monster, lay-to your fingers; help to bear 250
this away where my hogshead of wine is, or I'll
turn you out of my kingdom. Go to, carry this.

Trinculo. And this.

Stephano. Ay, and this.

231 **luggage** useless encumbrances   236 **jerkin** kind of jacket 237 **under the line** pun: (1) under the lime tree (2) under the equator   238 **bald jerkin** (sailors proverbially lost their hair from fevers contracted while crossing the equator)   239 **Do, do** fine, fine   239 **by line and level** by plumb line and carpenter's level; i.e., according to rule (with pun on "line")   239–40 **and't like** if it please   244 **pass of pate** sally of wit 245 **lime** birdlime (which is sticky; thieves have sticky fingers)   248 **barnacles** kind of geese supposed to have developed from shellfish

A noise of hunters heard. Enter divers Spirits in
shape of dogs and hounds, hunting them about;
Prospero and Ariel setting them on.

255 *Prospero.* Hey, Mountain, hey!

Ariel. Silver! There it goes, Silver!

Prospero. Fury, Fury! There, Tyrant, there! Hark,
hark!

[*Caliban, Stephano, and Trinculo are driven out.*]

Go, charge my goblins that they grind their joints
With dry convulsions,° shorten up their sinews
With agèd° cramps, and more pinch-spotted make
260   them
Than pard or cat o' mountain.°

Ariel.   Hark, they roar!

Prospero. Let them be hunted soundly. At this hour
Lies at my mercy all mine enemies.
Shortly shall all my labors end, and thou
265 Shalt have the air at freedom. For a little,
Follow, and do me service.   *Exeunt.*

ACT 5

Scene 1. [*In front of Prospero's cell.*]

Enter Prospero in his magic robes, and Ariel.

Prospero. Now does my project gather to a head.
My charms crack not, my spirits obey, and time
Goes upright with his carriage.° How's the day?

Ariel. On the sixth hour, at which time, my lord,

259 **dry convulsions** (such as come when the joints are dry from old age)
260 **agèd** i.e., such as old people have   261 **pard or cat o' mountain**
leopard or catamount 5.1.2–3 **time/ Goes upright with his carriage** time
does not stoop under his burden (because there is so little left to do)

You said our work should cease.

Prospero.   I did say so   5
When first I raised the tempest. Say, my spirit,
How fares the King and 's followers?

Ariel.   Confined together
In the same fashion as you gave in charge,
Just as you left them—all prisoners, sir,
In the line grove which weather-fends° your cell.   10
They cannot budge till your release.° The King,
His brother, and yours abide all three distracted,
And the remainder mourning over them,
Brimful of sorrow and dismay; but chiefly
Him that you termed, sir, the good old Lord
    Gonzalo.   15
His tears run down his beard like winter's drops
From eaves of reeds.° Your charm so strongly
    works 'em,
That if you now beheld them, your affections
Would become tender.

Prospero.   Dost thou think so, spirit?

Ariel. Mine would, sir, were I human.

Prospero.   And mine shall.   20
Hast thou, which art but air, a touch, a feeling
Of their afflictions, and shall not myself,
One of their kind, that relish all as sharply,
Passion° as they, be kindlier moved than thou art?
Though with their high wrongs I am struck to th'
    quick,   25
Yet with my nobler reason 'gainst my fury
Do I take part. The rarer action is
In virtue than in vengeance. They being penitent,
The sole drift of my purpose doth extend
Not a frown further. Go, release them, Ariel.   30
My charms I'll break, their senses I'll restore,
And they shall be themselves.

10 **weather-fends** protects from the weather   11 **till your release** until released by you   17 **eaves of reeds** i.e., a thatched roof   24 **Passion**
(verb)

Ariel.   I'll fetch them, sir.
                                                        Exit.

Prospero. Ye elves of hills, brooks, standing lakes,
        and groves,
     And ye that on the sands with printless foot
35   Do chase the ebbing Neptune, and do fly him°
     When he comes back; you demi-puppets that
     By moonshine do the green sour ringlets° make,
     Whereof the ewe not bites; and you whose pastime
     Is to make midnight mushrumps,° that rejoice
40   To hear the solemn curfew; by whose aid
     (Weak masters° though ye be) I have bedimmed
     The noontide sun, called forth the mutinous winds,
     And 'twixt the green sea and the azured vault
     Set roaring war; to the dread rattling thunder
45   Have I given fire and rifted Jove's stout oak
     With his own bolt; the strong-based promontory
     Have I made shake and by the spurs° plucked up
     The pine and cedar; graves at my command
     Have waked their sleepers, oped, and let 'em forth
50   By my so potent art. But this rough magic
     I here abjure; and when I have required°
     Some heavenly music (which even now I do)
     To work mine end upon their senses that°
     This airy charm is for, I'll break my staff,
55   Bury it certain fathoms in the earth,
     And deeper than did ever plummet sound
     I'll drown my book.   *Solemn music.*

*Here enters Ariel before; then Alonso, with a
frantic gesture, attended by Gonzalo; Sebastian
and Antonio in like manner, attended by Adrian
and Francisco. They all enter the circle which
Prospero had made, and there stand charmed;
which Prospero observing, speaks.*

35 **fly him** fly with him   37 **green sour ringlets** ("fairy rings," little cir-
cles of rank grass supposed to be formed by the dancing of fairies)
39 **mushrumps** mushrooms   41 **masters** masters of supernatural
power   47 **spurs** roots   51 **required** asked for   53 **their senses that**
the senses of those whom

A solemn air, and° the best comforter
To an unsettled fancy, cure thy brains,
Now useless, boiled within thy skull! There stand,   60
For you are spell-stopped.
Holy Gonzalo, honorable man,
Mine eyes, ev'n sociable to the show of thine,
Fall fellowly drops.° The charm dissolves apace;
And as the morning steals upon the night,   65
Melting the darkness, so their rising senses
Begin to chase the ignorant fumes that mantle
Their clearer reason. O good Gonzalo,
My true preserver, and a loyal sir
To him thou follow'st, I will pay thy graces   70
Home° both in word and deed. Most cruelly
Didst thou, Alonso, use me and my daughter.
Thy brother was a furtherer in the act.
Thou art pinched for't now, Sebastian. Flesh and
    blood,
You, brother mine, that entertained ambition,   75
Expelled remorse° and nature;° whom, with
    Sebastian
(Whose inward pinches therefore are most strong),
Would here have killed your king, I do forgive thee,
Unnatural though thou art. Their understanding
Begins to swell, and the approaching tide   80
Will shortly fill the reasonable shore,
That now lies foul and muddy. Not one of them
That yet looks on me or would know me. Ariel,
Fetch me the hat and rapier in my cell.
I will discase° me, and myself present   85
As I was sometime Milan. Quickly, spirit!
Thou shalt ere long be free.
              [*Exit Ariel and returns immediately.*]

                Ariel sings and helps to attire him.

58 **and** which is   63–64 **sociable to the show ... drops** associat-
ing themselves with the (tearful) appearance of your eyes, shed
tears in sympathy   70–71 **pay thy graces/ Home** repay thy favors
thoroughly   76 **remorse** pity   76 **nature** natural feeling   85 **discase**
disrobe

Where the bee sucks, there suck I;
In a cowslip's bell I lie;
90 There I couch when owls do cry.
On the bat's back I do fly
After summer merrily.
Merrily, merrily shall I live now
Under the blossom that hangs on the bough.

Prospero. Why, that's my dainty Ariel! I shall miss
95   thee,
But yet thou shalt have freedom; so, so, so.
To the King's ship, invisible as thou art!
There shalt thou find the mariners asleep
Under the hatches. The master and the boatswain
100 Being awake, enforce them to this place,
And presently,° I prithee.

Ariel. I drink the air before me, and return
Or ere your pulse twice beat.   *Exit.*

Gonzalo. All torment, trouble, wonder, and amaze-
        ment
105 Inhabits here. Some heavenly power guide us
Out of this fearful country!

Prospero.   Behold, sir King,
The wrongèd Duke of Milan, Prospero.
For more assurance that a living prince
Does now speak to thee, I embrace thy body,
110 And to thee and thy company I bid
A hearty welcome.

Alonso.   Whe'r° thou be'st he or no,
Or some enchanted trifle° to abuse me,
As late I have been, I not know. Thy pulse
Beats, as of flesh and blood; and, since I saw thee,
115 Th' affliction of my mind amends, with which,
I fear, a madness held me. This must crave°
(And if this be at all)° a most strange story.
Thy dukedom I resign and do entreat

---

101 **presently** immediately   111 **Whe'r** whether   112 **trifle** apparition
116 **crave** require (to account for it)   117 **And if this be at all** if this is
really happening

Thou pardon me my wrongs. But how should Prospero
Be living and be here?

Prospero.   First, noble friend,   120
Let me embrace thine age, whose honor cannot
Be measured or confined.

Gonzalo.   Whether this be
Or be not, I'll not swear.

Prospero.   You do yet taste
Some subtleties° o' th' isle, that will not let you
Believe things certain. Welcome, my friends all.   125
[*Aside to Sebastian and Antonio*] But you, my
    brace of lords, were I so minded,
I here could pluck his Highness' frown upon you,
And justify° you traitors. At this time
I will tell no tales.

Sebastian. [*Aside*] The devil speaks in him.

Prospero.   No.
For you, most wicked sir, whom to call brother   130
Would even infect my mouth, I do forgive
Thy rankest fault—all of them; and require
My dukedom of thee, which perforce I know
Thou must restore.

Alonso.   If thou beest Prospero,
Give us particulars of thy preservation;   135
How thou hast met us here, whom three hours
    since
Were wracked upon this shore; where I have lost
(How sharp the point of this remembrance is!)
My dear son Ferdinand.

Prospero.   I am woe° for't, sir.

Alonso. Irreparable is the loss, and patience   140
Says it is past her cure.

___

124 **subtleties** deceptions (referring to pastries made to look like something else—e.g., castles made out of sugar)   128 **justify** prove   139 **woe** sorry

Prospero. I rather think
You have not sought her help, of whose soft grace
For the like loss I have her sovereign aid
And rest myself content.

Alonso. You the like loss?

145 *Prospero.* As great to me, as late,° and supportable°
To make the dear° loss, have I means much weaker
Than you may call to comfort you; for I
Have lost my daughter.

Alonso. A daughter?
O heavens, that they were living both in Naples,
150 The King and Queen there! That they were, I wish
Myself were mudded in that oozy bed
Where my son lies. When did you lose your
daughter?

Prospero. In this last tempest. I perceive these lords
At this encounter do so much admire°
155 That they devour their reason, and scarce think
Their eyes do offices° of truth, their words
Are natural breath. But, howsoev'r you have
Been justled from your senses, know for certain
That I am Prospero, and that very duke
160 Which was thrust forth of Milan, who most strangely
Upon this shore, where you were wracked, was
landed
To be the lord on't. No more yet of this;
For 'tis a chronicle of day by day,
Not a relation for a breakfast, nor
165 Befitting this first meeting. Welcome, sir;
This cell's my court. Here have I few attendants,
And subjects none abroad.° Pray you look in.
My dukedom since you have given me again,
I will requite you with as good a thing,
170 At least bring forth a wonder to content ye

145 **As great to me, as late** as great to me as your loss, and as
recent 145 **supportable** (pronounced "súpportable") 146 **dear** (intensifies the meaning of the noun) 154 **admire** wonder 156 **do offices** perform services 167 **abroad** i.e., on the island

As much as me my dukedom.

Here Prospero discovers° Ferdinand and Miranda playing at chess.

Miranda. Sweet lord, you play me false.

Ferdinand.   No, my dearest love,
I would not for the world.

Miranda. Yes, for a score of kingdoms you should
    wrangle,
And I would call it fair play.°

Alonso.   If this prove   175
A vision of the island, one dear son
Shall I twice lose.

Sebastian.   A most high miracle!

Ferdinand. Though the seas threaten, they are merciful.
I have cursed them without cause.   [*Kneels.*]

Alonso.   Now all the blessings
Of a glad father compass thee about!   180
Arise, and say how thou cam'st here.

Miranda.   O, wonder!
How many goodly creatures are there here!
How beauteous mankind is! O brave new world
That has such people in't!

Prospero.   'Tis new to thee.

Alonso. What is this maid with whom thou wast at
    play?   185
Your eld'st° acquaintance cannot be three hours.
Is she the goddess that hath severed us
And brought us thus together?

Ferdinand.   Sir, she is mortal;

---

171 s.d. **discovers** reveals (by opening a curtain at the back of the
stage)   174–75 **for a score of kingdoms . . . play** i.e., if we were playing for stakes just short of the world, you would protest as now; but then,
the issue being important, I would call it fair play so much do I love
you (?)   186 **eld'st** longest

But by immortal providence she's mine.
190 I chose her when I could not ask my father
For his advice, nor thought I had one. She
Is daughter to this famous Duke of Milan,
Of whom so often I have heard renown
But never saw before; of whom I have
195 Received a second life; and second father
This lady makes him to me.

Alonso.   I am hers.
But, O, how oddly will it sound that I
Must ask my child forgiveness!

Prospero.   There, sir, stop.
Let us not burden our remembrance with
A heaviness that's gone.

200 *Gonzalo.*   I have inly wept,
Or should have spoke ere this. Look down, you gods,
And on this couple drop a blessèd crown!
For it is you that have chalked forth the way
Which brought us hither.

Alonso.   I say amen, Gonzalo.

205 *Gonzalo.* Was Milan thrust from Milan that his issue
Should become kings of Naples? O, rejoice
Beyond a common joy, and set it down
With gold on lasting pillars. In one voyage
Did Claribel her husband find at Tunis,
210 And Ferdinand her brother found a wife
Where he himself was lost; Prospero his dukedom
In a poor isle; and all of us ourselves
When no man was his own.

Alonso. [*To Ferdinand and Miranda*] Give me your
    hands.
Let grief and sorrow still° embrace his heart
That doth not wish you joy.

215 *Gonzalo.*   Be it so! Amen!

214 **still** forever

Enter Ariel, with the Master and Boatswain amaz-
edly following.

O, look, sir; look, sir! Here is more of us!
I prophesied if a gallows were on land,
This fellow could not drown. Now, blasphemy,
That swear'st grace o'erboard,° not an oath on
  shore?
Hast thou no mouth by land? What is the news?   220

Boatswain. The best news is that we have safely found
Our king and company; the next, our ship,
Which, but three glasses° since, we gave out split,
Is tight and yare° and bravely rigged as when
We first put out to sea.

Ariel.   [*Aside to Prospero*] Sir, all this service   225
Have I done since I went.

Prospero.   [*Aside to Ariel*] My tricksy spirit!

Alonso. These are not natural events; they strengthen
From strange to stranger. Say, how came you hither?

Boatswain. If I did think, sir, I were well awake,
I'd strive to tell you. We were dead of sleep   230
And (how we know not) all clapped under hatches;
Where, but even now, with strange and several°
  noises
Of roaring, shrieking, howling, jingling chains,
And moe° diversity of sounds, all horrible,
We were awaked; straightway at liberty;   235
Where we, in all our trim, freshly beheld
Our royal, good, and gallant ship, our master
Cap'ring to eye° her. On a trice, so please you,
Even in a dream, were we divided from them
And were brought moping° hither.

Ariel. [*Aside to Prospero*]   Was't well done?   240

219 **That swear'st grace o'erboard** that (at sea) swearest enough to
cause grace to be withdrawn from the ship   223 **glasses** hours   224 **yare**
shipshape   232 **several** various   234 **moe** more   238 **Cap'ring to eye**
dancing to see   240 **moping** in a daze

Prospero. [*Aside to Ariel*] Bravely, my diligence.
   Thou shalt be free.

Alonso. This is as strange a maze as e'er men trod,
   And there is in this business more than nature
   Was ever conduct° of. Some oracle
   Must rectify our knowledge.

245 *Prospero.*   Sir, my liege,
   Do not infest your mind with beating on
   The strangeness of this business. At picked leisure,
   Which shall be shortly, single I'll resolve you
   (Which to you shall seem probable) of every
250   These happened accidents;° till when, be cheerful
   And think of each thing well. [*Aside to Ariel*]
     Come hither, spirit.
   Set Caliban and his companions free.
   Untie the spell. [*Exit Ariel.*] How fares my gracious
     sir?
   There are yet missing of your company
255   Some few odd lads that you remember not.

Enter Ariel, driving in Caliban, Stephano, and
Trinculo, in their stolen apparel.

Stephano. Every man shift for all the rest, and let no
   man take care for himself; for all is but fortune.
   Coragio,° bully-monster, *coragio!*

Trinculo. If these be true spies which I wear in my
260   head, here's a goodly sight.

Caliban. O Setebos,° these be brave spirits indeed!
   How fine my master is! I am afraid
   He will chastise me.

Sebastian.   Ha, ha!
   What things are these, my Lord Antonio?
   Will money buy 'em?

---

244 **conduct** conductor   248–50 **single I'll resolve . . . accidents** I myself will solve the problems (and my story will make sense to you) concerning each and every incident that has happened   258 **Coragio**
courage (Italian)   261 **Setebos** the god of Caliban's mother

Antonio.   Very like. One of them   265
  Is a plain fish and no doubt marketable.

Prospero. Mark but the badges° of these men, my
    lords,
  Then say if they be true.° This misshapen knave,
  His mother was a witch, and one so strong
  That could control the moon, make flows and ebbs,   270
  And deal in her command without her power.°
  These three have robbed me, and this demi-devil
  (For he's a bastard one) had plotted with them
  To take my life. Two of these fellows you
  Must know and own; this thing of darkness I   275
  Acknowledge mine.

Caliban.   I shall be pinched to death.

Alonso. Is not this Stephano, my drunken butler?

Sebastian. He is drunk now. Where had he wine?

Alonso. And Trinculo is reeling ripe. Where should
    they
  Find this grand liquor that hath gilded 'em?   280
  How cam'st thou in this pickle?

Trinculo. I have been in such a pickle, since I saw you
  last, that I fear me will never out of my bones. I
  shall not fear flyblowing.°

Sebastian. Why, how now, Stephano?   285

Stephano. O, touch me not! I am not Stephano, but
  a cramp.

Prospero. You'd be king o' the isle, sirrah?

Stephano. I should have been a sore° one then.

Alonso. This is a strange thing as e'er I looked on.   290

267 **badges** (worn by servants to indicate to whose service they belong;
in this case, the stolen clothes are badges of their rascality)   268 **true**
honest   271 **deal in her command without her power** i.e., dabble in the
moon's realm without the moon's legitimate authority   284 **flyblowing**
(pickling preserves meat from flies)   289 **sore** (1) tyrannical (2) aching

Prospero. He is as disproportioned in his manners
    As in his shape. Go, sirrah, to my cell;
    Take with you your companions. As you look
    To have my pardon, trim it handsomely.

295 *Caliban.* Ay, that I will; and I'll be wise hereafter,
    And seek for grace. What a thrice-double ass
    Was I to take this drunkard for a god
    And worship this dull fool!

Prospero.   Go to! Away!

Alonso. Hence, and bestow your luggage where you
    found it.

300 *Sebastian.* Or stole it rather.
          [*Exeunt Caliban, Stephano, and Trinculo.*]

Prospero. Sir, I invite your Highness and your train
    To my poor cell, where you shall take your rest
    For this one night; which, part of it, I'll waste°
    With such discourse as, I not doubt, shall make it
305   Go quick away—the story of my life,
    And the particular accidents° gone by
    Since I came to this isle. And in the morn
    I'll bring you to your ship, and so to Naples,
    Where I have hope to see the nuptial
310   Of these our dear-beloved solemnizèd;°
    And thence retire me to my Milan, where
    Every third thought shall be my grave.

Alonso.   I long
    To hear the story of your life, which must
    Take° the ear strangely.

Prospero.   I'll deliver° all;
315   And promise you calm seas, auspicious gales,
    And sail so expeditious that shall catch°
    Your royal fleet far off. [*Aside to Ariel*] My Ariel,
    chick,
    That is thy charge. Then to the elements

303 **waste** spend   306 **accidents** incidents   310 **solemnizèd** (pronounced "solémnizèd")   314 **Take** captivate   314 **deliver** tell   316
catch catch up with

Be free, and fare thou well! [*To the others*]
Please you, draw near.   *Exeunt omnes.*

EPILOGUE

Spoken by Prospero

Now my charms are all o'erthrown,
And what strength I have's mine own,
Which is most faint. Now 'tis true
I must be here confined by you,
Or sent to Naples. Let me not,   5
Since I have my dukedom got
And pardoned the deceiver, dwell
In this bare island by your spell;
But release me from my bands°
With the help of your good hands.°   10
Gentle breath° of yours my sails
Must fill, or else my project fails,
Which was to please. Now I want°
Spirits to enforce, art to enchant;
And my ending is despair   15
Unless I be relieved by prayer,°
Which pierces so that it assaults
Mercy itself and frees all faults.
As you from crimes would pardoned be,
Let your indulgence set me free.   *Exit.*   20

FINIS

Epi. 9 **bands** bonds   10 **hands** i.e., applause to break the spell   11
Gentle breath i.e., favorable comment   13 **want** lack   16 **prayer** i.e.,
this petition

Textual Note

The Tempest was first printed in the Folio of 1623, the First Folio. The Folio text has been carefully edited and punctuated, and it has unusually complete stage directions that are probably Shakespeare's own. *The Tempest* is perhaps the finest text in the Folio, which may be why the Folio editors placed it first in the volume.

The present division into acts and scenes is that of the Folio. The present edition silently modernizes spelling and punctuation, regularizes speech prefixes, translates into English the Folio's Latin designations of act and scene, and makes certain changes in lineation in the interest either of meter, meaning, or a consistent format. Other departures from the Folio are listed below, including changes in lineation that bear upon the meaning. The reading of the present text is given first, in italics, and then the reading of the Folio (F) in roman.

The Scene: an uninhabited island . . . Names of the Actors [appears at end of play in F]

1.1.38 s.d. *Enter Sebastian, Antonio, and Gonzalo* [in F occurs after "plague," line 37]

1.2.173 *princess'* Princesse   201 *lightnings* Lightning   271 *wast* was   282 *she* he   380 *the burden bear* beare / the burthen

2.1.5 *master* Masters   38–39 *Antonio . . . Sebastian* [speakers reversed in F]

3.1.2 *sets* set   15 *busiest* busie lest   93 *withal* with all

3.2.126   *scout* cout

3.3.17 *Sebastian: I say tonight. No more* [appears in F after stage direction]   29 *islanders* Islands

4.1.9 *off* of   13 *gift* guest   124 s.d. *Juno and .... employment* [follows line 127 in F]   193 *them on* on them   231 *Let't* let's

5.1.60 *boiled* boile   72 *Didst* Did   75 *entertained* entertaine 82 *lies* ly   199 *remembrance* remembrances

The Sources of *The Tempest*

There is no known source for the plot of *The Tempest*. As far as we know, *The Tempest* and *Love's Labor's Lost* are Shakespeare's two original plots. Attempts have been made to locate the source of *The Tempest* in the German comedy *Die Schöne Sidea* by Jakob Ayrer, who died in 1605;[1] in certain scenarios of the Italian *commedia dell' arte*;[2] in two Spanish romances.[3] The differences, however, between these plots and the plot of *The Tempest* seem more significant than the similarities. The things these plots have in common with each other and with the plot of *The Tempest* are folk-tale motifs that have long been the common property of storytellers and playwrights.[4]

If there is no source for *The Tempest*, there are documents that are relevant to it. The names of many of the characters probably derive from Thomas' *History of Italy* (1549), and the name "Setebos" derives from Robert Eden's *History of Travaile* (1577), which mentions the "great devill Setebos" worshiped by the Patagonians. Shakespeare paraphrases a passage from John Florio's translation (1603) of Montaigne's

[1] See H. H. Furness' Variorum Edition of *The Tempest*, Philadelphia: Lippincott, 1897, pp. 324–43, which includes a translation of Ayrer's comedy.

[2] See H. D. Gray, "The Sources of *The Tempest*," *Modern Language Notes* XXXV (1920): 321–30.

[3] Antonio de Eslava's *Noches de Invierno* (1609), Chap. IV. (See Hardin Craig, *Interpretation of Shakespeare*, Columbia, Missouri: Lucas Brothers, 1948, pp. 344–45. And Diego Ortuñez de Calahorra's *Espejo de Principes y Caballeros* [1562; English translation, 1578–1601].) (See Joseph de Perott, "The Probable Source of the Plot of Shakespeare's *Tempest*," *Publications of the Clark University Library* I [1903–1905]: 209–16.)

[4] See W. W. Newell, "Sources of Shakespeare's *Tempest*," *Journal of American Folk-Lore* XVI (1905): 234–57.

essay on the American Indians, "Of the Caniballes" (Caliban's name may derive from "cannibal"); and he paraphrases a speech of the witch, Medea, in Ovid's *Metamorphoses*—using Arthur Golding's translation (1567), which he apparently checked against the Latin original. There is good reason to believe that Shakespeare had in mind, and may even have had on his desk, when he wrote *The Tempest,* certain reports that appeared in 1610 of a tempest and a shipwreck that took place off the Bermudas in 1609. I shall print—in modernized spelling and punctuation, and with some indication of their relevance—extracts from Montaigne, Ovid, and the so-called "Bermuda pamphlets." These last require a word of explanation.

On June 2, 1609, a fleet of nine ships set sail from Plymouth for Virginia, carrying more than five hundred colonists. On July 24, a tempest off the Bermudas separated from the rest of the fleet the flagship, the *Sea-Venture,* which carried the admiral, Sir George Somers, and the new governor of the colony, Sir Thomas Gates. In the course of the next several weeks, the other ships straggled into the port at Jamestown, but the occupants of the *Sea-Venture* were given up for lost. Then, miraculously, almost a year later, on May 23, 1610, the castaways arrived in Jamestown in two small ships they had built for the journey. Their deliverance, when the news of it reached London in September, was regarded as providential. But the beneficent hand of providence emerged even more clearly when the reports of the shipwreck began to appear. For the reports showed the stormy Bermudas, which mariners had shunned as an "Ile of Divels," to be actually an island paradise.

Since Shakespeare was closely connected with the leaders of the Virginia Company (e.g., the earls of Southampton and Pembroke) that had sponsored the expedition, he would have had good reason to read the reports of the shipwreck that appeared in 1610. The first to appear was *A Discovery of the Barmudas, otherwise called the Ile of Divels,* by Sylvester Jourdain,[5] who was with Somers. A month later there ap-

[5] Facsimile edition, ed. J. Q. Adams, New York: Scholars' Facsimiles and Reprints, 1940.

peared *The True Declaration of the estate of the Colonie in Virginia,* which was the report of the Virginia Company.[6] Most important for our purposes is a long letter by William Strachey, who was also with Somers, which is dated July 15, 1610, but which doubtless came over to London with Gates in September. Strachey's letter was not published until 1625, in *Purchas His Pilgrimes.*[7] But it seems to have circulated in manuscript among the leaders of the Virginia Company, and we may be reasonably sure that Shakespeare read it, since it bears most closely of all the reports on *The Tempest.* It is called *A true repertory of the wracke, and redemption of Sir Thomas Gates Knight; upon, and from the Ilands of the Bermudas: his comming to Virginia, and the estate of that Colonie then, and after.*

William Strachey: from *True Repertory of the Wrack,* 1610.

[*Description of the tempest*]

A dreadful storm and hideous began to blow from out the northeast, which swelling and roaring as it were by fits, some hours with more violence than others, at length did beat all light from heaven; which like an hell of darkness turned black upon us, so much the more fuller of horror, as in such cases horror and fear use to overrun the troubled and over-mastered senses of all, which (taken up with amazement) the ears lay so sensible to the terrible cries and murmurs of the winds, and distraction of our company, as who was most armed and best prepared was not a little shaken.

For four and twenty hours the storm in a restless tumult had blown so exceedingly, as we could not apprehend in our imaginations any possibility of greater violence, yet did we still find it, not only more terrible, but more constant, fury added to fury, and one storm urging a second more outrageous than the former; whether it so wrought upon our fears

---

[6] Reprinted in *Tracts and Other Papers,* collected by Peter Force. Washington: Force, 1844, Vol. III.

[7] Glasgow: MacLehose; New York: Macmillan, 1906, Vol. XIX.

or indeed met with new forces. Sometimes strikes [shrieks?] in our ship amongst women and passengers not used to such hurly and discomforts made us look one upon the other with troubled hearts and panting bosoms; our clamors drowned in the winds, and the winds in thunder. Prayers might well be in the heart and lips, but drowned in the outcries of the officers. Nothing heard that could give comfort, nothing seen that might encourage hope.... It could not be said to rain, the waters like whole rivers did flood in the air.... Here the glut of water (as if throttling the wind erewhile) was no sooner a little emptied and qualified, but instantly the winds (as having gotten their mouths now free and at liberty) spake more loud and grew tumultuous and malignant.... There was not a moment in which the sudden splitting or instant oversetting of the ship was not expected.

Howbeit this was not all. It pleased God to bring a greater affliction yet upon us; for in the beginning of the storm we had received likewise a mighty leak. And the ship ... was grown five foot suddenly deep with water above her ballast, and we almost drowned within whilst we sat looking when to perish from above. This, imparting no less terror than danger, ran through the whole ship with much fright and amazement, startled and turned the blood, and took down the braves of the most hardy mariner of them all, insomuch as he that before happily felt not the sorrow of others, now began to sorrow for himself when he saw such a pond of water so suddenly broken in, and which he knew could not (without present avoiding) but instantly sink him....

Once, so huge a sea brake upon the poop and quarter upon us, as it covered our ship from stern to stem, like a garment or a vast cloud, it filled her brim full for a while within, from the hatches up to the spar deck.... with much clamor encouraged and called upon others; who gave her now up, rent in pieces and absolutely lost. ["All lost!".... "We split, we split!" 1.1.52,61]

[St. Elmo's fire; Ariel: "I flamed amazement." 1.2.198]

During all this time, the heavens looked so black upon us that it was not possible the elevation of the pole might be observed; nor a star by night, not sunbeam by day was to be seen. Only upon the Thursday night, Sir George Somers, being upon the watch, had an apparition of a little round light, like a faint star, trembling, and streaming along with a sparkling blaze, half the height upon the mainmast, and shooting sometimes from shroud to shroud, tempting to settle as it were upon any of the four shrouds. And for three or four hours together, or rather more, half the night it kept with us; running sometimes along the mainyard to the very end, and then returning. At which, Sir George Somers called divers about him and showed them the same, who observed it with much wonder and carefulness. But upon a sudden, toward the morning watch, they lost the sight of it and knew not what way it made. The superstitious seamen make many constructions of this sea fire, which nevertheless is usual in storms: the same (it may be) which the Grecians were wont in the Mediterranean to call Castor and Pollux, of which, if one only appeared without the other, they took it for an evil sign of great tempest. The Italians, and such, who lie open to the Adriatic and Tyrrhene Sea, call it (a sacred Body) *Corpo sancto*; the Spaniards call it Saint Elmo, and have an authentic and miraculous legend for it. Be it what it will, we laid other foundations of safety or ruin, then in the rising or falling of it, could it have served us now miraculously to have taken our height by, it might have struck amazement, and a reverence in our devotions, according to the due of a miracle. But it did not light us any whit the more to our known way, who ran now (as do hoodwinked men) at all adventures, sometimes north, and northeast, then north and by west, and sometimes half the compass.

[*Providence*]

... Sir George Somers, when no man dreamed of such happiness, had discovered and cried land.... We were enforced to run her ashore as near the land as we could, which brought us within three-quarters of a mile of shore....

We found it to be the dangerous and dreaded island, or rather islands of the Bermuda; whereof let me give your Ladyship a brief description before I proceed to my narration. And that the rather, because they be so terrible to all that ever touched on them, and such tempests, thunders, and other fearful objects are seen and heard about them, that they be called commonly the Devil's Islands, and are feared and avoided of all sea travelers alive above any other place in the world. Yet it pleased our merciful God to make even this hideous and hated place both the place of our safety and means of our deliverance.

And hereby also, I hope to deliver the world from a foul and general error: it being counted of most that they can be no habitation for men, but rather given over to devils and wicked spirits. Whereas indeed we find them now by experience to be as habitable and commodious as most countries of the same climate and situation; insomuch as if the entrance into them were as easy as the place itself is contenting, it had long ere this been inhabited as well as other islands. Thus shall we make it appear that Truth is the daughter of Time, and that men ought not to deny everything which is not subject to their own sense. [Gonzalo's speech on travelers' tales, 3.3.43–49]

[*Caliban: "I'll not show him / Where the quick freshes are."* 3.2.70–71]

Sure it is that there are no rivers nor running springs of fresh water to be found upon any of them. When we came first, we digged and found certain gushings and soft bubblings which, being either in bottoms or on the side of hanging ground, were only fed with rain water which nevertheless soon sinketh into the earth and vanisheth away, or emptieth itself out of sight into the sea without any channel above or upon the superficies of the earth. For according as their rains fell, we had wells and pits (which we digged) either half full, or absolute exhausted and dry, howbeit some low bottoms (which the continual descent from the hills filled full, and in those flats could have no passage away) we found to continue as fishing ponds [Caliban: "dams ... for fish" (?). 2.2.188], or standing pools, continually summer and winter full of fresh water.

[*Caliban: "I'll get thee / Young scamels from the rock"* (?). 2.2.179–80*]

A kind of webfooted fowl there is, of the bigness of an English green plover, or seamew, which all the summer we saw not, and in the darkest nights of November and December (for in the night they only feed) they would come forth, but not fly far from home, and hovering in the air, and over the sea, made a strange hollow and harsh howling ... which birds with a light bough in a dark night (as in our lowbelling [similar to "a-batfowling," 2.1.189]) we caught. I have been at the taking of three hundred in an hour, and we might have laden our boats. Our men found a pretty way to take them, which was by standing on the rocks or sands by the seaside, and hollowing, laughing, and making the strangest outcry that possibly they could. With the noise whereof the birds would come flocking to that place, and settle upon the very arms and head of him that so cried, and still creep nearer and nearer, answering the noise themselves; by which our men would weigh them with their hand, and which weighed heaviest they took for the best and let the others alone, and so our men would take twenty dozen in two hours of the chiefest of them; and they were a good and well-relished fowl, fat and full as a partridge ... which birds for their blindness (for they see weakly in the day) and for their cry and hooting, we called the sea owl.

[*Mutinies*]

In these dangers and devilish disquiets (whilst the almighty God wrought for us and sent us, miraculously delivered from the calamities of the sea, all blessings upon the shore to content and bind us to gratefulness) thus enraged amongst ourselves, to the destruction each of other, into what a mischief and misery had we been given up, had we not had a governor with his authority to have suppressed the same? Yet was there a worse practice, faction, and conjuration afoot, deadly and bloody, in which the life of our governor with many others were threatened and could not but miscarry in his fall. But such is ever the will of God (who in the execution of His judgments, breaketh the firebrands upon the head of him who first kindleth them) there were, who conceived that our governor indeed neither durst, nor had authority to put in execution, or pass the act of justice upon anyone, how treacherous or impious so ever. . . . They persevered therefore not only to draw unto them such a number and associates as they could work in to the abandoning of our governor and to the inhabiting of this island. They had now purposed to have made a surprise of the storehouse. . . .

But as all giddy and lawless attempts have always something of imperfection, and that as well by the property of the action, which holdeth of disobedience and rebellion (both full of fear) as through the ignorance of the devisers themselves; so in this (besides those defects) there were some of the association, who not strong enough fortified in their own conceits, brake from the plot itself, and (before the time was ripe for the execution thereof) discovered the whole order, and every agent and actor thereof, who nevertheless were not suddenly apprehended, by reason the confederates were divided and separated in place, some with us, and the chief with Sir George Somers.

*[Caliban: "on whose nature / Nurture can never stick."
4.1.188–89]*

[After the castaways have arrived in Virginia:] Certain Indians (watching the occasion) seized the poor fellow [one of Sir Thomas Gates's men] and led him up into the woods and sacrificed him. It did not a little trouble the lieutenant governor, who since his first landing in the country (how justly soever provoked) would not by any means be wrought to a violent proceeding against them for all the practices of villainy with which they daily endangered our men, thinking it possible by a more tractable course to win them to a better condition. But now being startled by this, he well perceived how little a fair and noble entreaty works upon a barbarous disposition, and therefore in some measure purposed to be revenged.

[Purchas has the following marginal comment: "Can a leopard change his spots? Can a savage remaining savage be civil? Were not we ourselves made and not born civil in our progenitors' days? And were not Caesar's Britons as brutish as Virginians? The Roman swords were best teachers of civility to this and other countries near us."]

Sylvester Jourdain: from A Discovery of the
Barmudas, 1610.

[*Ariel: "Safely in harbor / Is the King's ship; in the deep nook." 1.2.226–27*]

. . . All our men, being utterly spent, tired, and disabled for longer labor, were even resolved, without any hope of their lives, to shut up the hatches and to have committed themselves to the mercy of the sea (which is said to be merciless) or rather to the mercy of their mighty God and redeemer. . . . So that some of them, having some good and comfortable waters in the ship, fetched them and drunk the one to the other, taking their last leave one of the other, until their more joyful and happy meeting in a more blessed world; when it pleased God out of his most gracious and merciful providence, so to direct and guide our ship (being left to the mercy of the sea) for her most advantage; that Sir George Somers . . . most wishedly happily descried land; whereupon he most comfortably encouraged the company to follow their pumping, and by no means to cease bailing out of the water. . . . Through which weak means it pleased God to work so strongly as the water was stayed for that little time (which, as we all much feared, was the last period of our breathing) and the ship kept from present sinking, when it pleased God to send her within half an English mile of that land that Sir George Somers had not long before descried—which were the islands of the Barmudas. And there neither did our ship sink, but more fortunately in so great a misfortune fell in between two rocks, where she was fast lodged and locked for further budging.

[*An island paradise*]

But our delivery was not more strange in falling so opportunely and happily upon the land, as our feeding and preservation was beyond our hopes and all men's expectations most admirable. For the islands of the Barmudas, as every man knoweth that hath heard or read of them, were never inhabited by any Christian or heathen people, but ever esteemed and reputed a most prodigious and enchanted place affording nothing but gusts, storms, and foul weather; which made every navigator and mariner to avoid them, as Scylla and Charybdis, or as they would shun the Devil himself; and no man was ever heard to make for the place, but as against their will, they have by storms and dangerousness of the rocks, lying seven leagues into the sea, suffered shipwrack. Yet did we find there the air so temperate and the country so abundantly fruitful of all fit necessaries for the sustenation and preservation of man's life, that most in a manner of all our provisions of bread, beer, and victual being quite spoiled in lying long drowned in salt water, notwithstanding we were there for the space of nine months (few days over or under) not only well refreshed, comforted, and with good saiety contented but, out of the abundance thereof, provided us some reasonable quantity and proportion of provision to carry us for Virginia and to maintain ourselves and that company we found there, to the great relief of them, as it fell out in their so great extremities ... until it pleased God ... that their store was better supplied. And greater and better provisions we might have had, if we had had better means for the storing and transportation thereof. Wherefore my opinion sincerely of this island is, that whereas it hath been and is full accounted the most dangerous, unfortunate, and most forlorn place of the world, it is in truth the richest, healthfulest, and pleasing land (the quantity and bigness thereof considered) and merely natural, as ever man set foot upon.

Council of Virginia: from *The True Declaration of the Estate of the Colony in Virginia*, 1610.

[*Providence*]

... God that heard Jonas crying out of the belly of hell, He pitied the distresses of His servants. For behold, in the last period of necessity Sir George Somers descried land, which was by so much the more joyful by how much their danger was despairful. The islands on which they fell were the *Bermudos,* a place hardly accessible through the environing rocks and dangers. Notwithstanding, they were forced to run their ship on shore, which through God's providence fell betwixt two rocks, that caused her to stand firm and not immediately to be broken. . . .

Again, as in the great famine of Israel, God commanded Elias to fly to the brook Cedron, and there fed him by ravens; so God provided for our disconsolate people in the midst of the sea by fowls, but with an admirable difference. Unto Elias the ravens brought meat, unto our men the fowls brought themselves for meat. For when they whistled or made any strange noise, the fowls would come and sit on their shoulders; they would suffer themselves to be taken and weighed by our men, who would make choice of the fattest and fairest, and let fly the lean and lightest. . . .

Consider all these things together. At the instant of need, they descried land; half an hour more, had buried their memorial in the sea. If they had fell by night, what expectation of light from an uninhabited desert? They fell betwixt a labyrinth of rocks, which they conceive are moldered into the sea by thunder and lightning. This was not Ariadne's thread, but the direct line of God's providence. If it had not been so near land, their company or provision had perished by water; if they had not found hogs and fowls and fish, they had perished by famine; if there had not been fuel, they had perished by want of fire; if there had not been timber, they could not have transported themselves to Virginia, but must have been forgotten forever. *Nimium timet qui Deo non credit;* he is too impiously fearful that will not trust in God so powerful.

What is there in all this tragical comedy that should discourage us with impossibility of the enterprise? When of all the fleet, one only ship by a secret leak was endangered, and yet in the gulf of despair was so graciously preserved.

[*Order and disorder*]

[Disorder in Virginia:] The ground of all those miseries was the permissive providence of God, who, in the fore-mentioned violent storm, separated the head from the body, all the vital powers of regiment being exiled with Sir Thomas Gates in those infortunate (yet fortunate) islands. The broken remainder of those supplies made a greater shipwreck in the continent of Virginia, by the tempest of dissension: every man, overvaluing his own worth, would be a commander; every man, underprizing another's value, denied to be commanded.

Michel de Montaigne: from *Of the Cannibals*, translated by John Florio, 1603.

[*Nature vs. art: Gonzalo's ideal commonwealth, 2.1.148–73*]

... I find (as far as I have been informed) there is nothing in that nation [the American Indians], that is either barbarous or savage, unless men call that barbarism which is not common to them. As indeed, we have no other aim of truth and reason than the example and idea of the opinions and customs of the country we live in. There is ever perfect religion, perfect policy, perfect and complete use of all things. They are even savage, as we call those fruits wild which nature of herself and of her ordinary progress hath produced; whereas indeed, they are those which ourselves have altered by our artificial devices, and diverted from their common order, we should rather term savage. In those are the true and most profitable virtues and natural properties most lively and vigorous, which in these we have bastardized, applying them to the pleasure of our corrupted taste. And if notwithstanding, in divers fruits of those countries that were never tilled, we shall find that, in respect of ours, they are most excellent and as delicate unto our taste, there is no reason art should gain the point of honor of our great and puissant mother Nature.

We have so much by our inventions surcharged the beauties and riches of her works that we have altogether overchoked her; yet wherever her purity shineth, she makes our vain and frivolous enterprises wonderfully ashamed. . . .

All our endeavor or wit cannot so much as reach to represent the nest of the least birdlet, its contexture, beauty, profit and use, no nor the web of a seely [i.e., trivial] spider. "All things," saith Plato, "are produced either by nature, by fortune, or by art. The greatest and fairest by one or other of the two first, the least and imperfect by the last." Those nations seem therefore so barbarous unto me, because they have received very little fashion from human wit and are yet near their original naturality. The laws of nature do yet command them, which are but little bastardized by ours, and that with such purity, as I am sometimes grieved the knowledge of it came no sooner to light, at what time there were men that better than we could have judged of it. I am sorry Lycurgus and Plato had it not; for me seemeth that what in those nations we see by experience, doth not only exceed all the pictures wherewith licentious Poesy hath proudly embellished the golden age, and all her quaint inventions to fain a happy condition of man, but also the conception and desire of Philosophy. They could not imagine a genuity so pure and simple as we see it by experience; nor ever believe our society might be maintained with so little art and humane combination. It is a nation, would I answer Plato, that hath no kind of traffic, no knowledge of letters, no intelligence of numbers, no name of magistrate, nor of politic superiority; no use of service, of riches, or of poverty; no contracts, no successions, no partitions, no occupation but idle; no respect of kindred but common, no apparel but natural, no manuring of lands, no use of wine, corn, or metal. The very words that import lying, falsehood, treason, dissimulations, covetousness, envy, detraction, and pardon, were never heard of amongst them. How dissonant would he find his imaginary commonwealth from this perfection? . . .

Furthermore, they live in a country of so exceeding pleasant and temperate situation that, as my testimonies have told me, it is very rare to see a sick body amongst them; and they have further assured me they never saw any man there either shaking with the palsy, toothless, with eyes dropping, or crooked and stooping through age.

[On cannibalism itself:] I am not sorry we note the barbarous horror of such an action, but grieved that, prying so narrowly into their faults, we are so blinded in ours. I think there is more barbarism in eating men alive than to feed upon them being dead; to mangle by tortures and torments a body full of lively sense, to roast him in pieces, to make dogs and swine to gnaw and tear him in mammocks (as we have not only read but seen very lately, yea and in our own memory, not amongst ancient enemies but our neighbors and fellow citizens; and which is worse, under pretense of piety and religion) than to roast and eat him after he is dead.

Ovid: from *Metamorphoses*, Medea's speech, translated by Arthur Golding, 1567.

[*Magic and metamorphosis: Prospero's farewell to his art 5.1.33–57*]

Ye airs and winds, ye elves of hills, of brooks, of woods
    alone,
Of standing lakes, and of the night approach ye every-
    chone.
Through help of whom (the crooked banks much
    wond'ring at the thing)
I have compelled streams to run clean backward to their
    spring.
By charms I make the calm seas rough, and make the
    rough seas plain
And cover all the sky with clouds, and chase them
    thence again.
By charms I raise and lay the winds, and burst the
    viper's jaw,
And from the bowels of the earth both stones and trees
    do draw.
Whole woods and forests I remove; I make the
    mountains shake,
And even the earth itself to groan and fearfully to quake.

I call up dead men from their graves; and thee O
    lightsome Moon
I darken oft, though beaten brass abate thy peril soon.
Our sorcery dims the morning fair, and darks the sun at
    noon.

Commentaries

SAMUEL TAYLOR COLERIDGE

From The Lectures of 1811–1812, Lecture IX

Among the ideal plays, I will take *The Tempest*, by way of example. Various others might be mentioned, but it is impossible to go through every drama, and what I remark on *The Tempest* will apply to all Shakespeare's productions of the same class.

In this play Shakespeare has especially appealed to the imagination, and he has constructed a plot well adapted to the purpose. According to his scheme, he did not appeal to any sensuous impression (the word "sensuous" is authorized by Milton) of time and place, but to the imagination, and it is to be borne in mind that of old, and as regards mere scenery, his works may be said to have been recited rather than acted—that is to say, description and narration supplied the

From *Shakespearean Criticism* by Samuel Taylor Coleridge. 2nd ed., ed. Thomas Middleton Raysor. 2 vols. (New York: E. P. Dutton and Company, Inc., 1960; London: J. M. Dent & Sons, Ltd., 1961). The exact text of Coleridge's lecture does not exist; what is given here is the transcript of a shorthand report taken by an auditor, J. P. Collier.

place of visual exhibition: the audience was told to fancy that they saw what they only heard described; the painting was not in colors, but in words.

This is particularly to be noted in the first scene—a storm and its confusion on board the king's ship. The highest and the lowest characters are brought together, and with what excellence! Much of the genius of Shakespeare is displayed in these happy combinations—the highest and the lowest, the gayest and the saddest; he is not droll in one scene and melancholy in another, but often both the one and the other in the same scene. Laughter is made to swell the tear of sorrow, and to throw, as it were, a poetic light upon it, while the tear mingles tenderness with the laughter. Shakespeare has evinced the power, which above all other men he possessed, that of introducing the profoundest sentiments of wisdom, where they would be least expected, yet where they are most truly natural. One admirable secret of his art is that separate speeches frequently do not appear to have been occasioned by those which preceded, and which are consequent upon each other, but to have arisen out of the peculiar character of the speaker.

Before I go further, I may take the opportunity of explaining what is meant by mechanic and organic regularity. In the former the copy must appear as if it had come out of the same mold with the original; in the latter there is a law which all the parts obey, conforming themselves to the outward symbols and manifestations of the essential principle. If we look to the growth of trees, for instance, we shall observe that trees of the same kind vary considerably, according to the circumstances of soil, air, or position; yet we are able to decide at once whether they are oaks, elms, or poplars.

So with Shakespeare's characters: he shows us the life and principle of each being with organic regularity. The Boatswain, in the first scene of *The Tempest*, when the bonds of reverence are thrown off as a sense of danger impresses all, gives a loose to his feelings, and thus pours forth his vulgar mind to the old Counselor:

"Hence! What care these roarers for the name of king? To cabin! Silence! Trouble us not."

Gonzalo replies—"Good; yet remember whom thou hast

aboard." To which the Boatswain answers—"None that I more love than myself. You are a counselor: if you can command these elements to silence and work the peace of the present, we will not hand a rope more; use your authority: if you cannot, give thanks that you have lived so long, and make yourself ready in your cabin for the mischance of the hour, if it so hap.—Cheerly, good hearts!—Out of our way, I say."

An ordinary dramatist would, after this speech, have represented Gonzalo as moralizing, or saying something connected with the Boatswain's language; for ordinary dramatists are not men of genius: they combine their ideas by association, or by logical affinity; but the vital writer, who makes men on the stage what they are in nature, in a moment transports himself into the very being of each personage, and, instead of cutting out artificial puppets, he brings before us the men themselves. Therefore, Gonzalo soliloquizes,—"I have great comfort from this fellow: methinks, he hath no drowning mark upon him; his complexion is perfect gallows. Stand fast, good fate, to his hanging! make the rope of his destiny our cable, for our own doth little advantage. If he be not born to be hanged, our case is miserable."

In this part of the scene we see the true sailor with his contempt of danger, and the old counselor with his high feeling, who, instead of condescending to notice the words just addressed to him, turns off, meditating with himself and drawing some comfort to his own mind by trifling with the ill expression of the Boatswain's face, founding upon it a hope of safety.

Shakespeare had predetermined to make the plot of this play such as to involve a certain number of low characters, and at the beginning he pitched the note of the whole. The first scene was meant as a lively commencement of the story; the reader is prepared for something that is to be developed, and in the next scene he brings forward Prospero and Miranda. How is this done? By giving to his favorite character, Miranda, a sentence which at once expresses the violence and fury of the storm, such as it might appear to a witness on the land, and at the same time displays the tenderness of her feelings—the exquisite feelings of a female brought up in a desert, but with all the advantages of education, all that could be communicated by a wise and affectionate father. She possesses all the delicacy of innocence, yet with all the powers of her mind unweakened by the combats of life. Miranda exclaims:

> O! I have suffered
> With those that I saw suffer: a brave vessel,
> Who had, no doubt, some noble creatures in her,
> Dash'd all to pieces

The doubt here intimated could have occurred to no mind but to that of Miranda, who had been bred up in the island with her father and a monster only: she did not know, as others do, what sort of creatures were in a ship; others never would have introduced it as a conjecture. This shows that while Shakespeare is displaying his vast excellence, he never fails to insert some touch or other which is not merely characteristic of the particular person, but combines two things—the person, and the circumstances acting upon the person. She proceeds:

> O! the cry did knock
> Against my very heart. Poor souls! they perish'd.
> Had I been any god of power, I would
> Have sunk the sea within the earth, or e'er
> It should the good ship so have swallow'd, and
> The fraughting souls within her.

She still dwells upon that which was most wanting to the completeness of her nature—these fellow creatures from whom she appeared banished, with only one relict to keep them alive, not in her memory, but in her imagination.

Another proof of excellent judgment in the poet, for I am now principally adverting to that point, is to be found in the preparation of the reader for what is to follow. Prospero is introduced, first in his magic robe, which, with the assistance of his daughter, he lays aside, and we then know him to be a being possessed of supernatural powers. He then instructs Miranda in the story of their arrival in the island, and this is conducted in such a manner that the reader never conjectures the technical use the poet has made of the relation, by informing the auditor of what it is necessary for him to know.

The next step is the warning by Prospero that he means, for particular purposes, to lull his daughter to sleep; and here he exhibits the earliest and mildest proof of magical power. In ordinary and vulgar plays we should have had some person brought upon the stage, whom nobody knows or cares anything about, to let the audience into the secret. Prospero having cast a sleep upon his daughter, by that sleep stops the narrative at the very moment when it was necessary to break it off, in order to excite curiosity and yet to give the memory and understanding sufficient to carry on the progress of the history uninterruptedly.

Here I cannot help noticing a fine touch of Shakespeare's knowledge of human nature, and generally of the great laws of the human mind: I mean Miranda's infant remembrance. Prospero asks her—

> Canst thou remember
> A time before we came unto this cell?
> I do not think thou canst, for then thou wast not
> Out three years old.

Miranda answers,

> Certainly, sir, I can.

Prospero inquires,

> By what? by any other house or person?
> Of any thing the image tell me, that
> Hath kept with thy remembrance.

To which Miranda returns,

> 'Tis far off;
> And rather like a dream than an assurance
> That my remembrance warrants. Had I not
> Four or five women once, that tended me?

This is exquisite! In general, our remembrances of early life arise from vivid colors, especially if we have seen them in motion: for instance, persons when grown up will remember a bright green door, seen when they were quite young; but Miranda, who was somewhat older, recollected four or five women who tended her. She might know men from her father, and her remembrance of the past might be worn out by the present object, but women she only knew by herself, by the contemplation of her own figure in the fountain, and she recalled to her mind what had been. It was not that she had seen such and such grandees, or such and such peeresses, but she remembered to have seen something like the reflection of herself: it was not herself, and it brought back to her mind what she had seen most like herself.

In my opinion the picturesque power displayed by Shakespeare, of all the poets that ever lived, is only equaled, if equaled, by Milton and Dante. The presence of genius is not shown in elaborating a picture: we have had many specimens of this sort of work in modern poems, where all is so dutchified, if I may use the word, by the most minute touches, that the reader naturally asks why words, and not painting, are used? I know a young lady of much taste, who observed that in reading recent versified accounts of voyages and travels, she, by a sort of instinct, cast her eyes on the opposite page, for colored prints of what was so patiently and punctually described.

The power of poetry is, by a single word perhaps, to instill that energy into the mind which compels the imagination to produce the picture. Prospero tells Miranda,

> One midnight,
> Fated to the purpose, did Antonio open
> The gates of Milan; and i' the dead of darkness,
> The ministers for the purpose hurried thence
> Me, and thy crying self.

Here, by introducing a single happy epithet, "crying," in the last line, a complete picture is presented to the mind, and in the production of such pictures the power of genius consists.

In reference to preparation, it will be observed that the storm, and all that precedes the tale, as well as the tale itself, serve to develop completely the main character of the drama, as well as the design of Prospero. The manner in which the heroine is charmed asleep fits us for what follows, goes beyond our ordinary belief, and gradually leads us to the appearance and disclosure of a being of the most fanciful and delicate texture, like Prospero, preternaturally gifted.

In this way the entrance of Ariel, if not absolutely forethought by the reader, was foreshown by the writer: in addition, we may remark, that the moral feeling called forth by the sweet words of Miranda,

> Alack, what trouble
> Was I then to you!

in which she considered only the sufferings and sorrows of her father, puts the reader in a frame of mind to exert his imagination in favor of an object so innocent and interesting. The poet makes him wish that, if supernatural agency were to be employed, it should be used for a being so young and lovely. "The wish is father to the thought," and Ariel is introduced. Here what is called poetic faith is required and created, and our common notions of philosophy give way before it: this feeling may be said to be much stronger than historic faith, since for the exercise of poetic faith the mind is previously prepared. I make this remark, though somewhat digressive, in order to lead to a future subject of these lectures—the poems of Milton. When adverting to those, I shall have to explain further the distinction between the two.

Many scriptural poems have been written with so much of Scripture in them that what is not Scripture appears to be not true, and like mingling lies with the most sacred revelations. Now Milton, on the other hand, has taken for his subject that one point of Scripture of which we have the mere fact recorded, and upon this he has most judiciously constructed his whole fable. So of Shakespeare's *King Lear*: we have little historic evidence to guide or confine us, and the few facts handed down to us, and admirably employed by the poet, are sufficient, while we read, to put an end to all doubt as to the credibility of the story. It is idle to say that this or that incident is improbable, because history, as far as it goes, tells us that the fact was so and so. Four or five lines in the Bible include the whole that is said of Milton's story, and the Poet has called up that poetic faith, that conviction of the mind, which is necessary to make that seem true which otherwise might have been deemed almost fabulous.

But to return to *The Tempest*, and to the wondrous creation of Ariel. If a doubt could ever be entertained whether Shakespeare was a great poet, acting upon laws arising out of his own nature and not without law, as has sometimes been idly asserted, that doubt must be removed by the character of Ariel. The very first words uttered by this being introduce the spirit, not as an angel, above man; not a gnome or a fiend, below man; but while the poet gives him the faculties and the advantages of reason, he divests him of all mortal character, not positively, it is true, but negatively. In air he lives, from air he derives his being, in air he acts; and all his colors and properties seem to have been obtained from the rainbow and the skies. There is nothing about Ariel that cannot be conceived to exist either at sunrise or at sunset: hence all that belongs to Ariel belongs to the delight the mind is capable of receiving from the most lovely external appearances. His answers to Prospero are directly to the question and nothing beyond; or where he expatiates, which is not unfrequently, it is to himself and upon his own delights, or upon the unnatural situation in which he is placed, though under a kindly power and to good ends.

Shakespeare has properly made Ariel's very first speech characteristic of him. After he has described the manner in which he had raised the storm and produced its harmless consequences, we find that Ariel is discontented—that he has been freed, it is true, from a cruel confinement, but still that he is bound to obey Prospero and to execute any commands imposed upon him. We feel that such a state of bondage is almost unnatural to him, yet we see that it is delightful for him to be so employed. It is as if we were to command one of the winds in a different direction to that which nature dictates, or one of the waves, now rising and now sinking, to recede before it bursts upon the shore: such is the feeling we experience, when we learn that a being like Ariel is commanded to fulfill any mortal behest.

When, however, Shakespeare contrasts the treatment of Ariel by Prospero with that of Sycorax, we are sensible that the liberated spirit ought to be grateful, and Ariel does feel and acknowledge the obligation; he immediately assumes the airy being, with a mind so elastically corresponding that when once a feeling has passed from it, not a trace is left behind.

Is there anything in nature from which Shakespeare caught the idea of this delicate and delightful being, with such childlike simplicity, yet with such preternatural powers? He is neither born of heaven, nor of earth; but, as it were, between both, like a May blossom kept suspended in air by the fanning breeze, which prevents it from falling to the ground, and only finally, and by compulsion, touching earth. This reluctance of the sylph to be under the command even of Prospero is kept up through the whole play, and in the exercise of his admirable judgment Shakespeare has availed himself of it in order to give Ariel an interest in the event, looking forward to that moment when he was to gain his last and only reward—simple and eternal liberty.

Another instance of admirable judgment and excellent preparation is to be found in the creature contrasted with Ariel—Caliban, who is described in such a manner by Prospero as to lead us to expect the appearance of a foul, unnatural monster. He is not seen at once: his voice is heard; this is the preparation; he was too offensive to be seen first in all his deformity, and in nature we do not receive so much disgust from sound as from sight. After we have heard Caliban's voice he does not enter until Ariel has entered like a water nymph. All the strength of contrast is thus acquired without any of the shock of abruptness, or of that unpleasant sensation, which we experience when the object presented is in any way hateful to our vision.

The character of Caliban is wonderfully conceived: he is a sort of creature of the earth, as Ariel is a sort of creature of the air. He partakes of the qualities of the brute, but is distinguished from brutes in two ways: by having mere understanding without moral reason; and by not possessing the

instincts which pertain to absolute animals. Still, Caliban is in some respects a noble being: the poet has raised him far above contempt: he is a man in the sense of the imagination: all the images he uses are drawn from nature and are highly poetical; they fit in with the images of Ariel. Caliban gives us images from the earth, Ariel images from the air. Caliban talks of the difficulty of finding fresh water, of the situation of morasses, and of other circumstances which even brute instinct, without reason, could comprehend. No mean figure is employed, no mean passion displayed, beyond animal passion and repugnance to command.

The manner in which the lovers are introduced is equally wonderful, and it is the last point I shall now mention in reference to this, almost miraculous, drama. The same judgment is observable in every scene, still preparing, still inviting, and still gratifying, like a finished piece of music. I have omitted to notice one thing, and you must give me leave to advert to it before I proceed: I mean the conspiracy against the life of Alonzo. I want to show you how well the poet prepares the feelings of the reader for this plot, which was to execute the most detestable of all crimes, and which, in another play, Shakespeare has called "the murder of sleep."

Antonio and Sebastian at first had no such intention: it was suggested by the magical sleep cast on Alonzo and Gonzalo; but they are previously introduced scoffing and scorning at what was said by others, without regard to age or situation—without any sense of admiration for the excellent truths they heard delivered, but giving themselves up entirely to the malignant and unsocial feeling which induced them to listen to everything that was said, not for the sake of profiting by the learning and experience of others, but of hearing something that might gratify vanity and self-love, by making them believe that the person speaking was inferior to themselves.

This, let me remark, is one of the grand characteristics of a villain; and it would not be so much a presentiment as an anticipation of hell for men to suppose that all mankind were as wicked as themselves, or might be so, if they were not too great fools. Pope, you are perhaps aware, objected to this conspiracy; but in my mind, if it could be omitted, the play would lose a charm which nothing could supply.

Many, indeed innumerable, beautiful passages might be quoted from this play, independently of the astonishing scheme of its construction. Everybody will call to mind the grandeur of the language of Prospero in that divine speech, where he takes leave of his magic art; and were I to indulge myself by repetitions of the kind, I should descend from the character of a lecturer to that of a mere reciter. Before I terminate, I may particularly recall one short passage which has fallen under the very severe, but inconsiderate, censure of Pope and Arbuthnot, who pronounce it a piece of the grossest bombast. Prospero thus addresses his daughter, directing her attention to Ferdinand:

> The fringed curtains of thine eye advance,
> And say what thou seest yond.

Taking these words as a periphrase of—"Look what is coming yonder," it certainly may to some appear to border on the ridiculous and to fall under the rule I formerly laid down—that whatever, without injury, can be translated into a foreign language in simple terms, ought to be in simple terms in the original language; but it is to be borne in mind that different modes of expression frequently arise from difference of situation and education: a blackguard would use very different words, to express the same thing, to those a gentleman would employ, yet both would be natural and proper; difference of feeling gives rise to difference of language: a gentleman speaks in polished terms, with due regard to his own rank and position, while a blackguard, a person little better than half a brute, speaks like half a brute, showing no respect for himself nor for others.

But I am content to try the lines I have just quoted by the introduction to them; and then, I think, you will admit, that nothing could be more fit and appropriate than such language. How does Prospero introduce them? He has just told Miranda a wonderful story, which deeply affected her and filled her with surprise and astonishment, and for his own purposes he afterwards lulls her to sleep. When she awakes,

Shakespeare has made her wholly inattentive to the present, but wrapped up in the past. An actress who understands the character of Miranda would have her eyes cast down and her eyelids almost covering them, while she was, as it were, living in her dream. At this moment Prospero sees Ferdinand and wishes to point him out to his daughter, not only with great, but with scenic solemnity, he standing before her and before the spectator in the dignified character of a great magician. Something was to appear to Miranda on the sudden, and as unexpectedly as if the hero of a drama were to be on the stage at the instant when the curtain is elevated. It is under such circumstances that Prospero says, in a tone calculated at once to arouse his daughter's attention,

> The fringed curtains of thine eye advance,
> And say what thou seest yond.

Turning from the sight of Ferdinand to his thoughtful daughter, his attention was first struck by the downcast appearance of her eyes and eyelids; and, in my humble opinion, the solemnity of the phraseology assigned to Prospero is completely in character, recollecting his preternatural capacity, in which the most familiar objects in nature present themselves in a mysterious point of view. It is much easier to find fault with a writer by reference to former notions and experience than to sit down and read him, recollecting his purpose, connecting one feeling with another, and judging of his words and phrases in proportion as they convey the sentiments of the persons represented.

Of Miranda we may say that she possesses in herself all the ideal beauties that could be imagined by the greatest poet of any age or country; but it is not my purpose now so much to point out the high poetic powers of Shakespeare as to illustrate his exquisite judgment, and it is solely with this design that I have noticed a passage with which, it seems to me, some critics, and those among the best, have been unreasonably dissatisfied. If Shakespeare be the wonder of the ignorant, he is, and ought to be, much more the wonder of the learned: not only from profundity of thought, but from his astonishing and intuitive knowledge of what man must be at all times and under all circumstances, he is rather to be looked upon as a prophet than as a poet. Yet, with all these unbounded powers, with all this might and majesty of genius, he makes us feel as if he were unconscious of himself and of his high destiny, disguising the half god in the simplicity of a child.

E. M. W. TILLYARD

The Tragic Pattern: *The Tempest*

It is a common notion that *Cymbeline* and *The Winter's Tale* are experiments leading to the final success of *The Tempest*. I think it quite untrue of *The Winter's Tale*, which, in some ways though not in others, deals with the tragic pattern more adequately than the later play. Certainly it deals with the destructive portion more directly and fully. On the other hand, *The Tempest*, by keeping this destructive portion largely in the background and dealing mainly with regeneration, avoids the juxtaposition of the two themes, which some people (of whom I am not one) find awkward in *The Winter's Tale*. The simple truth is that if you cram a trilogy into a single play something has to be sacrificed. Shakespeare chose to make a different sacrifice in each of his two successful renderings of the complete tragic pattern: unity in *The Winter's Tale*, present rendering of the destructive part of the tragic pattern in *The Tempest*.

Many readers, drugged by the heavy enchantments of Prospero's island, may demur at my admitting the tragic element to the play at all. I can cite in support one of the latest studies of the play, Dover Wilson's[1] (although I differ somewhat in the way I think the tragic element is worked out). Of the storm scene he writes:

From *Shakespeare's Last Plays* by E. M. W. Tillyard (London: Chatto and Windus, Ltd., 1938). Reprinted by permission of Chatto and Windus, Ltd., and Barnes and Noble, Inc.
[1] *The Meaning of the Tempest,* the Robert Spence Watson Memorial Lecture for 1936, delivered before the Literary and Philosophical Society of Newcastle-upon-Tyne, on October 5th, 1936.

It is as if Shakespeare had packed his whole tragic vision of life into one brief scene before bestowing his new vision upon us.

But one has only to look at the total plot to see that in its main lines it closely follows those of *Cymbeline* and *The Winter's Tale*, and that tragedy is an organic part of it. Prospero, when one first hears of him, was the ruler of an independent state and beloved of his subjects. But all is not well, because the King of Naples is his enemy. Like Basilius in Sidney's *Arcadia*, he commits the error of not attending carefully enough to affairs of state. The reason for this error, his Aristotelian ἁμαρτία, is his love of study. He hands over the government to his brother Antonio, who proceeds to call in the King of Naples to turn Prospero out of his kingdom. Fearing the people, Antonio refrains from murdering Prospero and his infant daughter, but sets them adrift in a boat. Now, except for this last item, the plot is entirely typical of Elizabethan revenge tragedy. Allow Prospero to be put to death, give him a son instead of a daughter to live and to avenge him, and your tragic plot is complete. Such are the affinities of the actual plot of *The Tempest*. And in the abstract it is more typically tragic in the fashion of its age than *The Winter's Tale*, with its debt to the Greek romances.

In handling the theme of regeneration, Shakespeare in one way alters his method. Although a royal person had previously been the protagonist, it had been only in name. Cymbeline had indeed resembled Prospero in having his enemies at his mercy and in forgiving them, but he owed his power not to himself, but to fortune and the efforts of others. As for Leontes, he has little to do with his own regeneration; for it would be perverse to make too much of his generosity in sheltering Florizel and Perdita from the anger of Polixenes. But Prospero is the agent of his own regeneration, the parent and tutor of Miranda; and through her and through his own works he changes the minds of his enemies. It was by this centering of motives in Prospero as well as by subordinating the theme of destruction that Shakespeare gave *The Tempest* its unified structure.

In executing his work, Shakespeare chose a method new

to himself but repeated by Milton in *Samson Agonistes*. He began his action at a point in the story so late that the story was virtually over; and he included the total story either by narrating the past or by re-enacting samples of it: a complete reaction from the method of frontal attack used in *The Winter's Tale*.

For the re-enactment of tragedy it is possible to think with Dover Wilson that the storm scene does this. But it does nothing to re-enact the specific tragic plot in the play, the fall of Prospero; and one of its aims is to sketch (as it does with incomparable swiftness) the characters of the ship's company. The true re-enactment is in the long first scene of the second act where Antonio, in persuading Sebastian to murder Alonso, personates his own earlier action in plotting against Prospero, thus drawing it out of the past and placing it before us in the present. This long scene, showing the shipwrecked king and courtiers and the conspiracy, has not had sufficient praise nor sufficient attention. Antonio's transformation from the cynical and lazy badgerer of Gonzalo's loquacity to the brilliantly swift and unscrupulous man of action is a thrilling affair. Just so Iago awakes from his churlish "honesty" to his brilliant machinations. Antonio is indeed one of Shakespeare's major villains:

Antonio.   Will you grant with me
    That Ferdinand is drowned?

Sebastian.   He's gone.

Antonio.   Then tell me,
    Who's the next heir of Naples?

Sebastian.   Claribel.

Antonio. She that is Queen of Tunis; she that dwells
    Ten leagues beyond man's life; she that from Naples
    Can have no note—unless the sun were post;
    The man i' the moon's too slow—till newborn chins
    Be rough and razorable; she that from whom
    We all were sea-swallowed, though some cast again,
    And, by that destiny, to perform an act
    Whereof what's past is prologue, what to come,

In yours and my discharge.

Sebastian.   What stuff is this? How say you?
'Tis true my brother's daughter's Queen of Tunis;
So is she heir of Naples; 'twixt which regions
There is some space.

Antonio.   A space whose ev'ry cubit
Seems to cry out "How shall that Claribel
Measure us back to Naples? Keep in Tunis,
And let Sebastian wake!" Say this were death
That now hath seized them, why, they were no worse
Than now they are. There be that can rule Naples
As well as he that sleeps; lords that can prate
As amply and unnecessarily
As this Gonzalo; I myself could make
A chough of as deep chat. O, that you bore
The mind that I do! What a sleep were this
For your advancement! Do you understand me?

                                   (2.1.247–72)

We should do wrong to take the conspiracy very seriously in itself. We know Prospero's power, and when Ariel enters and wakes the intended victims we have no fears for their future safety. But all the more weight should the scene assume as recalling the past.

Dover Wilson[2] greatly contributes to a right understanding of the play by stressing the first lines of the fifth act, when Prospero declares to Ariel that he will pardon his enemies, now quite at his mercy:

Ariel.   Your charm so strongly works 'em,
That if you now beheld them, your affections
Would become tender.

Prospero.   Dost thou think so, spirit?

Ariel. Mine would, sir, were I human.

Prospero.   And mine shall.
Hast thou, which art but air, a touch, a feeling

[2]*Op.cit.*, pp. 14–18.

> Of their afflictions, and shall not myself,
> One of their kind, that relish all as sharply,
> Passion as they, be kindlier moved than thou art?
> Though with their high wrongs I am struck to th' quick,
> Yet with my nobler reason 'gainst my fury
> Do I take part. The rarer action is
> In virtue than in vengeance. They being penitent,
> The sole drift of my purpose doth extend
> Not a frown further.   (5.1.17–30)

But when Dover Wilson would have this to represent Prospero's sudden conversion from a previously intended vengeance, I cannot follow him. It is true that Prospero shows a certain haste of temper up to that point of the play, and that he punishes Caliban and the two other conspirators against his life with some asperity; but his comments on them, after his supposed conversion, have for me the old ring:

> Mark but the badges of these men, my lords,
> Then say if they be true. This misshapen knave,
> His mother was a witch, and one so strong
> That could control the moon, make flows and ebbs,
> And deal in her command without her power.
> These three have robbed me; and this demi-devil
> (For he's a bastard one) had plotted with them
> To take my life. Two of these fellows you
> Must know and own; this thing of darkness I
> Acknowledge mine.   (267–76)

The last words express all Prospero's old bitterness that Caliban has resisted him and refused to respond to his nature.[3] Indeed, Prospero does not change fundamentally during the play, though, like Samson's, his own accomplished regeneration is put to the test. If he had seriously intended vengeance, why should he have stopped Sebastian and Antonio murdering Alonso? That he did stop them is proof of his already achieved regeneration from vengeance to mercy. This act,

[3]See the admirable discussion of "nature" and "nurture" in *The Tempest* in Middleton Murry's *Shakespeare*, pp. 396 ff.

and his talk to Ariel of taking part with his reason against his fury, are once again a re-enactment of a process now past, perhaps extending over a period of many years. I do not wish to imply that the re-enactment is weak or that the temptation to vengeance was not there all the time. Prospero's fury at the thought of Caliban's conspiracy, which interrupts the masque, must be allowed full weight. It is not for nothing that Miranda says that—

> Never till this day
> Saw I him touched with anger so distempered.
>
> (4.1.144–45)

We must believe that Prospero felt thus, partly because Caliban's conspiracy typifies all the evil of the world which has so perplexed him, and partly because he is still tempted to be revenged on Alonso and Antonio. He means to pardon them, and he will pardon them. But beneath his reason's sway is this anger against them, which, like Satan's before the sun in *Paradise Lost,* disfigures his face. When Dover Wilson calls Prospero

> a terrible old man, almost as tyrannical and irascible as Lear at the opening of his play,

he makes a valuable comparison, but it should concern Prospero as he once was, not the character who meets us in the play, in whom these traits are mere survivals.

The advantage of this technique of re-enactment was economy, its drawback an inevitable blurring of the sharp outline. The theme of destruction, though exquisitely blended in the whole, is less vivid than it is in *The Winter's Tale.* Having made it so vivid in that play, Shakespeare was probably well content to put the stress on the theme of re-creation. And here he did not work solely by re-enactment. He strengthened Prospero's re-enacted regeneration by the figures of Ferdinand and Miranda. I argued above that, in view of his background of Elizabethan chivalrous convention, Ferdinand need not have been as insignificant as he is usually supposed. Similarly, Miranda's character has been unduly diminished in recent years. Today, under the stress of the new psychology, men have become nervous lest they should be caught illicitly attaching their daydreams of the perfect woman to a character in fiction. They laugh at the Victorians for falling unawares into this error, and Miranda may have been one of the most popular victims. Hence the anxiety not to admire her too much. E. K. Chambers has written:

> Unless you are sentimentalist inveterate, your emotions will not be more than faintly stirred by the blameless loves at first sight of Ferdinand and Miranda.

Schücking[4] goes further and considers Miranda a poor imitation of Beaumont and Fletcher's idea of the chaste female, an idea that could be dwelt on so lovingly and emphatically only in a lascivious age. In depicting her with her talk of "modesty, the jewel in my dower" and her protests that if Ferdinand will not marry her, "I'll die your maid," and in making Prospero so insistent that she should not lose her maidenhead before marriage, Shakespeare, according to Schücking, is yielding to the demands of his age against his own better judgment. But Miranda is sufficiently successful a symbolic figure for it to matter little if she makes conventional and, in her, unnatural remarks. And even this defense may be superfluous. Since Miranda had never seen a young man, it might reasonably be doubted whether she would behave herself with entire propriety when she did. Prospero, too, had made enough mistakes in his life to be very careful to make no more. Further, Miranda was the heiress to the Duchy of Milan and her father hoped she would be Queen of Naples. What most strikingly emerged from the abdication of our late King was the strong "anthropological" feeling of the masses of the people concerning the importance of virginity in a king's consort. The Elizabethans were not less superstitious than ourselves and would have sympathized with Prospero's anxiety that the future Queen of Naples should keep her maidenhead till marriage: otherwise ill luck would be sure to follow.

[4]*Character Problems in Shakespeare's Plays*, pp. 249–50.

To revert to Miranda's character, like Perdita she is both symbol and human being, yet in both capacities somewhat weaker. She is the symbol of "original virtue," like Perdita, and should be set against the devilish figure of Antonio. She is the complete embodiment of sympathy with the men she thinks have been drowned: and her instincts are to create, to mend the work of destruction she has witnessed. She is— again like Perdita, though less clearly—a symbol of fertility. Stephano asks of Caliban, "Is it so brave a lass?" and Caliban answers,

> Ay, lord. She will become thy bed, I warrant,
> And bring thee forth brave brood.   (3.2.108–9)

Even if *The Tempest* was written for some great wedding, it need not be assumed that the masque was inserted merely to fit the occasion. Like the goddesses in Perdita's speeches about the flowers, Juno and Ceres and the song they sing may be taken to reinforce the fertility symbolism embodied in Miranda:

Juno.   Honor, riches, marriage blessing,
                 Long continuance, and increasing,
                 Hourly joys be still upon you!
                 Juno sings her blessings on you.

Ceres.   Earth's increase, foison plenty,
                 Barns and garners never empty,
                 Vines with clust'ring bunches growing,
                 Plants with goodly burden bowing;
                 Spring come to you at the farthest
                 In the very end of harvest!
                 Scarcity and want shall shun you,
                 Ceres' blessing so is on you.   (4.1.106–17)

The touches of ordinary humanity in Miranda—her siding with Ferdinand against a supposedly hostile father, for instance—are too well known to need recalling. They do not amount to a very great deal and leave her vaguer as a human being than as a symbol. Middleton Murry is not at his happiest when he says that "they are so terribly, so agonizingly real, these women of Shakespeare's last imagination." As far as Miranda is concerned, any agonizing sense of her reality derives from the critic and not from the play. But this does not mean that, judged by the play's requirements (which are not those of brilliant realism), Miranda is not perfection. Had she been more weakly drawn, she would have been insignificant, had she been more strongly, she would have interfered with the unifying dominance of Prospero.

Not only do Ferdinand and Miranda sustain Prospero in representing a new order of things that has evolved out of destruction; they also vouch for its continuation. At the end of the play Alonso and Prospero are old and worn men. A younger and happier generation is needed to secure the new state to which Prospero has so painfully brought himself, his friends, and all his enemies save Caliban.

BERNARD KNOX

The Tempest and the Ancient Comic Tradition

In *The Tempest* Shakespeare abandons the three familiar *milieux* in which most of his plays are set (classical antiquity, medieval England, and Renaissance Europe)[1] for a nameless island which is remote even from that Tunis which is itself, according to Antonio, "ten leagues beyond man's life." This island is not only uncharted, it is one on which anything can happen: "All torment, trouble, wonder, and amazement Inhabits heere." The poet places his characters in a world which seems to be purely of his own creating; it seems in this respect significant that, in spite of prodigies of *Quellenforschung*, no satisfactory source of *The Tempest* has yet been identified.

In the so-called "romances" of Shakespeare's last period there is an accelerated flight from probability; it is a movement beyond the "probable impossibility" to the complete impossibility. In *The Tempest* the laws which govern objects existing in space and time as we know them are imperiously suspended. Until the solemn moment when Prospero abjures his rough magic, the action develops in a world which defies nature: "These are not naturall events, they strengthen From strange, to stranger." One wonders how Prospero can keep his promise to the bewildered Alonso—"I'le resolve you (Which to you shall seeme probable) of every These happend accidents."

From *English Stage Comedy*. English Institute Essays, 1954, ed. W. K. Wimsatt, Jr. (New York, Columbia University Press, 1955, pp. 52–73). Reprinted by permission of Columbia University Press.

[1] Cf. Gilbert Highet, *The Classical Tradition* (Oxford, 1949), p. 194.

A recent production by the Yale Dramatic Association presented *The Tempest* as "science fiction"; the shipwreck scene took place in a space ship, and the action which takes place away from Prospero's cell was seen on a gigantic television screen, tuned in by a Prospero who sat before a control board which buzzed and flashed green light. The point was well taken: Shakespeare has in fact done what the modern science-fictioneers do—substituted for the normal laws of the operation of matter a new set of laws invented for the occasion.

Such a substitution creates great possibilities for what Aristotle called "Spectacle," and if the Yale Dramatic Association developed those possibilities somewhat exuberantly along modern lines they at least did no worse than Dryden and Davenant in 1667, whose stage direction for Act 1, scene 1, reads, in part: "This Tempest . . . has many dreadful Objects in it, as several Spirits in horrid shapes flying down among the Sailers, then rising and crossing in the Air. And when the Ship is sinking, the whole House is darken'd, and a shower of Fire falls upon 'em."

But novel and fantastic effects (and in this play it is clear that Shakespeare was interested in producing them) have their dangerous side; they may, by trading too much on it, destroy that willing suspension of disbelief on which every dramatic performance depends—the audience may come to feel, with Gonzalo, "Whether this be Or be not, I'le not sweare." The dramatist, by asking too much, may lose everything. Such a defiance of the normal laws of cause and effect in the operations of nature is especially dangerous in comedy, for comedy's appeal, no matter how contrived the plot may be, is to the audience's sense of solid values in a real world, to a critical faculty which can recognize the inappropriate. Tragedy, which questions normal human assumptions, may introduce the super- and the hypernatural more safely than comedy, which depends on the solidity of those assumptions for a response. A comic poet who sets his characters in action, not in the world as we know it but in one which defies our expectation, must compensate for the strangeness of the events by making the essences and relationships of the characters immediately and strikingly familiar. To put it another way, the fantasy and originality of the setting must be balanced and disciplined by a rigid adherence to tradition in character and plot.

This, I suggest, is a valid formula for *The Tempest*. It has certainly the most extraordinary and fantastic setting, for the sorcery of Prospero is a stranger thing than the familiar English fairy magic of *A Midsummer Night's Dream*. But in other ways it is the most rigidly traditional of all Shakespeare's comedies—with one exception. The exception is *The Comedy of Errors*, which is however apprentice work, a typical Renaissance *remaniement* of a Plautine original. *The Tempest* is as original as *The Comedy of Errors* is imitative; and yet they are the beginning and end of the same road. For the traditional foundation on which *The Tempest*'s cloud-capped towers are raised is the ancient comedy of Plautus, Terence, and (though the name would not have meant much to Shakespeare) Menander.

Like all proper foundations, this one is not conspicuous. But there are odd corners where its outline is visible in the superstructure. This, for example:

> *Prospero.* [*To Ariel*] She did confine thee
>   By helpe of her more potent Ministers,
>   And in her most unmittigable rage,
>   Into a cloven Pyne, within which rift,
>   Imprison'd, thou didst painefully remaine
>   A dozen yeeres: within which space she di'd,
>   And left thee there: where thou didst vent thy groanes
>   As fast as Mill-wheeles strike.

The groans of a disobedient spirit imprisoned in a cloven pine by a "blew ey'd hag" come "as fast as Mill-wheels strike": the simile illustrates the unfamiliar by appeal to an aspect of ordinary experience. Yet not, presumably, Ariel's ordinary experience: there are no mills in the strange economy of Prospero's island. The simile illustrates by an appeal from one world to another, with an anachronism the reverse of those Homeric similes which compare conditions of the heroic age to those of the poet's own time. (Homer compares the voice of Achilles to a trumpet, an instrument which the embattled heroes of his poem never mention or use, almost certainly because it had not yet been invented.) The mill wheels of Shakespeare's simile come not from his own world but from the world of Plautine comedy, where with monotonous frequency the rebellious slave is threatened or actually punished with an assignment to the brutal labor of the mill. And in this fantastic context, where Ariel ("my slave, as thou reportst thyselfe") is reminded of his punishment for former disobedience and threatened with even worse punishment for present disobedience, the simile gives a touch of familiarity and proportion to the outlandish details of Ariel's nature and status.

Here the classical precedent is for a moment distinctly visible, but in general it does its work the more efficiently because it is not obtrusive. Below the strange and brilliant surface composed of medieval magic and Renaissance travel tales, the initial situation, the nature and relationships of most of the characters, the development of the action and its final solution are all conjugations of the basic paradigms of classical comedy.

One of the most influential of these paradigms relates to the existence in ancient society of a dividing line stricter and more difficult to cross than any social barrier has been since: the distinction between slave and free. The free man could not imagine a misfortune worse than slavery, nor the slave a greater blessing than freedom. Slave and free were not so much separate classes as separate worlds: Aristotle could go so far as to claim that they were separate natures. This division was the most important sociological datum of ancient society, affecting men's attitude toward each other with a power almost as great as that of natural differences of sex or color. Among other things it provided a fixed contrast of condition and standards on which comedy would be based.

Ancient tragedy at the height of its development ignores the division and deals only with free men; Attic tragedy did not deal with slaves until Euripides introduced them, and this innovation was one of the main grounds for the conservative attack on him. The place for slaves was comedy, which, says Aristotle, "is an imitation of characters of a lower type"; and the lowest type imaginable was the slave. Comic slaves

could be beaten, could curse, lie, cheat, be drunken, lecherous, and cowardly to the limit of the free audience's capacity
for laughter without offending its sense of propriety and human dignity. Such an exhibition might in fact be considered
to have a moral effect; in Plutarch's "Life of Lycurgus"
(Chap. 28) we are told that at Sparta the ephors introduced
into the military dining halls Helots who had been deliberately inebriated as a spectacle to teach the young what
drunkenness was like; they also made the Helots learn songs
and dances that were, to quote Plutarch again, "ignoble and
ridiculous."

This was, of course, not a real dramatic performance
(though there is evidence of some kind of comic performance at Sparta from quite early times); at Athens the picture
is clearer. It is perhaps only a coincidence that the chorus of
satyrs in the only two surviving specimens of the humorous
satyr play are, in the plot of the plays, temporarily enslaved,
but it is evident that typical Athenian Old Comedy depended
heavily on the laughter to be extracted from the low pro-
clivities and activities of slaves. Aristophanes is not typical,
but he indicates what is typical in a famous passage of self-
congratulation which sets forth his claim to have ennobled
comedy. Among other things he claims to have "liberated the
slaves, whom the poets always brought on stage howling, all
for the sake of the same old joke, so that a fellow slave could
make fun of their stripes and ask them, 'What happened to
your hide, poor devils? Were your sides assaulted by a whip-
lash army that cut down the trees on your back?' " Aristophanes did not, of course, dispense entirely with servile
humor, rather he seems to have adapted it to subtler purposes
by introducing witty contrasts between slave and free. In *The
Knights*, for instance, he brings on stage all the prominent
Athenian politicians of the day as slaves in the house of a
bad-tempered old man called Demos: in this comedy Demos-
thenes, Nicias and Cleon fight, cheat, drink, spy, play the
coward, curse, bawl, lie, and rant as valiantly as any slave
ever born. Here the humorous aspects of servile behavior are
used to make a satiric point, that the free men behave like
slaves; *The Frogs* makes the opposite point by ringing the
changes on the contrast between the master Dionysus and his

slave Xanthias, who repeatedly exchange identities—with the surprising result that the slave emerges as his master's superior in wit, courage, and, incidentally, literary taste, for Xanthias cannot abide Euripides.

In the comedy of the fourth century the magnificent fantasy and political wit of Aristophanes are sadly lacking, but the theme of contrast between slave and free remains. In the domestic comedy of Menander and his contemporaries (the models of the Roman comic poets) the theme crystallizes into a variety of stock patterns, which have exerted enormous influence on comedy ever since.

In this comedy the master design is always more or less the same. A domestic problem involving the free members of the household (usually, in Menander, a marriage or a seduction—sometimes both) is eventually solved through complicated intrigues which involve the slave members of the household. The comedy proceeds on two social levels which interpenetrate, often on two plot levels as well, which also interpenetrate. The slave characters (and a host of technically free but hardly distinguishable lower-class types such as parasites, butlers, cooks, and pimps) have their own problems (the attainment of freedom, a free meal or a free drink), the solution of which is artfully made to depend on the solution of the problem of the free characters. A typical paradigm is the plot in which a clever slave, by intelligent initiative and intrigue (often directed against his less intelligent fellow slaves) solves his master's problem (which may range from finding a wife to marrying off a child) and, as a reward for his services, gains his private objective, his liberty.

This is a slave who has the intelligence of, and eventually attains the status of, a free man; but there is another type of slave who is a convenient vehicle for the traditional servile humor. This one provides the sullen bad temper, the cursing, the drunkenness, the indecency, thievishness, and cowardice which are the traditional characteristics of the comic slave. He may have the same ambition as his cleverer fellow, but not the same capacity; he forms grand designs, but through stupidity (often through the direct intervention of the clever slave) he fails miserably, and is humiliated and punished with blows or a stint at the mill.

While the slaves, in aspiration and action, trespass on the confines of the free world, the freeborn may find themselves, as foundlings, kidnapped children, or prisoners of war, temporary denizens of the slave world; their identification and restoration to freedom (and usually marriage) is the play's denouement, and usually coincides with, and balances, the liberation of the clever slave or the restoration of the stupid slave to his proper station, or both. Together with these contrasts of condition there are deeper contrasts of nature; free men can think and act like slaves and slaves rise superior in intelligence or emotion to their masters. One of the most searching and profound of Roman comedies is Lessing's favorite, *The Captives* of Plautus, in which master and slave, both enslaved as prisoners of war, exchange identities so that the master (as the slave) can be released to take the ransom demand home, while the slave remains in slavery (as the master), risking and, as it turns out, suffering terrible punishment when the truth is discovered. The nobility displayed by the slave is, characteristically enough, justified at the end of the play by the discovery that he was really born free, and his liberation is balanced by the punishment of the slave who originally kidnapped and sold him into slavery. In this and in practically all Roman comedy, the finale is a restoration of the characters to their proper status; in the typical pattern, the restoration of one of the two young lovers to freedom makes possible their marriage, and the stern father releases the clever and independent slave who has been instrumental in bringing about the happy conclusion.

When the dramatists of the Renaissance began to imitate the Roman comedies, slavery was a thing of the past in Europe (though not a few Elizabethan worthies made their fortunes by introducing it into the West Indies), but the ancient comic design was easily adapted to the conditions of a society which, like that of Elizabethan England, was based, however insecurely, on hierarchical social categories. Shakespearean comedy abounds in brilliant adaptations of the basic formula: the cruel reduction to his proper station suffered by Malvolio, who had "greatnesse thrust" upon him;

the exposure of Parolles "the gallant militarist" as a "past-saving slave"; above all the magnificent interpenetration of the two worlds of court and tavern in *Henry IV.* Falstaff acts the role of the King in the Boar's Head, runs his sword through Hotspur's corpse at Shrewsbury, and sets out for London crying, "The Lawes of England are at my command-ment," only to be brusquely restored to his proper station as a "Foole and Jester." Prince Hal, like some foundling, as his father suggests, begins as "sworn brother to a leash of Draw-ers," sounding "the very base-string of humility," but in the end restores himself to his proper station, "to mock the ex-pectation of the world."

But in *The Tempest*, a Utopia which Shakespeare invented for himself (as Gonzalo invents his in the play), there is no need to translate the classic form: it can be used literally. Prospero is master (and incidentally an irritable old man with a marriageable daughter) and Ariel and Caliban are slaves. Prospero as sorcerer has the power to enslave and release the free men too: this contrast is relevant for all the characters of the play—one of its main components is what Brower has called "the slavery-freedom continuity." "The 'slaves' and 'servants' of the play," he points out, "suffer various kinds of imprisonment, from Ariel in his 'cloven pine' to Ferdinand's mild confinement, and before the end of Act 4 everyone except Prospero and Miranda has been imprisoned in one way or another. During the course of Act 5 all the prisoners ex-cept Ferdinand (who has already been released) are set free. . . ."[2]

After the long expository scene between Prospero and Miranda (itself a typical Plautine delayed prologue) we are presented with an interview between master and intelligent slave:

> All haile, great Master, grave Sir, haile: I come
> To answer Thy best pleasure; be't to fly,
> To swim, to dive into the fire: to ride
> On the curld clowds: to thy strong bidding, taske
> Ariel, and all his Qualitie.

[2] R. A. Brower, *The Fields of Light* (Oxford, 1951), p. 110.

This is servile enough, and comparable to many a hyperbolic declaration of availability made by Roman comic slaves; its comic tone is pointed up by the fact that the moment Ariel is asked to make good some of these fine promises, he rebels. "Is there more toyle?" he asks,

> Since thou dost give me pains,
> Let me remember thee what thou hast promis'd
> Which is not yet perform'd me.

Prospero.   How now? moodie?
  What is't thou canst demand?

Ariel. My Libertie.

Some critics have been disturbed at the vehemence of Prospero's reaction; and it is true that phrases such as "Thou liest, malignant Thing"—"my slave, as thou reportst thy selfe"—and "Dull thing, I say so" sound more suited for Caliban than delicate Ariel. Yet it is not really surprising that Prospero should display what Wilson calls "ebullitions of imperious harshness" toward a slave who, after such an enthusiastic declaration of willingness to serve him, balks at the first mention of "more worke."

Prospero does more than chide; he threatens punishment. Sycorax punished Ariel with confinement in a cloven pine—"it was a torment To lay upon the damn'd"—but Prospero threatens to go one step farther: "I will rend an Oake And peg—thee in his knotty entrailes. . . ." Ariel begs for pardon and promises to be "correspondent to command." He is rewarded with a fresh promise of freedom—"after two daies I will discharge thee"—and sent about his master's business with renewed imperiousness:

> goe take this shape
> And hither come in 't: goe: hence
> With diligence.

"Exit," reads the stage direction.

From this point on Ariel is correspondent to command, and his first service is to bring Ferdinand into the presence of Miranda. It is the traditional role of the intelligent slave to further his master's marriage projects, and Ariel fully regains Prospero's favor and gets a renewed promise of the traditional reward. "Delicate Ariel, Ile set thee free for this." In fact, Ariel gains a remission of part of his stated time: "Ile free thee Within two dayes for this."

Throughout the rest of the play Ariel acts as Prospero's eyes and ears, but, as befits the clever slave, with a certain initiative too. He rescues Alonso and Gonzalo from the conspirators, and his words suggest that, though he has a general commission to protect Gonzalo at any rate, the methods have been left to him. "Prospero my Lord, shall know what I have done." His mischievous action against Caliban and the two Neapolitans is apparently his own idea, for Prospero later asks him where they are, and Ariel gives a full report of the chase he has led them. Yet the comic aspects of the relationship between master and slave are not neglected in the swift action of the play's central section. Ariel, ordered to produce spirits for the masque, replies:

> Before you can say come, and goe,
> And breathe twice: and cry so, so:
> Each one tripping on his Toe,
> Will be here with mop, and mowe.

This sounds remarkably like the half-ironical servile exaggeration of the Plautine slave promising miracles of speed. Charmides orders his slave to go from Athens to Piraeus—*I, i, ambula, actutum redi,* "Go on, go on, start walking, come back right away"—and gets the answer, *Illic sum atque hic sum,* "I'm there and back again." And that same Ariel who asks "Doe you love me Master? no?" at the end of the jingle quoted above, can also admit that he fears his master's temper.

Prospero. Spirit: We must prepare to meet with Caliban.

Ariel. I my Commander, when I presented *Ceres*
   I thought to have told thee of it, but I fear'd
   Least I might anger thee.

The comic aspects of Ariel's slavery are balanced by those of Prospero's mastery. This is not the only reference to Prospero's short temper. "Why speakes my father so ungently?"—"he's compos'd of harshnesse"—"your father's in some passion"—"never till this day Saw I him touch'd with anger, so distemper'd"—these observations only confirm the impression made by Prospero's outbursts of fury against his slaves. There is more than a touch in him of the Plautine old man, the irascible *senex* (*severus, difficilis, iratus, saevus,* as Donatus describes him),[3] who may in the end turn out to have a heart of gold, but who for the first four acts has only a noticeably short temper and a rough tongue.

This anger of Prospero is of course much more than a reminiscence of the irascibility of the stock comic figure: he is a man who has been grievously wronged, and who now, with his enemies at his mercy, intends to revenge himself. That this has been his intention is made perfectly clear in the speech in which that intention is forever renounced:

> Thogh with their high wrongs I am strook to th' quick
> Yet, with my nobler reason, gainst my furie
> Doe I take part: the rarer Action is
> In vertue, then in vengeance.

And this renunciation takes place when the slave rises superior to his master, setting an example of noble compassion:

> *Ariel.* . . . your charm so strongly works 'em
>   That if you now beheld them, your affections
>   Would become tender.
>
> *Prospero.* Dost thou thinke so, Spirit?
>
> *Ariel.* Mine would, Sir, were I humane.
>
> *Prospero.* And mine shall.

This is a magnificently imaginative version of the scenes in which the comedy slave surpasses the master in qualities

---

[3] Cf. George F. Duckworth, *The Nature of Roman Comedy* (Princeton, 1952), p. 242, n. 14.

which are traditionally those of the free man—in intelligence, courage, self-sacrifice. Here the nonhuman slave surpasses his human master in humanity.

As the play draws to a close, the recognition of Ariel's services and the renewed promises of liberation increase in frequency to become an obsessive burden:

>   thou
> Shalt have the ayre at freedome: for a little
> Follow, and doe me service.
>   quickly Spirit,
> Thou shalt ere long be free.
>   I shall misse
> Thee, but yet thou shalt have freedome.
> Bravely (my diligence) thou shalt be free.

"The reluctance of the sylph to be under the command even of Prospero," says Coleridge, "is kept up through the whole play, and in the exercise of his admirable judgment Shakespeare has availed himself of it in order to give Ariel an interest in the event, looking forward to that moment when he was to gain his last and only reward—simple and eternal liberty." He might have added that what Shakespeare "has availed himself of" is a dramatic design as old as European comedy.

Ariel, the slave whose nature is free, is balanced by Ferdinand, the free man and prince, who is enslaved. Accused as "spy" and "traitor," he is subdued by Prospero's magic: but there is nothing magical about the entertainment he is promised.

> Ile manacle thy necke and feete together:
> Sea water shalt thou drinke: thy food shall be
> The fresh-brooke Mussels, wither'd roots, and huskes
> Wherein the Acorne cradled. Follow.

This is a Shakespearean version of the chains and prison diet with which the ancient comic slave is so often threatened, and of which he so often complains. And Ferdinand's next appearance shows him performing servile tasks:

> I must remove
> Some thousands of these Logs, and pile them up,
> Upon a sore injunction.

The work he is doing is in fact Caliban's work (*"Enter Caliban with a burthen of wood"* is the stage direction for the preceding scene), and Ferdinand himself describes it as "wodden slaverie." But whereas Caliban has just declared his independence, and Ariel longs to be free, Ferdinand the free man is for the moment content to be a slave:

> all corners else o' th' Earth
> Let liberty make use of: space enough
> Have I in such a prison.

The service which he so willingly accepts is of course not that of his master, but that of his mistress:

> The verie instant that I saw you, did
> My heart flie to your service, there resides
> To make me slave to it, and for your sake
> Am I this patient Logge-man.

And the multiple wit of these variations on the theme is dazzlingly displayed when he and Miranda plight their troth:

Miranda.   to be your fellow
   You may denie me, but Ile be your servant
   Whether you will or no.

Ferdinand. My Mistris (deerest)
   And I thus humble ever.

Miranda. My husband then?

Ferdinand. I, with a heart as willing
   As bondage ere of freedome: heere's my hand.

He accepts marriage (that is, bondage) with a heart "as willing as bondage ere of freedome" (as willingly as Ariel, for example, would accept his liberty), but this acceptance, overheard by Prospero, is the signal for his release from the "wodden slaverie" in which he is now bound.

Ferdinand, as we have seen, is contrasted to Ariel, but Ariel's real opposite is Caliban, "my slave, who never Yeelds us kinde answere." Caliban's employment is menial: while Ariel treads "the Ooze of the salt deepe," Caliban "do's make our fire Fetch in our wood, and serves in Offices That profit us." It is remarkable that on an island where spirits can be made to produce banquets and perform masks, Prospero should need the services of Caliban to "fetch in firing ... scrape trenchering" and "wash dish," but so it is. "We cannot misse him."

Caliban, besides being a "Tortoys," "Hag-seed," a "delicate Monster," a "Moone-calfe," a "debosh'd Fish," and a "borne Devill," is also a slave, a poisonous, lying, and abhorred slave, to quote Prospero. His first speech (offstage)— "There's wood enough within"—and the onstage curses which follow it are enough to suggest a familiar frame of reference for the first appearance of this outlandish figure: he is the surly, cursing slave of the old tradition.

Caliban's curses are highly original in expression— "language as hobgoblin as his person," says Dryden justly. Shakespeare has created a special vocabulary of invective appropriate to the savage apprehension of nature, but the expressions have the same dramatic characteristics as their venerable ancestors. The cursing seems to be a thing in and for itself—it violates plausibility, for one thing. Why should Prospero put up with it, and counter it with threats of punishment that sound curiously like it? And Caliban is made to refer to another aspect of this improbability; "his Spirits heare me, And yet I needes must curse." He "needes must curse" because his cursing is vital to the comic essence of his nature; the scene in which he exchanges curses for Prospero's threats of punishment is a traditional feature of the comedy of master and slave.

Caliban is a sullen slave (a Sceparnio), a cursing slave (a Toxilus), and he is also a lecherous one. The only touch of low sexual humor in *The Tempest* is Caliban's unrepentant laughter when reminded of his attempt on Miranda's virtue: but that one laugh is enough to remind us that he has an ancestry reaching back through scurrilous Plautine slaves and Aristophanic comic actors wearing a leather *phallos* to the ithyphallic satyrs of the Greek vase paintings.

Caliban's meeting with Trinculo and Stephano is a servile parallel and parody of Miranda's meeting with Ferdinand; both mistress and slave are overcome with wonder at the vision of their counterparts in Neapolitan society. Miranda's worshiping remark, "I might call him A thing divine," is echoed in Caliban's "that's a brave God, and beares Celestiall liquor"; while Ferdinand's "My Language? Heavens" finds a base echo in Stephano's "where the divell should he learne our language?" Stephano and Trinculo—"two *Neapolitanes* scap'd"—are to Ferdinand as Caliban is to Miranda; creatures of a lower order. And Stephano the "drunken butler" is a familiar figure; the slave in charge of his master's wine who drinks most of it himself is a standard character of the old comedy. In one of the better-known Plautine plays, the *Miles Gloriosus*, there is a scene with not one but two drunken butlers, one dead drunk on his back inside the house, the other drunk on his feet outside.

But the drunkenness of Stephano is surpassed by that of Caliban. His extravagant admiration of Stephano, as Trinculo perceives, is more than savage simplicity: "The poore Monster's in drinke." In his drunken fit he thinks of the primary objective of all slaves, his freedom. Unlike Ariel, he cannot hope to win it by delicate service; he can gain his freedom only by working against his master or by running away from him. He deserts Prospero, "the Tyrant that I serve," for Stephano, and the service of this new master turns out to be perfect freedom, which he proceeds to celebrate in song and dance: "Freedome, high-day, high-day, freedome." It is the traditional servile drunken exhibition and it is grotesquely funny, but it is only the other side of the coin which shows us Ariel, moody, demanding his liberty. Ariel and Caliban are opposite as earth and air, but they are both enslaved, and in this they are alike. One suspects that Caliban speaks something close to the truth when he tells Stephano that Prospero's power depends on one thing only, his "Bookes":

> without them
> Hee's but a Sot, as I am; nor hath not
> One Spirit to command: they all do hate him
> As rootedly as I.

"They say there's but five upon this Isle," says Trinculo. "We are three of them, if th' other two be brain'd like us, the State totters." Of the three of them, the one with the most brains is Caliban. With servile flattery and cunning he supplants Trinculo in Stephano's graces, securing a series of reprimands and eventually a beating for his fellow slave.

> Beate him enough: after a little time
> Ile beate him too.

He is now Stephano's "lieutenant," but he knows what must be done to guarantee his new-found dignity: he must encompass Prospero's death. And so the "foule Conspiracy" is formed. The slaves indulge their exaggerated fantasies of freedom and sovereignty: "Monster, I will kill this man: his daughter and I will be King and Queene, save our Graces: and *Trinculo* and Thy selfe shall be Vice-royes." It is a servile parody of the more serious conspiracy of the free men, Antonio and Sebastian.

The drunken butler dreams of a kingdom; he is not the first. It is instructive to compare his plans with those of Gripus, the Plautine slave who has fished a treasure out of the sea and intends to hang on to it:

> When I'm once free, I'll equip myself with property, an
> estate, a house. I'll go into trade with great ships; I'll be
> considered a King among Kings. . . . I'll build a great city,
> and call it Gripus, after myself, a monument to my fame
> and doings. And in it I'll set up a great Kingdom . . . And
> yet, King though I am, I must make my breakfast on sour wine
> and salt, no relish for my bread.

This comic incongruity between the present and the imagined future, between station and ambition, is carried to hilarious lengths in the climactic appearance of Caliban and his associates. They "do smell all horse-pisse," but Stephano's royal dignity is undisturbed. "Wit shall not goe unrewarded while I am King of this Country," he says, and Trinculo hails him in the titles of the old ballad, "O King *Stephano,* O Peere: O worthy *Stephano.*" Standing at the entrance to Prospero's cell King Stephano talks like a tragic hero: "I do begin to have bloody thoughts." And Caliban's urgent warnings are rejected in royal style: "Monster, lay to your fingers . . . or Ile turne you out of my Kingdome."

A few seconds later Stephano's kingdom melts into thin air. And on his last appearance he and Trinculo are ordered off with Caliban to perform menial tasks; no distinction is made between them.

> Goe Sirha, to my Cell,
> Take with you your Companions: as you looke
> To have my pardon, trim it handsomely.

The stupid slaves, their wild ambitions foiled and their presumption suitably punished, are restored to their proper place and function.

Prospero has already been recognized as "sometime *Millaine*" and restored to *his* proper station—"thy dukedom I resigne"—the marriage of Ferdinand and Miranda is arranged; all that remains is to free the clever slave—"to the elements Be free, and fare thou well"—and the play, except for a version of the conventional Plautine request for applause, is over, the traditional paradigm complete. Gonzalo is given the speech in which the loose ends are tied together and the pattern of restoration spelled out:

> In one voyage
> Did *Claribell* her husband finde at *Tunis,*
> And *Ferdinand* her brother, found a wife,
> Where he himselfe was lost: *Prospero* his Dukedome
> In a poore Isle:

So far we are still within the recognizable limits of the ancient plan, but Gonzalo's closing words (though they continue the metaphor of liberation) can serve to remind us that this plan is only the bare outline of a poetic structure which in feeling and imagination as far surpasses Plautine comedy as "great'st do's least":

> —*Prospero* his Dukedome
> In a poore Isle: and all of us, our selves,
> When no man was his owne.

LORIE JERRELL LEININGER

The Miranda Trap

Sexism and Racism
in Shakespeare's *Tempest*

Shakespeare's *Tempest* was first performed before King
James I at Whitehall in November of 1611. It was presented
a second time at the court of King James early in 1613, as
part of the marriage festivities of James's daughter Elizabeth,
who, at the age of sixteen, was being married to Frederick
the Elector Palatine. The marriage masque within *The Tempest* may have been added for this occasion. In any case, the
goddess Ceres' promise of a life untouched by winter
(*"Spring come to you at the farthest / In the very end of harvest!"* 4.1.114–15)[1] and all the riches the earth can provide
(*"Earth's increase, foison plenty"* 110) was offered to the living royal couple as well as to Ferdinand and Miranda.

Elizabeth had fallen dutifully in love with the bridegroom
her father had chosen for her, the youthful ruler of the rich
and fertile Rhineland and the leading Protestant prince of
central Europe. Within seven years Frederick was to become
"Frederick the Winter King" and "The Luckless Elector," but
in 1613 he was still the living counterpart of Ferdinand in
The Tempest, even as Elizabeth was the counterpart of
Miranda. Like Miranda, Elizabeth was beautiful, loving,
chaste, and obedient. She believed her father to be incapable
of error, in this sharing James's opinion of himself. Miranda

From *The Woman's Part: Feminist Criticism of Shakespeare,* eds., Carolyn R. S.
Lenz, Gayle Green, and Carol T. Neely (Urbana, Illinois: University of Illinois Press,
1980). Reprinted by permission of University of Illinois Press, pp. 285–94.

in the play is "admired Miranda," "perfect," "peerless," one who "outstrips all praise"; Elizabeth was praised as "the eclipse and glory of her kind," a rose among violets.[2]

What was the remainder of her life to be like? Elizabeth, this flesh-and-blood Miranda, might have found it difficult to agree that "We are such stuff / As dreams are made on; and our little life / Is rounded with a sleep" (156–58). The future held thirteen children for her, and forty years as a landless exile. Her beloved Frederick died of the plague at the age of thirty-six, a plague spreading through battle camps and besieged cities in a Europe devastated by a war which appeared endless—the Thirty Years War, in which whole armies in transit disappeared through starvation and pestilence. The immediate cause of this disastrous war had been Frederick and Elizabeth's foolhardy acceptance of the disputed throne of Bohemia. Politically inept, committed to a belief in hierarchical order and Neoplatonic courtliness, the new king and queen failed to engage the loyalty of the Bohemians or to prepare adequately for the inevitable attack by the previously deposed king.

While the happiness of the young lovers in *The Tempest* depended upon their obedience to Miranda's father, the repeated political and military failures of Elizabeth and Frederick were exacerbated by their dependence upon the shifting promises of King James. Elizabeth experienced further tragedy when two of her sons drowned, the eldest at the age of fifteen in an accident connected with spoils from the New World, the fourth son in a tempest while privateering in the New World. There was no Prospero-figure to restore them to life magically.

The Princess Elizabeth, watching *The Tempest* in 1613, was incapable of responding to clues which might have warned her that being Miranda might prove no unmixed blessing: that even though Miranda occupies a place next to Prospero in the play's hierarchy and appears to enjoy all of the benefits which Caliban, at the base of that hierarchy, is denied, she herself might prove a victim of the play's hierarchical values. Elizabeth would be justified in seeing Miranda as the royal offspring of a ducal father, as incomparably beautiful (her external beauty mirroring her inward virtue, in keeping with Neoplatonic idealism), as lovingly educated and gratefully responsive to that education, as chaste (her chastity symbolic of all human virtue), obedient and, by the end of the play, rewarded with an ideal husband and the inheritance of two dukedoms. Caliban, at the opposite pole, is presented as the reviled offspring of a witch and the Devil, as physically ugly (his ugly exterior mirroring his depraved inner nature), as racially vile, intrinsically uneducable, uncontrollably lustful (a symbol of all vice), rebellious, and, being defined as a slave by nature, as justly enslaved.

Modern readers have become more attentive than Elizabeth could have been in 1613 to clues such as Prospero's address to Miranda, "What! I say, / My foot my tutor?" (1.2.469–70). The crucial line is spoken near the end of the scene which begins with Prospero's and Ariel's delighted revelation that the tempest was raised through Prospero's magic powers and then continues with the demonstration of Prospero's ability to subjugate the spirit Ariel, the native Caliban, and finally the mourning Prince Ferdinand to his will. Miranda's concern is engaged when Prospero accuses Ferdinand of being a spy, a traitor and usurper; Prospero threatens to manacle Ferdinand's head and feet together and to force him to drink salt water. When Ferdinand raises his sword to resist Prospero's threats, Prospero magically deprives him of all strength. Miranda, alarmed, cries,

> O dear father,
> Make not too rash a trial of him, for
> He's gentle, and not fearful. (467–69)

Prospero's response is,

> What! I say,
> My foot my tutor? (469–70)

Miranda is given to understand that she is the foot in the family organization of which Prospero is the head. Hers not to reason why, hers but to follow directions: indeed, what kind of body would one have (Prospero, or the play, asks) if one's foot could think for itself, could go wherever it pleased, independent of the head?

Now it is true that Prospero is acting out a role which he knows to be unjust, in order to cement the young couple's love by placing obstacles in their way. Miranda, however, has no way of knowing this. Prospero has established the principle that stands whether a father's action be just or unjust: the daughter must submit to his demand for absolute unthinking obedience.

But might not being a "foot" to another's "head" prove advantageous, provided that the "head" is an all-powerful godlike father who educates and protects his beloved daughter? Some ambiguous answers are suggested by the play, particularly in the triangular relationship of Prospero, Miranda, and Caliban.

When Prospero says to Miranda,

> We'll visit Caliban my slave, who never
> Yields us kind answer,   (306–7)

Miranda's response is,

> 'Tis a villain, sir,
> I do not love to look on.
>   (308–9)

Miranda fears Caliban, and she has reason to fear him. The play permits either of two interpretations to explain the threat which Caliban poses. His hostility may be due to his intrinsically evil nature, or to his present circumstances: anyone who is forced into servitude, confined to a rock, kept under constant surveillance, and punished by supernatural means would wish his enslavers ill.[3] Whatever Caliban's original disposition may have been when he lived alone on the isle—and we lack disinterested evidence—he must in his present circumstances feel hostility toward Prospero and Miranda. Miranda is far more vulnerable to Caliban's ill will than is her all-powerful father.

Prospero responds to Miranda's implicit plea to be spared exposure to Caliban's hostility with the *practical* reasons for needing a slave:

> But, as 'tis,
> We cannot miss him. He does make our fire,
> Fetch in our wood, and serves in offices
> That profit us. What, ho! Slave! Caliban!   (310–13)

A daughter might conceivably tell her loving father that she would prefer that they gather their own wood, that in fact no "profit" can outweigh the uneasiness she experiences. Miranda, however, is not free to speak, since a father who at any time can silence his daughter with "What! My foot my tutor?" will have educated that "foot" to extreme sensitivity toward what her father does or does not wish to hear from her. Miranda dare not object to her enforced proximity to a hostile slave, for within the play's universe of discourse any attempt at pressing her own needs would constitute both personal insubordination and a disruption of the hierarchical order of the universe of which the "foot/head" familial organization is but one reflection.

Miranda, admired and sheltered, has no way out of the cycle of being a dependent foot in need of protection, placed in a threatening situation which in turn calls for more protection, and thus increased dependence and increased subservience.

Miranda's presence as the dependent, innocent, feminine extension of Prospero serves a specific end in the play's power dynamics. Many reasons are given for Caliban's enslavement: the one which carries greatest dramatic weight is Caliban's sexual threat to Miranda. When Prospero accuses Caliban of having sought "to violate / The honor of my child" (348–49), Caliban is made to concur in the accusation:

> O ho, O ho! Would't had been done!
> Thou didst prevent me; I had peopled else
> This isle with Calibans.   (349–51)

We can test the element of sexual politics at work here by imagining, for a moment, that Prospero had been cast adrift with a small son instead of a daughter. If, twelve years later, a ship appeared bearing King Alonso and a marriageable daughter, the play's resolution of the elder generation's hatreds through the love of their offspring could still have been effected. What would be lost in such a reconstruction would be the sexual element in the enslavement of the native. No son would serve. Prospero needs Miranda as sexual bait, and then needs to protect her from the threat which is inescapable given his hierarchical world—slavery being the ultimate extension of the concept of hierarchy. It is Prospero's needs—the Prosperos of the world—not Miranda's, which are being served here.

The most elusive yet far-reaching function of Miranda in the play involves the role of her chastity in the allegorical scheme. Most critics agree that the chastity of Miranda and Ferdinand in the fourth act symbolizes all human virtue ("Chastity is the quality of Christ, the essential symbol of civilization"[4]), while Caliban's lust symbolizes all human vice.

The first result of this schematic representation of all virtue and vice as chastity and lust is the exclusion from the field of moral concern the very domination and enslavement which the play vividly dramatizes. The exclusion is accomplished with phenomenal success under the guise of religion, humanism, and Neoplatonic idealism, by identifying Prospero with God (or spirit, or soul, or imagination), and Caliban with the Devil (or matter, body, and lust). Within the Christian-humanist tradition, the superiority of spirit over matter, or soul over body, was commonplace: body existed to serve soul, to be, metaphorically, enslaved by soul. In a tradition which included the *Psychomachia*, medieval morality plays, and Elizabethan drama, the "higher" and "lower" selves existing within each person's psyche had been represented allegorically in the form of Virtues and Vices. A danger inherent in this mode of portraying inner struggle lay in the possibility of identifying certain human beings with the Vice-figures, and others (oneself included) with the representatives of Virtue. Such identification of self with Virtue and others with Vice led to the great Christian-humanist inversion: the warrant to plunder, exploit and kill in the name of God—Virtue destroying Vice.

It was "only natural" that the educated and privileged be identified with virtue and spirit, and that those who do society's dirty work, and all outsiders, be identified with vice and matter. Ellen Cantarow has analyzed the tendency of allegory to link virtue with privilege and sin with misfortune, making particular power relationships appear inevitable, "natural" and just within a changeless, "divinely ordained" hierarchical order;[5] Nancy Hall Rice has analyzed the manner in which the artistic process of embodying evil in one person and then punishing or destroying that person offers an ersatz solution to the complex problem of evil, sanctioning virulent attacks on social minorities or outcasts;[6] and Winthrop D. Jordan has discussed the tendency of Western civilization to link African natives, for example, with preconceived concepts of sexuality and vice. Jordan speaks of "the ordered hierarchy of [imputed] sexual aggressiveness": the lower one's place on the scale of social privilege, the more dangerously lustful one is perceived as being.[7]

Thus in *The Tempest*, written some fifty years after England's open participation in the slave trade,[8] the island's native is made the embodiment of lust, disobedience, and irremediable evil, while his enslaver is presented as a God-figure. It makes an enormous difference in the expectations raised, whether one speaks of the moral obligations of Prospero-the-slave-owner toward Caliban-his-slave, or speaks of the moral obligations of Prospero-the-God-figure toward Caliban-the-lustful-Vice-figure. In the second instance (the allegorical-symbolic), the only requirement is that Prospero be punitive toward Caliban and that he defend his daughter Miranda's chastity—that daughter being needed as a pawn to counterbalance Caliban's lust. In this symbolic scheme, Miranda is deprived of any possibility of human freedom, growth or thought. She need only *be* chaste—to exist as a walking emblem of chastity. This kind of symbolism is damaging in that it deflects our attention away from the fact that real counterparts to Caliban, Prospero, and Miranda exist— that real slaves, real slave owners, and real daughters existed in 1613 for Shakespeare's contemporaries and have continued to exist since then.

To return to one of those daughters, Miranda's living counterpart Elizabeth Stuart, at whose wedding festivities *The Tempest* was performed: it appears likely that King James's daughter and her bridegroom were influenced in their unrealistic expectations of their powers and rights as future rulers by the widespread Jacobean attempt to equate unaccountable aristocratic power with benevolent infallibility and possibly by the expression of that equation in *The Tempest.* In our own century the play apparently continues to reflect ongoing societal confusions that may seduce women—and men—into complicity with those who appear to favor them while oppressing others. Can we envision a way out? If a twentieth-century counterpart to Miranda were to define, and then confront, *The Tempest's* underlying assumptions—as, obviously, neither the Miranda created by Shakespeare nor her living counterpart in the seventeenth century could do—what issues would she need to clarify? Let us invent a modern Miranda, and permit her to speak a new Epilogue:

"My father is no God-figure. No one is a God-figure. My father is a man, and fallible, as I am. Let's put an end to the fantasy of infallibility.

"There is no such thing as a 'natural slave.' No sub-human laborers exist. Let's put an end to *that* fantasy. I will not benefit from such a concept presented in any guise, be it Aristotelian, biblical, allegorical, or Neoplatonic. Three men are reminded of Indians when first they see Caliban; he might be African, his mother having been transported from Algiers. I will not be used as the excuse for his enslavement. If either my father or I feel threatened by his real or imputed lust, we can build a pale around our side of the island, gather our own wood, cook our own food, and clean up after ourselves.

"I cannot give assent to an ethical scheme that locates all virtue symbolically in one part of my anatomy. My virginity has little to do with the forces that will lead to good harvest or to greater social justice.

"Nor am I in any way analogous to a foot. Even if I were, for a moment, to accept my father's hierarchical mode, it is difficult to understand his concern over the chastity of his *foot*. There is no way to make that work. Neither my father, nor my husband, nor any one alive has the right to refer to me as his foot while thinking of himself as the head— making me the obedient mechanism of his thinking. What I do need is the opportunity to think for myself; I need practice in making mistakes, in testing the consequences of my actions, in becoming aware of the numerous disguises of economic exploitation and racism.

"Will I succeed in creating my 'brave new world' which has people in it who no longer exploit one another? I cannot be certain. I will at least make my start by springing 'the Miranda-trap,' being forced into unwitting collusion with domination by appearing to be a beneficiary. I need to join forces with Caliban—to join forces with all those who are exploited or oppressed—to stand beside Caliban and say,

> As we from crimes would pardon'd be,
> Let's work to set each other free."

NOTES

1. This quotation and subsequent ones are from *The Tempest*, Arden Shakespeare, ed. Frank Kermode (Cambridge, Mass.: Harvard University Press, 1958).

2. "The eclipse and glory of her kind" is the closing line of Sir Henry Wotton's poem "On His Mistress, The Queen of Bohemia," in *The Poems of Sir Walter Raleigh . . . with those of Sir Henry Wotton and other Courtly Poets from 1540–1650*, ed. John Hannah (London: Bell and Sons, 1892), pp. 95–96. "A rose among violets" is a paraphrase of the third verse of that poem; the compliment was often quoted.

3. That the spirit Ariel, the figure contrasted to Caliban in the allegorical scheme, is a purely imaginary construct for whom no human counterparts exist helps to obscure the fact that human counterparts for Caliban did indeed exist. A community of free blacks had been living in London for over fifteen years at the time of the writing of *The Tempest*. The first Indian to have been exhibited in England had been brought to London during the reign of Queen Elizabeth's grandfather, Henry VII. For a full discussion of the historical background see Chapter II of my dissertation, "The Jacobean Bind: A Study of *The Tempest, The Revenge of Bussy D'Ambois, The Atheist's Tragedy, A King and No King* and *The Alchemist*, the Major Plays of 1610 and 1611, in the Context of Renaissance Expansion and Jacobean Absolutism," University of Massachusetts/Amherst,

1975. For more on the effects of the ambiguity surrounding the definition of Caliban as an abstract embodiment of evil and as an inhabitant of a newly discovered island see Chapter III of the same work, which considers *The Tempest* in relation to seventeenth- and twentieth-century imperialism.

Four critics, among others, who have dealt with the colonial aspects of *The Tempest* and have focused upon Caliban and his enslavement as moral concerns are O. Mannoni, *Prospero and Caliban: The Psychology of Colonization*, trans. Pamela Powesland (New York: Praeger, 1956); Philip Mason, *Prospero's Magic: Some Thoughts on Class and Race* (London: Oxford University Press, 1962), pp. 75–97; Roberto Fernández Retamar, "Caliban," *Massachusetts Review* 15 (Winter–Spring 1974): 7–72; and Kermode, "Introduction," *The Tempest*. While Kermode observes that Shakespeare, and more generally Renaissance writers, held contradictory attitudes toward Indians, viewing them on one hand as inhabitants of a golden age, with no *meum* or *tuum*, and on the other hand as human beasts in whom one could place no trust, he nevertheless arrives at the conclusion that "the confusion of interests characteristic of the subject is harmoniously reflected in Shakespeare's play" (p. xxxi)—a "harmony" more likely to be acceptable to those who are at ease with the historical reality of conquest and enslavement than by those who, like Caliban's living counterparts, have been conquered, enslaved, or colonized. It is puzzling that even an article as sensitive as Harry Berger, Jr.'s "Miraculous Harp: A Reading of Shakespeare's *Tempest*," in *Shakespeare Studies* 5 (1969): 253–83, in its exploration of the contradictory elements in Prospero's character—his tendency to see himself as a god, his limited knowledge of human nature, his pleasure in dominating others, and his preference for, and success in, dealing with projected embodiments of pure evil—falls short of focusing upon the dramatization of enslavement itself as an ethical concern. I explore this question, posed in general terms, in my "Cracking the Code of *The Tempest*," *Bucknell Review* 25 (Spring 1979), issue on "Shakespeare: Contemporary Critical Approaches," ed. Harry R. Garvin and Michael D. Payne.

4. Irving Ribner, "Introduction" to Shakespeare's *Tempest*, ed. George Lyman Kittredge, rev. Ribner (Waltham, Mass.: Blaisdell, 1966), p. xv.

5. Ellen Cantarow, "A Wilderness of Opinions Confounded: Allegory and Ideology," *College English* 34 (1972): 215–16.

6. Nancy Hall Rice, "Beauty and the Beast and the Little Boy: Clues about the Origins of Sexism and Racism from Folklore and Literature," Diss. University of Massachusetts/Amherst, 1974, p. 207.

7. Winthrop D. Jordan, *The White Man's Burden: Historical Origins of Racism in the United States* (New York: Oxford University Press, 1974), p. 196.

8. See, for example, accounts of the 1562–68 slaving voyages of Sir John Hawkins (one with Sir Francis Drake) which appear in Richard Hakluyt's *Principall Navigations Voiages and Discoveries of the English Nation* (London, 1589; facs. rpt. Cambridge: Cambridge University Press, 1965), Part Two, 521–22, 526–29, 531–32, 553–54, 562–64.

STEPHEN GREENBLATT

The Use of Salutary Anxiety in *The Tempest*

When near the close of his career Shakespeare reflected upon his own art with still greater intensity and self-consciousness than in *Measure for Measure*, he once again conceived of the playwright as a princely creator of anxiety. But where in *Measure for Measure* disguise is the principal emblem of this art, in *The Tempest* the emblem is the far more potent and disturbing power of magic. Prospero's chief magical activity throughout *The Tempest* is to harrow the other characters with fear and wonder and then to reveal that their anxiety is his to create and allay. The spectacular storm in the play's first scene gives way to Miranda's empathic agitation: "O! I have suffered / With those that I saw suffer.... O, the cry did knock / Against my very heart" (1.2.5–6, 8–9). "The direful spectacle of the wrack," replies Prospero,

> which touched
> The very virtue of compassion in thee,
> I have with such provision in mine art
> So safely ordered that there is no soul—
> No, not so much perdition as an hair
> Betid to any creature in the vessel
> Which thou heard'st cry, which thou saw'st sink.
>
> (26–32)

Miranda has been treated to an intense experience of suffering and to a still more intense demonstration of her father's

From Stephen Greenblatt, *Shakespearean Negotiations* (Univ. of California Press, 1988). Used by permission of the publisher and the author. The title of this extract is the editor's.

power, the power at once to cause such suffering and to cancel it. Later in the play the threat of "perdition"—both loss and damnation—will be concentrated against Prospero's enemies, but it is important to recall that at the start the management of anxiety through the "provision" of art is practiced upon Prospero's beloved daughter. Her suffering is the prelude to the revelation of her identity, as if Prospero believes that this revelation can be meaningful only in the wake of the amazement and pity he artfully arouses. He is setting out to fashion her identity, just as he is setting out to refashion the inner lives of his enemies, and he employs comparable disciplinary techniques.

With his daughter, Prospero's techniques are mediated and softened: she suffers at the sight of the sufferings of unknown wretches. With his enemies the techniques are harsher and more direct—the spectacle they are compelled to watch is not the wreck of others but of their own lives. In one of the play's most elaborate scenes, Prospero stands above the stage, invisible to those below him, and conjures up a banquet for Alonso, Antonio, Sebastian, and their party; when they move toward the table, Ariel appears like a Harpy and, with a clap of his wings and a burst of thunder and lightning, makes the table disappear. Ariel then solemnly recalls their crimes against Prospero and sentences the guilty in the name of the powers of Destiny and Fate:

> Thee of thy son, Alonso,
> They have bereft; and do pronounce by me
> Ling'ring perdition (worse than any death
> Can be at once). (3.3.75–78)

Prospero is delighted at Ariel's performance:

> My high charms work,
> And these, mine enemies, are all knit up
> In their distractions. They now are in my pow'r.
> (88–90)

To compel others to be "all knit up / In their distractions," to cause a paralyzing anxiety, is the dream of power, a dream perfected over bitter years of exile.[1] But as we have already seen, the artful manipulation of anxiety is not only the manifestation of aggression; it is also a strategy for shaping the inner lives of others and for fashioning their behavior. Hence we find Prospero employing the strategy not only upon those he hates but upon his daughter and upon the man whom he has chosen to be his daughter's husband. Ferdinand and Miranda fall in love instantly—"It goes on, I see, / As my soul prompts it" (1.2.420–21), remarks Prospero—but what is missing from their love is precisely the salutary anxiety that Prospero undertakes to impose: "this swift business / I must uneasy make, lest too light winning / Make the prize light" (451–53). To Miranda's horror, he accuses Ferdinand of treason and employs his magic charms once again to cause a kind of paralysis: "My spirits," exclaims Ferdinand, "as in a dream, are all bound up" (487). The rituals of humiliation and suffering through which Prospero makes Ferdinand and Miranda pass evidently have their desired effect: at the end of the play the couple displayed to the amazed bystanders are revealed to be not only in a state of love but in a state of symbolic war. The lovers, you will recall, are discovered playing chess, and Miranda accuses Ferdinand of cheating. The deepest happiness is represented in this play as a state of playful tension.

Perhaps the supreme representation of this tension in *The Tempest* is to be found not in Prospero's enemies or in his daughter and son-in-law but in himself. The entire action of the play rests on the premise that value lies in controlled uneasiness, and hence that a direct reappropriation of the usurped dukedom and a direct punishiment of the usurpers has less moral and political value than an elaborate inward restaging of loss, misery, and anxiety. Prospero directs this restaging not only against the others but also—even principally—against himself. That is, he arranges for the reenactment in a variety of registers and through different symbolic agents of the originary usurpation, and in the play's most memorable yet perplexing moment, the princely artist puts himself through the paralyzing uneasiness with which he has afflicted others. The moment to which I refer is that of the interrupted wedding masque. In the midst of the climactic demonstration of Prospero's magical powers, the celebration of the paradisal "green land" where spring comes at the very end of harvest, Prospero suddenly starts, breaks off the masque, and declares that he had "forgot that foul conspiracy / Of the beast Caliban and his confederates / Against my life" (4.1.139–41).

In recalling the conspiracy, Prospero clearly exhibits signs of extreme distress: Ferdinand is struck by the "passion / That works him strongly," and Miranda says that "never till this day" has she seen him "touch'd with anger, so distemper'd" (143–45). Noticing that Ferdinand looks "in a mov'd sort," as if he were "dismay'd," Prospero tells him to "be cheerful" and informs him that "Our revels now are ended." The famous speech that follows has the effect of drastically evacuating the masque's majestic vision of plenitude. "Let me live here ever," the delighted Ferdinand had exclaimed, enchanted by the promise of an aristocrat's equivalent of the Land of Cockaigne:

> Honor, riches, marriage-blessing,
> Long continuance, and increasing,
> Hourly joys be still upon you! (106–8)

But Prospero now explains that the beneficent goddesses "Are melted into air, into thin air" (150). What had seemed solid is "baseless"; what had seemed enduring ("the great globe itself")

> shall dissolve,
> And like this insubstantial pageant faded
> Leave not a rack behind. (154–56)

Prospero offers this sublime vision of emptiness to make Ferdinand feel "cheerful"—secure in the consciousness that life is a dream. It is difficult to believe in the effectiveness of these professed attempts at reassurance: like Duke

Vincentio's religious consolations in *Measure for Measure*, they seem suited more to heighten anxiety than to allay it. The ascetic security Prospero articulates has evidently not stilled his own "beating mind":

> Sir, I am vex'd;
> Bear with my weakness, my old brain is troubled.
> Be not disturb'd with my infirmity.   (158–60)

Since Prospero's art has in effect created the conspiracy as well as the defense against the conspiracy, and since the profession of infirmity comes at the moment of his greatest strength, we may conclude that we are witnessing the practice of salutary anxiety operating at the center of the play's world, in the consciousness of Prospero himself, magician, artist, and prince. This does not mean that Prospero's anxiety about the conspiracy, about his enemies and servants and daughter, about his own inward state is not genuinely felt, nor does it mean that he is in absolute, untroubled control either of the characters whom he has brought onto the island or of himself. Rapt in his own magical vision of bounteousness, he has forgotten a serious threat to his life: "The minute of their plot / Is almost come" (141–42). But it is important to take seriously his deep complicity in his present tribulations, for only by actively willing them can he undo the tribulations that he unwillingly and unwittingly brought about years before. At that time, absorbed in his occult studies, he had been unaware of the dangers around him; now as the condition of a return to his dukedom, he himself brings those dangers to the center of his retreat. This center, whether we regard it as emblematic of the dominant religious, aesthetic, or political institution, is not the still point in a turbulent world but the point at which the anxieties that shape the character of others are screwed up to their highest pitch. Precisely from that point—and as a further exemplification of the salutary nature of anxiety—reconciliation and pardon can issue forth. This pardon is not a release from the power in which Prospero holds everyone around him but, as with Latimer and James I, its ultimate expression.[2]

Shakespeare goes beyond Latimer and James, however, in envisaging a case in which anxiety does not appear to have its full redeeming effect, a case in which the object of attention refuses to be fashioned inwardly, refuses even to acknowledge guilt, and yet is pardoned. The generosity of the pardon in this instance is inseparable from a demonstration of supreme force. "For you, most wicked sir," Prospero says to his brother Antonio,

> whom to call brother
> Would even infect my mouth, I do forgive
> Thy rankest fault—all of them; and require
> My dukedom of thee, which perforce, I know
> Thou must restore. (5.1.130–34)

Antonio's silence at this point suggests that he remains unrepentant, but it also expresses eloquently the paralysis that is the hallmark of extreme anxiety. It has been argued convincingly that the truculence of the villains at the close of the play marks the limit of Prospero's power—as Prospero's failure to educate Caliban has already shown, the strategy of salutary anxiety cannot remake the inner life of everyone—yet at the very moment the limit is marked, the play suggests that it is relatively inconsequential. It would no doubt be preferable to receive the appropriate signs of inward gratitude from everyone, but Prospero will have to content himself in the case of Antonio with the full restoration of his dukedom.[3]

What I have been describing here is the theatrical appropriation and staging of a sixteenth- and seventeenth-century social practice. But the strategy of salutary anxiety is not simply reflected in a secondhand way by the work of art, because the practice itself is already implicated in the artistic traditions and institutions out of which this particular representation, *The Tempest*, has emerged. Latimer may have been indifferent or hostile to the drama and to literature in general, but his tale of the Cambridge prisoner seems shaped by literary conventions, earlier tales of wronged innocence and royal pardons. And if the practice he exemplifies helps to empower theatrical representations, fictive representations have themselves helped to empower his practice.[4] So too Dudley Carleton, watching men about to go to their deaths, thinks of the last act of a play, and when a pardon is granted, the spectators applaud. This complex circulation between the social dimension of an aesthetic strategy and the aesthetic dimension of a social strategy is difficult to grasp because the strategy in question has an extraordinarily long and tangled history, one whose aesthetic roots go back at least as far as Aristotle's *Poetics*. But we may find a more manageable, though still complex, model in the relation between *The Tempest* and one of its presumed sources, William Strachey's account of the tempest that struck an English fleet bound for the fledgling colony at Jamestown.[5]

Strachey's account, with its bravura description of a violent storm at sea and its tale of Englishmen providentially cast ashore on an uninhabited island rumored to be devil haunted, is likely, along with other New World materials, to have helped shape *The Tempest*. The play was performed long before Strachey's narrative was printed in Purchas's *Pilgrims* as "A true reportory of the wrack, and redemption of Sir Thomas Gates Knight," but scholars presume that Shakespeare read a manuscript version of the work, which takes the form of a confidential letter written to a certain "noble lady."[6] My interest is not the particular verbal echoes, which have been painstakingly researched since Malone in 1808 first called attention to them, but the significance of the relation between the two texts, or rather between the institutions that the texts serve. For it is important to grasp that we are dealing not with the reflections of isolated individuals musing on current events but with expressions whose context is corporate and institutional.

William Strachey was a shareholder and secretary of the Virginia Company's colony at Jamestown; his letter on the events of 1609–10 was unpublished until 1625, not for want of interest but because the Virginia Company was engaged in a vigorous propaganda and financial campaign on behalf of the colony, and the company's leaders found Strachey's report too disturbing to allow it into print. Shakespeare too was a shareholder in a joint-stock company, the King's Men, as well as its principal playwright and sometime actor; *The Tempest* also remained unpublished for years, again presumably not for want of interest but because the theater company resisted losing control of its playbook. Neither joint-stock company was a direct agent of the crown: despite the legal fiction that they were retainers of the monarch, the King's Men could not have survived through royal patronage alone, and they were not in the same position of either dependence or privilege as other household servants; the crown had deliberately withdrawn from the direction of the Virginia Company. Royal protection and support, of course, remained essential in both cases, but the crown would not assume responsibility, nor could either company count on royal financial support in times of need. Committed for their survival to attracting investment capital and turning a profit, both companies depended on their ability to market stories that would excite, interest, and attract supporters. Both Strachey and Shakespeare were involved in unusually direct and intricate ways in every aspect of their companies' operations: Strachey as shareholder, adventurer, and eventually secretary; Shakespeare as shareholder, actor, and playwright. Because of these multiple positions, both men probably identified intensely with the interests of their respective companies.

I want to propose that the relation between the play and its alleged source is a relation between joint-stock companies.[7] I do not mean that there was a direct, contractual connection.[8] As we have already seen with Latimer, the transfer of cultural practices and powers depends not upon contracts but upon networks of resemblance. In the case of Strachey· and Shakespeare, there *are*, in point of fact, certain intriguing institutional affiliations: as Charles Mills Gayley observed many years ago, a remarkable number of social and professional connections link Shakespeare and the stockholders and directors of the Virginia Company; moreover, Strachey in 1605 wrote a prefatory sonnet commending Jonson's *Sejanus* and in 1606 is listed as a shareholder in an acting company known as the Children of the Queen's Revels, the company that had taken over the Blackfriars Theatre from Richard Burbage.[9] Still, I should emphasize that these affiliations do not amount to a direct transfer of properties; we are dealing with a system of mimetic rather than contractual exchange. The conjunction of Strachey's unpublished letter and Shakespeare's play signals an institutional circulation of culturally significant narratives. And as we shall see, this circulation has as its central concern the public management of anxiety.

Strachey tells the story of a state of emergency and a crisis of authority. The "unmerciful tempest" that almost sank Sir Thomas Gates's ship, the *Sea Venture,* provoked an immediate collapse of the distinction between those who labor and those who rule, a distinction, we should recall, that is at the economic and ideological center of Elizabethan and Jacobean society: "Then men might be seen to labour, I may well say, for life, and the better sort, even our Governour, and Admiral themselves, not refusing their turn. . . . And it is most true, such as in all their life times had never done hours work before (their minds now helping their bodies) were able twice forty eight hours together to toil with the best" (in Purchas, 19:9–11). "The best"—the violence of the storm has turned Strachey's own language upside down: now it is the common seamen, ordinarily despised and feared by their social superiors, who are, as the Romans called their aristocrats, the *optimi viri,* the best of men.[10] Indeed the storm had quite literally a leveling force: while the governor was "both by his speech and authority heartening every man unto his labour," a great wave "struck him from the place where he sat, and groveled him, and all us about him on our faces, beating together with our breaths all thoughts from our bosoms, else then that we were now sinking" (10).

Even after the ship had run aground in the Bermudas and the one hundred fifty men, women, and children on board had been saved, the crisis of authority was not resolved; indeed it only intensified then, not because of a leveling excess of anxiety but because of its almost complete absence in the colonists. The alarm of the rulers makes itself felt in quirks of Strachey's style. He reports, for example, that many palmettos were cut down for their edible tops, but the report has a strange nervous tone, as the plants are comically turned into wealthy victims of a popular uprising: "Many an ancient Burgher was therefore heaved at, and fell not for his place, but for his head: for our common people, whose bellies never had ears, made it no breach of Charity in their hot bloods and tall stomachs to murder thousands of them" (19).

The strain registered here in the tone stands for concerns that are partially suppressed in the published text, concerns that are voiced in a private letter written in December 1610 by Richard Martin, secretary of the Virginia Company in London, to Strachey, who was by then in Jamestown. Martin asks Strachey for a full confidential report on "the nature & quality of the soil, & how it is like to serve you without help from hence, the manners of the people, how the Barbarians are content with your being there, but especially how our own people do brook their obedience, how they endure labor, whether willingly or upon constraint, how they live in the exercise of Religion, whether out of conscience or for fashion, And generally what ease you have in the government there, & what hope of success."[11]

Here the deepest fears lie not with the human or natural resources of the New World but with the discipline of the English colonists and common seamen. And the principal questions—whether obedience is willing or forced, whether religious observance is sincere or feigned—suggest an interest in inner states, as if the shareholders in the Virginia Company believed that only with a set of powerful inward restraints could the colonists be kept from rebelling at the first sign of the slippage or relaxation of authority. The company had an official institutional interest in shaping and controlling the minds of its own people. But the Bermuda shipwreck revealed the difficulty of this task as well as its importance: set apart from the institutional and military safeguards established at Jamestown, Bermuda was an experimental space, a testing ground where the extent to which disciplinary anxiety had been internalized by the ordinary venturers could be measured.

The results were not encouraging. As Strachey and others remark, Bermuda was an extraordinarily pleasant surprise: the climate was healthful, the water was pure, there were no native inhabitants to contend with, and, equally important, there was no shortage of food. Tortoises—"such a kind of meat, as a man can neither absolutely call Fish nor Flesh"

$(24)^{12}$—were found in great number, and the skies were dark with great flocks of birds:

> Our men found a pretty way to take them, which was by standing on the Rocks or Sands by the Sea side, and hollowing, laughing, and making the strangest out-cry that possibly they could: with the noise whereof the Birds would come flocking to that place, and settle upon the very arms and head of him that so cried, and still creep nearer and nearer, answering the noise themselves: by which our men would weigh them with their hands, and which weighed heaviest they took for the best and let the others alone. (Purchas, 19:22–23)

Even to us, living for the most part in the confident expectation of full bellies, this sounds extraordinary enough; to seventeenth-century voyagers, whose ordinary condition was extreme want and who had dragged themselves from the violent sea onto an unknown shore with the likely prospect of starvation and death, such extravagant abundance must have seemed the fantastic realization of old folk dreams of a land where the houses were roofed with pies and the pigs ran about with little knives conveniently stuck in their precooked sides. In this Land of Cockaigne setting, far removed not only from England but from the hardships of Jamestown, the authority of Sir Thomas Gates and his lieutenants was anything but secure. For the perception that Bermuda was a providential deliverance contained within it a subversive corollary: why leave? why press on to a hungry garrison situated in a pestiferous swamp and in grave tension with the surrounding Algonquian tribesmen?[13]

According to Strachey, Gates was initially concerned less about his own immediate authority than about the possible consequences of his absence in Virginia. The *Sea Venture* had come to grief in the tempest, but Gates thought (correctly, as it happened) that the other two vessels might have reached their destination, and this thought brought not only consolation but anxiety, which focused, in characteristic Renaissance fashion, on the ambitions of the younger generation. Fearful about "what innovation and tumult might happily (haply) arise, among the younger and ambitious spirits of the new companies to arrive in Virginia" (26) in his absence, Gates wished to construct new ships as quickly as possible to continue on to Jamestown, but the sailors and the colonists alike began to grumble at this plan. In Virginia, they reasoned, "nothing but wretchedness and labour must be expected, with many wants and a churlish entreaty"; in Bermuda, all things "at ease and pleasure might be enjoyed" (29) without hardship or threatening. There is, at least as Strachey reports it, virtually no internalization of the ideology of colonialism; the voyagers appear to think of themselves as forced to endure a temporary exile from home. As long as "they were (for the time) to lose the fruition both of their friends and Country, as good, and better it were for them, to repose and seat them where they should have the least outward wants the while" (29). And to this dangerous appeal—the appeal, in Strachey's words, of "liberty, and fulness of sensuality" (35)—was added a still more dangerous force: religious dissent.

Arguments against leaving Bermuda began to be voiced not only among the "idle, untoward, and wretched number of the many" (29) but among the educated few. One of these, Stephen Hopkins, "alleged substantial arguments, both civil and divine (the Scripture falsely quoted) that it was no breach of honesty, conscience, nor Religion, to decline from the obedience of the Governour, or refuse to go any further, led by his authority (except it so pleased themselves) since the authority ceased when the wrack was committed, and with it, they were all then freed from the government of any man" (30–31). Hopkins evidently accepted the governor's authority as a contractual obligation that continued only so long as the enterprise remained on course. Once there was a swerve from the official itinerary, that authority, not granted a general or universal character, lapsed, and the obedience of the subject gave way to the will and pleasure of each man.[14] We cannot know, of course, if Hopkins said anything so radical, but this is how his "substantial arguments, both civil and divine," sounded to those in command. In Strachey's account, at least, the shipwreck had led to a profound questioning of authority that seems to anticipate the challenge posed by mid-seventeenth-century radicals like Winstanley.

What are the boundaries of authority? What is the basis of its claim to be obeyed? How much loyalty does an individual owe to a corporation?

When the seditious words were reported to Gates, the governor convened a martial court and sentenced Hopkins to death, but the condemned man was so tearfully repentant that he received a pardon. This moving scene—the saving public display of anxiety—evidently did not settle the question of authority, however, for shortly after, yet another mutiny arose, this time led by a gentleman named Henry Paine. When Paine was warned that he risked execution for "insolency," he replied, Strachey reports, "with a settled and bitter violence, and in such unreverent terms, as I should offend the modest ear too much to express it in his own phrase; but its contents were, how that the Governour had no authority of that quality, to justify upon any one (how mean soever in the colony) an action of that nature, and therefore let the Governour (said he) kiss, &c." (34). When these words, "with the omitted additions," were reported, the governor, "who had now the eyes of the whole Colony fixed upon him," condemned Paine "to be instantly hanged; and the ladder being ready, after he had made many confessions, he earnestly desired, being a Gentleman, that he might be shot to death, and towards the evening he had his desire, the Sun and his life setting together" (34). "He had his desire"— Strachey's sarcasm is also perhaps the representation of what those in authority regarded as an intolerable nonchalance, a refusal to perform those rituals of tearful repentance that apparently saved Hopkins's life. In effect Paine is killed to set an example, condemned to die for cursing authority, for a linguistic crime, for violating discursive decorum, for inadequate anxiety in the presence of power.

In his narrative, Strachey represents the norms Paine has challenged by means of his "&c"—the noble lady to whom he is writing, like Mr. Kurtz's intended, must be sheltered from the awful truth, here from the precise terms of the fatal irreverent challenge to authority. The suppression of the offending word enacts in miniature the reimposition of salutary anxiety by a governor "so solicitous and careful, whose both example . . . and authority, could lay shame, and command upon our people" (28). The governor is full of care—therefore resistant to the lure of the island—and he manages, even in the midst of a paradisal plenty, to impose this care upon others. When the governor himself writes to a fellow officer explaining why all of the colonists must be compelled to leave the island, he invokes not England's imperial destiny or Christianity's advancement but the Virginia Company's investment: "The meanest in the whole Fleet stood the Company in no less than twenty pounds, for his own personal Transportation, and things necessary to accompany him" (36). On the strength of this compelling motive, new ships were built, and in an impressive feat of navigation, the whole company finally reached Jamestown.

Upon their arrival Gates and his people found the garrison in desperate condition—starving, confused, terrorized by hostile and treacherous Indians, and utterly demoralized. In Gates's view, the problem was almost entirely one of discipline, and he addressed it by imposing a set of "orders and instructions" upon the colony that transformed the "government" of Jamestown "into an absolute command." The orders were published in 1612 by Strachey as the *Laws Divine, Moral, and Martial*, an exceptionally draconian code by which whipping, mutilation, and the death penalty might be imposed for a wide range of offenses, including blasphemy, insubordination, even simple criticism of the Virginia Company and its officers. These orders, the first martial law code in America, suspended the traditional legal sanctions that governed the lives of Englishmen, customary codes based on mutual constraints and obligations, and instituted in their stead the grim and self-consciously innovative logic of a state of emergency. The company's claim upon the colonists had become total. The group that had been shipwrecked in Bermuda passed from dreams of absolute freedom to the imposition of absolute control.

Such then were the narrative materials that passed from Strachey to Shakespeare, from the Virginia Company to the King's Men: a violent tempest, a providential shipwreck on a strange island, a crisis in authority provoked by both danger and excess, a fear of lower-class disorder and upper-class ambition, a triumphant affirmation of absolute control linked to the manipulation of anxiety and to a departure from the island. But the swerve away from these materials in *The Tempest* is as apparent as their presence: the island is not in America but in the Mediterranean; it is not uninhabited—Ariel and Caliban (and, for that matter, Sycorax) were present before the arrival of Prospero and Miranda; none of the figures are in any sense colonists; the departure is for home rather than a colony and entails not an unequivocal heightening of authority but a partial diminution, signaled in Prospero's abjuration of magic.

> I'll break my staff,
> Bury it certain fathoms in the earth,
> And deeper than did ever plummet sound
> I'll drown my book.   (5.1.54–57)

If the direction of Strachey's narrative is toward the promulgation of the martial law codes, the direction of *The Tempest* is toward forgiveness. And if that forgiveness is itself the manifestation of supreme power, the emblem of that power remains marriage rather than punishment.

The changes I have sketched are signs of the process whereby the Bermuda narrative is made negotiable, turned into a currency that may be transferred from one institutional context to another. The changes do not constitute a coherent critique of the colonial discourse, but they function as an unmooring of its elements so as to confer upon them the currency's liquidity. Detached from their context in Strachey's letter, these elements may be transformed and recombined with materials drawn from other writers about the New World who differ sharply from Strachey in their interests and motives—Montaigne, Sylvester Jourdain, James Rosier, Robert Eden, Peter Martyr—and then integrated in a dramatic text that draws on a wide range of discourse, including pastoral and epic poetry, the lore of magic and witchcraft, literary romance, and a remarkable number of Shakespeare's own earlier plays.

The ideological effects of the transfer to *The Tempest* are ambiguous. On the one hand, the play seems to act out a fantasy of mind control, to celebrate absolute patriarchal rule, to push to an extreme the dream of order, epic achievement, and ideological justification implicit in Strachey's text. The lower-class resistance Strachey chronicles becomes in Shakespeare the drunken rebellion of Stephano and Trinculo, the butler and jester who, suddenly finding themselves freed from their masters, are drawn to a poor man's fantasy of mastery: "the King and all our company else being drown'd, we will inherit here" (2.2.182–83). Similarly, the upper-class resistance of Henry Paine is transformed into the murderous treachery of Sebastian, in whom the shipwreck arouses dreams of an escape from subordination to his older brother, the king of Naples, just as Antonio had escaped subordination to his older brother Prospero:

> *Sebastian.*   I remember
>   You did supplant your brother Prospero.
> *Antonio.*   True.
>   And look how well my garments sit upon me,
>   Much feater than before. My brother's servants
>   Were then my fellows, now they are my men.
>
>   (2.1.274–78)

By invoking fratricidal rivalry here Shakespeare is not only linking the Strachey materials to his own long-standing theatrical preoccupations but also supplementing the contractual authority of a governor like Sir Thomas Gates with the familial and hence culturally sanctified authority of the eldest son. To rise up against such a figure, as Claudius had against old Hamlet or Edmund against Edgar, is an assault not only on a political structure but on the moral and natural order of things: it is an act that has, as Claudius says, "the primal eldest curse upon't." The assault is magically thwarted by Ariel, the indispensable agent of Prospero's "art"; hence that art, potentially a force of disorder, spiritual violence, and darkness, is confirmed as the agent of legitimacy. Through his mastery of the occult, Prospero withholds food from his enemies, spies upon them, listens to their secret conversations, monitors their movements, blocks their actions, keeps track of their dealings with the island's native inhabitant, torments and disciplines his servants, defeats conspiracies against his life. A crisis of authority—deposition from power, exile, impotence—gives way through the power of his art to a full restoration. From this perspective Prospero's magic is the romance equivalent of martial law.

Yet *The Tempest* seems to raise troubling questions about this authority. The great storm with which the play opens has some of the leveling force of the storm that struck the *Sea Venture*. To be sure, unlike Strachey's gentlemen, Shakespeare's nobles refuse the boatswain's exasperated demand that they share the labor, "Work you then," but their snarling refusal—"Hang, cur! hang, you whoreson, insolent noise-maker!" (1.1.42–44)—far from securing their class superiority, represents them as morally beneath the level of the common seamen.[16] Likewise, Shakespeare's king, Alonso, is not "groveled" by a wave, but—perhaps worse—he is peremptorily ordered below by the harried boatswain: "What cares these roarers for the name of king? To cabin! silence! trouble us not" (16–18). And if we learn eventually that these roarers are in fact produced *by* a king—in his name and through his command of a magical language—this knowledge does not altogether cancel our perception of the storm's indifference to the ruler's authority and the idle aristocrat's pride of place.

The perception would perhaps be overwhelmed by the display of Prospero's power were it not for the questions that are raised about this very power. A Renaissance audience might have found the locus of these questions in the ambiguous status of magic, an ambiguity deliberately heightened by the careful parallels drawn between Prospero and the witch Sycorax and by the attribution to Prospero of claims made by Ovid's witch Medea. But for a modern audience, at least, the questions center on the figure of Caliban, whose claim to the legitimate possession of the island—"This island's mine by Sycorax my mother" (1.2.331)—is never really answered, or rather is answered by Prospero only with hatred, torture, and enslavement.[17] Though he treats Caliban as less than human, Prospero finally expresses, in a famously enigmatic phrase, a sense of connection with his servant-monster, standing anxious and powerless before him: "this thing of darkness

I / Acknowledge mine" (5.1.275–76). He may intend these words only as a declaration of ownership, but it is difficult not to hear in them some deeper recognition of affinity, some half-conscious acknowledgment of guilt. At the play's end the princely magician appears anxious and powerless before the audience to beg for indulgence and freedom.

As the epilogue is spoken, Prospero's magical power and princely authority—figured in the linked abilities to raise winds and to pardon offenders—pass, in a startling display of the circulation of social energy, from the performer onstage to the crowd of spectators. In the play's closing moments the marginal, vulnerable actor, more than half-visible beneath the borrowed robes of an assumed dignity, seems to acknowledge that the imaginary forces with which he has played reside ultimately not in himself or in the playwright but in the multitude. The audience is the source of his anxiety, and it holds his release quite literally in its hands: without the crowd's applause his "ending is despair" (Epilogue, 15). This admission of dependence includes a glance at the multitude's own vulnerability:

> As you from crimes would pardon'd be,
> Let your indulgence set me free.
>
> (Epilogue, 19–20)

But it nonetheless implicates the prince as well as the player in the experience of anxiety and the need for pardon.

Furthermore, even if we may argue that such disturbing or even subversive reflections are contained within the thematic structure of the play, a structure that seems to support the kind of authority served by Strachey, we must acknowledge that the propagandists for colonization found little to admire in the theater. That is, the most disturbing effects of the play may have been located not in what may be perceived in the text by a subtle interpreter—implied criticisms of colonialism or subversive doubts about its structures of authority—but in the phenomenon of theatrical representation itself. In 1593 Sir Thomas Smith reminded each captain in Virginia that his task was "to lay the foundation of a good and . . . an eternal colony for your posterity, not a May game or stage play."[18]

Festive, evanescent, given over to images of excess, stage plays function here as the symbolic opposite to the lasting colony. So too in a sermon preached in London in 1610 to a group of colonists about to set out for Virginia, William Crashaw declared that the enemies of the godly colony were the devil, the pope, and the players—the latter angry "because we resolve to suffer no Idle persons in Virginia."[19] Similarly, at the end of the martial law text, Strachey records an exceptionally long prayer that he claims was "duly said Morning and Evening upon the Court of Guard, either by the Captain of the watch himself, or by some one of his principal officers." If Strachey is right, twice a day the colonists would have heard, among other uplifting sentiments, the following: "Whereas we have by undertaking this plantation undergone the reproofs of the base world, insomuch as many of our own brethren laugh us to scorn, O Lord we pray thee fortify us against this temptation: let *Sanballat*, & *Tobias*, Papists & players, & such other *Ammonites* & *Horonites* the scum & dregs of the earth, let them mock such as help to build up the walls of Jerusalem, and they that be filthy, let them be filthy still."[20] Even if the content of a play seemed acceptable, the mode of entertainment itself was the enemy of the colonial plantation.

What then is the relation between the theater and the surrounding institutions? Shakespeare's play offers us a model of unresolved and unresolvable doubleness: the island in *The Tempest* seems to be an image of the place of pure fantasy, set apart from surrounding discourses; and it seems to be an image of the place of power, the place in which all individual discourses are organized by the half-invisible ruler. By extension art is a well-demarcated, marginal, private sphere, the realm of insight, pleasure, and isolation; and art is a capricious, central, public sphere, the realm of proper political order made possible through mind control, coercion, discipline, anxiety, and pardon. The aesthetic space—or, more accurately, the commercial space of the theatrical joint-stock company—is constituted by the simultaneous appropriation of and swerving from the discourse of power.

And this doubleness in effect produces two different accounts of the nature of mimetic economy. In one account, aesthetic representation is unlike all other exchanges because it takes nothing; art is pure plenitude. Everywhere else there is scarcity: wretches cling to "an acre of barren ground, long heath, brown furze, any thing" (1.1.66–67), and one person's gain is another's loss. In works of art, by contrast, things can be imitated, staged, reproduced without any loss or expense; indeed what is borrowed seems enhanced by the borrowing, for nothing is used up, nothing fades. The magic of art resides in the freedom of the imagination and hence in liberation from the constraints of the body. What is produced elsewhere only by intense labor is produced in art by a magical command whose power Shakespeare figures in Ariel's response to Prospero's call:

> All hail, great master, grave sir, hail! I come
> To answer thy best pleasure; be't to fly,
> To swim, to dive into the fire, to ride
> On the curl'd clouds. To thy strong bidding, task
> Ariel, and all his quality.   (1.2.189–93)

This account of art as pure plenitude is perhaps most perfectly imaged in Prospero's wedding masque, with its goddesses and nymphs and dancing reapers, its majestic vision of

> Barns and garners never empty;
> Vines with clust'ring bunches growing,
> Plants with goodly burthen bowing.   (4.1.111–13)

But the prayer at the end of the martial law code reminds us that there is another version of mimetic economy, one in which aesthetic exchanges, like all other exchanges, always involve loss, even if it is cunningly hidden; in which aesthetic value, like all other value, actively depends upon want, craving, and absence; in which art itself—fantasy ridden and empty—is the very soul of scarcity. This version too finds its expression in *The Tempest* in the high cost Prospero has paid for his absorption in his secret studies, in Ariel's grumblings about his "pains" and "toil," and in the sudden vanishing—"to a strange, hollow, and confused noise"—of the masque that had figured forth plenitude and in Prospero's richly anxious meditation on the "baseless fabric" of his own glorious vision.

It is this doubleness that Shakespeare's joint-stock company bequeathed to its cultural heirs. And the principal beneficiary in the end was not the theater but a different institution, the institution of literature. Shakespeare served posthumously as a principal shareholder in this institution as well—not as a man of the theater but as the author of the book. During Shakespeare's lifetime, the King's Men showed no interest in and may have actually resisted the publication of a one-volume collection of their famous playwright's work; the circulation of such a book was not in the interests of their company. But other collective enterprises, including the educational system in which this study is implicated, have focused more on the text than on the playhouse.

For if Shakespeare himself imagined Prospero's island as the great Globe Theatre, succeeding generations found that island more compactly and portably figured in the bound volume. The passage from the stage to the book signals a larger shift from the joint-stock company, with its primary interest in protecting the common property, to the modern corporation, with its primary interest in the expansion and profitable exploitation of a network of relations. Unlike the Globe, which is tied to a particular place and time and community, unlike even the traveling theater company, with its constraints of personnel and stage properties and playing space, the book is supremely portable. It may be readily detached from its immediate geographical and cultural origins, its original producers and consumers, and endlessly reproduced, circulated, exchanged, exported to other times and places.[21]

The plays, of course, continue to live in the theater, but Shakespeare's achievement and the cult of artistic genius erected around the achievement have become increasingly identified with his collected works. Those works have been widely acknowledged as the central literary achievement of English culture. As such they served—and continue to serve—as a fetish of Western civilization, a fetish Caliban curiously anticipates when he counsels Stephano and Trinculo to cut Prospero's throat:[22]

> Remember
> First to possess his books; for without them
> He's but a sot, as I am; nor hath not
> One spirit to command: they all do hate him
> As rootedly as I. Burn but his books. (3.2.95–99)

NOTES

1. Recall Carleton's description of the expression on the faces of the Bye Plot conspirators as they were assembled together on the scaffold.
2. On the significance of pardon as a strategy in Renaissance monarchies, see Natalie Zemon Davis, *Fiction in the Archives* (Stanford: Stanford University Press, forthcoming). Davis's wonderful book, which she graciously allowed me to read in manuscript, shows that the system of pardons in France generated a remarkable range of narratives. Though the English legal system differed in important ways from the French, pardon played a significant, if more circumscribed, role. Shakespeare seems to have deliberately appropriated for *The Tempest* the powerful social energy of princely pardons.
3. In this regard Prospero resembles less a radical reformer like Latimer than a monarch like Queen Elizabeth: a ruler who abjured the complete inquisitorial control of the inner life and settled when necessary for the outward signs of obedience.

    For a brilliant discussion of Prospero's relations with Antonio, see the introduction to the Oxford Shakespeare edition of *The Tempest*, ed. Stephen Orgel (Oxford: Oxford University Press, 1987). Throughout this essay, I have profited from Orgel's introduction, which he kindly showed me in advance of its publication.
4. I am trying to resist here the proposition that Latimer's story is the actual practice that is then represented in works of art, and hence that in it we encounter the basis in reality of theatrical fictions. Even if we assume that the events in Cambridge occurred exactly as Latimer related them—and this is a large assumption based on a reckless act of faith—those events seem saturated with narrative conventions. It is not only that Latimer lives his life as if it were material for the stories he will tell in his sermons but that the actions he reports are comprehensible only if already fashioned into a story.
5. On Strachey's career, see S. G. Culliford, *William Strachey, 1572–1621* (Charlottesville: University Press of Virginia, 1965). See also Charles Richard Sanders, "William Strachey, the Virginia Colony, and Shakespeare," *Virginia Magazine* 57 (1949): 115–32. Sanders notes that "many

of the eighteenth century Stracheys became servants of the East India Company" (118).

6. William Strachey, in Samuel Purchas, *Hakluytus Posthumus or Purchas His Pilgrimes*, 20 vols. (Glasgow: James Maclehose and Sons, 1905–7), 19:5–72. It seems worth remarking the odd coincidence between this circumstance and Latimer's presenting his sermon also to a noble lady. Men in this period often seem to shape their experiences in the world to present them as instruction or entertainment to powerfully placed ladies. The great Shakespearean exploration of this social theme is *Othello*.

7. On joint-stock companies in the early modern period, see William Robert Scott, *The Constitution and Finance of English, Scottish, and Irish Joint-Stock Companies to 1720*, 3 vols. (Cambridge: Cambridge University Press, 1912). On the theater and the marketplace, see the excellent book by Jean-Christophe Agnew, *Worlds Apart: The Market and the Theater in Anglo-American Thought, 1550–1750* (Cambridge: Cambridge University Press, 1986).

8. Indeed the demand for such connections, a demand almost always frustrated in the early modern period, has strengthened the case for the formalist isolation of art.

9. Charles Mills Gayley, *Shakespeare and the Founders of Liberty in America* (New York: Macmillan, 1917); William Strachey, *The Historie of Travell into Virginia Britannia* (1612), ed. Louis B. Wright and Virginia Freund, Hakluyt Society 2d ser., no. 103 (London, 1953), p. xix.

10. Detestation of the sailors is a common theme in the travel literature of the period. One of the strongest elements of an elitist utopia in *The Tempest* is the fantasy that the sailors will in effect be put to sleep for the duration of the stay on the island, to be awakened only to labor on the return voyage.

11. Quoted in the introduction to *The Historie of Travell into Virginia Britannia*, p. xxv.

12. I quote these lines because they may have caught Shakespeare's attention: "What have we here?" asks Trinculo, catching sight of Caliban, "a man or a fish? dead or alive? A fish, he smells like a fish" (2.2.25–26). Prospero in exasperation calls Caliban a tortoise (1.2.316).

13. The promotional literature written on behalf of the Virginia Company prior to the voyage of 1609 makes it clear that there was already widespread talk in England about the hardships of the English colonists. No one on the *Sea Venture* is likely to have harbored any illusions about the conditions at Jamestown.

14. The office of governor was created by the royal charter of 1609. The governor replaced the council president as the colony's chief executive. He was granted the right to "correct and punishe, pardon, governe, and rule all such the subjects of us . . . as shall from time to time adventure themselves . . . thither," and he was empowered to impose martial law in cases of mutiny or rebellion (quoted in *The Three Charters of the Virginia Company of London, with Seven Related Documents, 1606–1621*, ed. S. F. Bemiss, Jamestown 350th Anniversary Historical Booklet 4 [Williamsburg, Va., 1957], p. 52). See Warren M. Billings, "The Transfer of English Law to Virginia, 1606–1650," in *The Westward Enterprise: English Activities in Ireland, the Atlantic, and America, 1480–1650*, ed.

K. R. Andrews, N. P. Canny, and P. E. H. Hair (Liverpool: Liverpool University Press, 1978), pp. 214ff.

15. Leaving the island is not in itself, as is sometimes claimed, an abjuration of colonialism: as we have seen in the case of Bermuda, the enforced departure from the island signals the resumption of the colonial enterprise. On the other hand, insofar as *The Tempest* conflates the Bermuda and Virginia materials, the departure for Italy—and by implication England—would necessitate abandoning the absolute rule that had been established under martial law.

16. The noblemen's pride is related to the gentlemanly refusal to work that the leaders of the Virginia Company bitterly complained about. The English gentlemen in Jamestown, it was said, preferred to die rather than lift a finger to save themselves. So too when the boatswain urges Antonio and Sebastian to get out of the way or to work, Antonio answers, "We are less afraid to be drown'd than thou art" (1.1.45–46).

17. For acute observations on the parallels with Sycorax, see Stephen Orgel, "Prospero's Wife," *Representations* 8 (1985): 1–13; among the many essays on Caliban is one of my own: "Learning to Curse: Aspects of Linguistic Colonialism in the Sixteenth Century," in *First Images of America: The Impact of the New World on the Old*, 2 vols., ed. Fredi Chiappelli (Berkeley: University of California Press, 1976), 2:561–80.

18. Quoted in Nicholas Canny, "The Permissive Frontier: The Problem of Social Control in English Settlements in Ireland and Virginia, 1550–1650," in *The Westward Enterprise*, p. 36.

19. William Crashaw, *A sermon preached in London before the right honorable the Lord Lawarre, Lord Governour and Captaine Generall of Virginia . . . at the said Lord Generall his leave taking of England . . . and departure for Virginea, Febr. 21, 1609* (London, 1610), pp. H1v–H1r. The British Library has a copy of Strachey's *Lawes Diuine, Morall and Martiall* with a manuscript inscription by the author to Crashaw; see Sanders, "William Strachey, the Virginia Colony, and Shakespeare," p. 121.

20. William Strachey, *For the Colony in Virginia Britannia. Lawes Diuine, Morall and Martiall, &c.* (London: Walter Burre, 1612), in Peter Force, *Tracts and Other Papers, Relating Principally to the Origin, Settlement, and Progress of the Colonies in North America, from the Discovery to the Year 1776*, 4 vols. (Washington, D.C., 1836–46), 3:67.

21. In our century the market for Shakespeare as book has come to focus increasingly upon adolescents in colleges and universities who are assigned expensive texts furnished with elaborate critical introductions and editorial apparatus. On the ideological implications of Shakespeare in the curriculum, see Alan Sinfield, "Give an account of Shakespeare and Education, showing why you think they are effective and what you have appreciated about them. Support your comments with precise references," in *Political Shakespeare: New Essays in Cultural Materialism*, ed. Jonathan Dollimore and Alan Sinfield (Manchester: Manchester University Press, 1985), pp. 134–57.

22. But if Shakespeare's works have become a fetish, they are defined for their possessors not by their magical power to command but by their freedom from the anxieties of rule. They are the emblems of cultivation, civility, recreation, but they are not conceived of as direct agents in the work of empire.

SYLVAN BARNET

The Tempest on Stage and Screen

> These our actors,
> As I foretold you, were all spirits and
> Are melted into air, into thin air.

Although performances of plays are illusive and elusive, we do have some evidence about even the earliest productions of Shakespeare—for instance in original stage directions—and we have detailed descriptions of many later productions.

Shakespeare's company played chiefly at the Globe Theatre, an open-air playhouse that served the London public, and although there is every likelihood that *The Tempest* was produced there, in fact no document specifies that it was. The earliest reference to a performance tells us that *The Tempest* was given before King James I on November 1, 1611, at the Banqueting House in Whitehall. The second reference (May 20, 1613) is to yet another performance at court, asserting that the play was staged as part of the wedding celebrations of Princess Elizabeth, daughter of James I. Court performances, especially performances of the highly allegorical dramatic works called masques, customarily made great use of spectacular effects, some of which would be particularly suited to *The Tempest*. Consider, for example, descriptions of nautical effects. Ben Jonson's *Masque of Blackness*, staged in the Banqueting House in 1605, began when a curtain decorated with a landscape painting dropped to the floor (the hall was not equipped to elevate the curtain): "An artificial sea was seen to shoot forth, ... raised with waves which seemed to move, and in some places the billow to break." Jonson's next production at court, *Masque of Beauty* (1608), required an "island floating on a calm water." As the introduction to the present volume indicates, *The Tempest* itself in some ways resembles a masque, and Prospero stages what is in effect a masque, when in 4.1.118*ff.* he conjures up Iris, Ceres, and Juno in "a most majestic vision." An original stage direction says that Juno "descends," but this action would cause no difficulty even at the Globe, which was equipped to let a deity descend in a throne from above the stage. Still, perhaps when *The Tempest* was staged at court some visual effects were heightened or added. For instance, a production in the Banqueting House would have used artificial illumination, making possible lighting effects that could not have been achieved at the open-air Globe Theatre and that perhaps could not have been equaled even in the indoors Blackfriars Theatre used by Shakespeare's company in the winter. On the other hand, nothing specified in *The Tempest* was beyond the facilities available at the Globe.

Whatever the original productions were like, we can roughly classify most subsequent productions as either plain or fancy, that is, either relatively simply staged productions of the text or, on the other hand, relatively elaborately staged productions of a text altered to accommodate the machinery necessary to produce spectacular effects. Justifications can be offered for both kinds. Briefly, advocates of fancy, spectacular productions point to the court records we have just noticed, and argue that the production of *The Tempest* must have resembled other court productions. Advocates of plain production, on the other hand, argue that the records merely record but do not describe productions of *The Tempest*, and, moreover, that *The Tempest* was surely not written simply to be produced only twice at court. Shakespeare must have written the play for regular production at the Globe (though, again, there are no extant references to any production there).

This much can certainly be said, based on the evidence of the stage directions in the first printed version of the play (and reprinted in the present text): Shakespeare valued auditory and visual effects. Thus, the play begins with "Thunder and lightning," and a little later in the first scene we encounter a stage direction that says, "Enter mariners wet." In the next scene Prospero says to Ariel, "Go make thyself like a nymph o' th' sea. Be subject / To no sight but thine and mine, invisible / To every eyeball else," and a few lines later we get this stage direction: "Enter Ariel like a water nymph." If Ariel is "invisible to every eyeball" other than Prospero's and Ariel's, why the costume of a sea nymph? Because, obviously, Shakespeare wanted to feast the spectators' eyes with unusual visual material. Later (3.3.52) we get a stage direction calling for spectacle and magic: "Thunder and lightning. Enter Ariel, like a harpy; claps his wings upon the table; and with a quaint device the banquet vanishes." Although a later stage direction calls for "Shapes" to enter and carry out the table, thus indicating that only the food on the table vanishes, not the table itself, the effect nevertheless must have been wonderful, and whatever the "quaint device" was—perhaps a table whose top flipped over—we seem to be in a world of masquelike machinery. Less complex, but no less indicative of Shakespeare's use of visual effects, is the stage direction at the beginning of the last act: "Enter Prospero in his magic robes." It seems reasonable to assume that these robes were something extraordinary.

Fancy versions of *The Tempest* were common in the late seventeenth century, and in the first half of the eighteenth. "Versions" is perhaps too generous; these adaptations were so extensive that they should be considered independent works rather than productions of Shakespeare's play. In 1667 William Davenant's and John Dryden's *The Tempest: or the Enchanted Island* was staged, a play which added (to balance Miranda) Hippolito, a handsome young man who had never seen a woman. There were other additions, too: Miranda was given a younger sister, Dorinda, who would marry Hippolito; Caliban also was given a sister, Sycorax; and Ariel was paired with a female sprite, Milcha, who was pursued by two new comic sailors. Other changes included a good many cuts, especially in Prospero's lines. Shakespeare's play was thus made more symmetrical—more orderly, so to speak—

and at the same time more fanciful, thus suiting the taste of an age that regarded itself as rational or classical and also as willing to enjoy the most extreme flights of a poet's imagination.

In 1674 Thomas Shadwell, adapting the adaptation, converted the piece into an opera. He added songs, a chorus of devils, and ballets of winds and Tritons, and in 1695 this opera was done with music by Henry Purcell. But the Davenant-Dryden version, too, continued to be immensely popular. It was produced at the Theatre Royal, Drury Lane, almost every year between 1701 and 1756, virtually driving Shakespeare's play from the stage. In 1745–1746, however, Shakespeare's original play was given six performances at Drury Lane, and though the Davenant-Dryden version was again revived, its days were numbered. In 1757 David Garrick put on Shakespeare's play, cutting only 432 lines and (more remarkable, in an age that felt free to "improve" Shakespeare) adding only 14. Although this relatively faithful version of Shakespeare's play was regularly staged during much of the rest of the eighteenth century, in 1787 John Philip Kemble, the noted classical actor, restored Hippolito and Dorinda. Because Dorinda's role was larger than Miranda's, it was much preferred by actresses in the last decade of the century. Operatic treatments, too, continued in the early nineteenth century, but in 1838 William Charles Macready, manager of Covent Garden, played Prospero in a text remarkably close to Shakespeare's. Still, it should be noted that although Macready rejected the accretions, his production employed a good deal of machinery, beginning with a huge ship, and continuing with Ariel flying around.

Charles Kean's production in 1857, which cut much of Shakespeare's text, was remarkable for its mechanically contrived spectacular effects, especially the storm and the other magic. It was boasted of this production: "The scenic appliances are of a more extensive nature than have been attempted in any theater in Europe." But whereas Davenant and Dryden believed that they had to refine Shakespeare's rather primitive plays for a more sophisticated age, the Victorian and Edwardian producers could with some reason believe they were fulfilling Shakespeare's intention when they provided as much splendor and magic as the theater (equipped with gaslight in 1817, and with limelight twenty years later) could produce. When electricity was introduced, in the third quarter of the nineteenth century, even more wonderful illusions became possible. This was an age when the theaters concentrated on splendid visual effects, and if the effects went far beyond anything that was possible in Shakespeare's own day it can nevertheless be argued that Shakespeare, with his thunder and lightning, his unusual costumes for Ariel and for Prospero, his masque of goddesses, and even his "wet" mariners, had himself sought to provide both realism and marvelous spectacles.

Probably the most notable Edwardian spectacular production was staged by Herbert Beerbohm Tree in 1904, when Tree played Caliban. An amazingly realistic shipwreck, in the Kean tradition, was followed by a blackout, then by the expository scene between Prospero and Miranda, and then by a scene, behind a gauze, of nymphs in a purple light playing on the water (they were suspended by wires) and on the sand. The light gradually turned amber, and the sands became gold, to the strains of "Come unto These Yellow Sands." Tree transposed some scenes, and made some heavy cuts, reducing the last act to less than half its original length, but he added elaborate pantomimes. Thus, he deleted the material that follows Prospero's speech beginning "Ye elves of hills, brooks, standing lakes, and groves" (5.1.33–57), in which Prospero breaks his staff and vows to drown his book. Tree then added lightning, thunder, another vision of nymphs singing about their yellow sands, and a final pantomime. In a souvenir playbill Tree describes the end:

> Caliban creeps from his cave, and watches the departing ship bearing away the freight of humanity which for a brief spell has gladdened and saddened his island home, and taught him to "seek for grace." For the last time Ariel appears, singing the song of the bee.... The voice of the sprite rises higher and higher until it is merged into the note of the lark—Ariel is now as free as a bird. Caliban listens for the last time to the sweet air, then turns sadly in the direction of the departing ship. The play is ended. As the curtain rises again, the ship is seen on the ho-

rizon, Caliban stretching out his arms towards it in mute despair. The night falls, and Caliban is left on the lonely rock. He is a King once more.

But if most nineteenth-century productions strove to make Shakespeare real by means of elaborate sets and illusionistic lighting effects, the period also saw the rise of a counter-movement. As early as 1811 Ludwig Tieck, the German critic and translator of Shakespeare, pleaded for an Elizabethan-like theater in which the plays could be staged as they had been staged in Shakespeare's day. In 1894 William Poel founded the Elizabethan Stage Society, dedicated to restoring Elizabethan stage conditions. Poel saw that the use of cumbersome sets (encouraged by the proscenium stage) destroyed the continuity of Shakespeare's scenes; since elaborate sets could not be quickly struck, directors tended to delete or transpose scenes that in the text intervened between scenes requiring a given massive set. Moreover, Poel believed that attempts at illusionism were futile. In 1897 he staged *The Tempest* on what was thought to be an Elizabethan stage erected in the hall of the Mansion House. Bernard Shaw, in a review of the production, gives us a good idea of Poel's aims:

Mr. Poel says frankly, "See that singers' gallery up there! Well, let's pretend that it's the ship." We agree; and the thing is done. But how could we agree to such a pretence with a stage ship? Before it we should say, "Take that thing away: if our imagination is to create a ship, it must not be contradicted by something that apes a ship so vilely as to fill us with denial and repudiation of its imposture." The singing gallery makes no attempt to impose on us: it disarms criticism by unaffected submission to the facts of the case, and throws itself honestly on our fancy, with instant success.

Poel dressed his players in Elizabethan costume, basing Prospero's costume on a print in a Renaissance book about magic, and basing the costumes for the magical "Shapes" on prints illustrating court masques. He made some cuts—notably the bawdry—but because the stage itself provided a permanent set, and because the spectators were expected to imagine the locales, he did not have to cut scenes that otherwise, requiring a change of set, would have been deleted. Poel's efforts to present Shakespeare without illusion were to have an enormous effect on the staging of Shakespeare, but they did not immediately banish Victorian spectacular, illusionistic productions. As we have seen, one of the most spectacular, Tree's, was given in 1904.

It is worth noting, by the way, that Tree played Caliban. This role has, of course, been played in several ways, sometimes as a drunken beast, sometimes as a noble savage, sometimes as the missing link (an 1890s interpretation based on Darwinism), and, recently, as a detribalized victim of colonial power. In the late seventeenth century, and in the eighteenth, Caliban was chiefly a minor comic figure, but with the rise of Romanticism he could become a "natural" man, a creature of sensibility. In 1806, in Kemble's production, he was not only a comic lout but also a pitiful victim; in 1811–1812, Samuel Taylor Coleridge, in a series of lectures, spoke of Caliban as a "noble being; a man in the sense of the imagination, all the images he utters are drawn from nature, and are highly poetical." A viewer of Macready's production of 1838 saw in Caliban one who "arouses our sympathies" because he resists a tyrannical oppressor. The late nineteenth-century Darwinian versions persisted into the first third of the twentieth century, in their way helping to make Caliban sympathetic, for, though a beast, he supposedly aspired to become a man. Beerbohm Tree, calling attention to Caliban's "love of music and his affinity with the unseen world," said that in Caliban "we discern in the soul which inhabits this elemental man the germs of a sense of beauty, in the dawn of art."

In our own time, Caliban has been variously presented— for example, as an American Indian, as a militant black, and (in Peter Brook's production at Stratford-upon-Avon in 1963 and especially in his production at the Round House in London in 1968) as a prehistoric man, the incarnation of bestial sexuality. In a production at the Mermaid Theatre in London, in 1970, Jonathan Miller, advancing a view that could not have been imagined before the middle of our century, saw the play as being about the destructive effects of colonialism, and he therefore depicted Caliban (played by a black actor) as the uneducated field hand, juxtaposed against Ariel (also played by a black actor), the cunning house slave. Prospero, of course, was the brutal local governor. (In 1945 in the United States, by the way, Canada Lee became the first black actor to play Caliban, but the production did not advance a view about colonialism.) Miller dressed his courtiers in black and introduced an attendant dwarf, thus evoking the world of Velasquez, i.e., the world of the Spanish conquistadores. Miller has said that the underlying idea is the tragic destruction consequent upon a white assault on a tribal culture. Gone was Beerbohm Tree's Caliban, who at the end extended his hands toward the departing ship "in mute despair"; instead, Miller's *Tempest* ended with Caliban shaking his fist in rage, and Ariel—ever the alert opportunist—picking up the staff that their master had abandoned. But this view already shows signs of having worn thin; several productions in the last decade have returned to Caliban the noble savage, and, on the other hand, to Caliban as part of Prospero's own passionate (or even monstrous) nature.

Probably the most memorable Prospero of modern times has been John Gielgud, who has performed the role in four productions: 1930, 1940, 1957, and 1973. By the way, the 1930 production, directed by Harcourt Williams, is a landmark in the stage history of the play because Ariel, who since the early eighteenth century had always been played by a woman—usually a singer who could also dance—now was played by a male, the boyish Leslie French. Occasional productions in the 1930s and 40s reverted to a female Ariel, but the male Ariel is now standard.

Gielgud in 1930 was twenty-six; he played the part without a beard, and did not seek to convey the impression of an old man. (In fact, although Prospero is often played as elderly, apart from one reference to his "old brain," nothing in the text requires that he be beyond middle age.) In 1940 Gielgud wore a small goatee, but again he did not seem old. The productions of 1957 (at Stratford-upon-Avon, and later at Drury Lane, directed by Peter Brook), were on the whole bleak, though some scenes showed a stifling tropical jungle, but whatever the set, it was conceived as a metaphor of Prospero's agitated mind. There was lots of magic—trapdoors and dissolving gauzes—but the masque was eerie rather than beautiful, and the costumes (except for Ferdinand's, which was orange, green, and white) were relatively drab. Except at the end, when he was again the duke, Gielgud wore not an elaborate magician's robe but a simple saronglike garment. To several reviewers he was a haunted figure out of El Greco, a man filled with anguish, struggling to rise above the memory of the "high wrongs" he had endured. He finally conquered his passions, and, at the end, armed with a sword, set out for Milan, not as one who would live in easy retirement but as one who would continue to struggle against evil.

In 1973, directed by Peter Hall at the National Theatre, Gielgud again played a Prospero whose mind was beating through most of the play, though the harshness (which Brook wanted in 1957) was somewhat modified by the music of the great organ voice for which Gielgud is famous, and the settings were magical and dreamlike. At the end of this version, when he appeared not in silks but in ordinary Elizabethan attire, the audience perceived a resemblance to Shakespeare. In other ways, too, Hall sought to emphasize the Renaissance origin of the work. The production employed Inigo Jones-like symbolism: half of Caliban's face was monstrous, the other half that of the noble savage, and the stage balanced Prospero's cave (civilization) against Caliban's (primitivism).

But in talking about Gielgud's Prosperos we have gotten a bit ahead of our story, though we will return to Gielgud in a moment. In 1968 Peter Brook directed *The Tempest* at the Round House in London, a converted station house for trains at the end of the line. This production, like the Davenant-Dryden adaptation that ruled the stage in the late seventeenth century and the first half of the eighteenth, made the play into something utterly new. Brook began with actors and audience milling on the floor (there was no stage, except for some low platforms and for some scaffolding under a white tent that hung from the high ceiling), and then the actors (in work clothes, except for Prospero, who wore a white karate suit, and Ariel, who wore a kimono) started to do warm-up exercises. Next, the actors stiffened their faces into masks, uttered unintelligible sounds, and the play began. Some of the audience sat on boxes or chairs along three sides of the auditorium, others sat on the scaffolding. The gist of Shakespeare's plot was retained, but with much cutting (Alonso, Antonio, Gonzalo, and Sebastian were dropped); the surviving lines were chiefly muttered or intoned without pauses at the ends of lines or sentences. Caliban's mother, Sycorax (mentioned in Shakespeare's text but not a character in the play) was presented, a monstrous giant, and Caliban's birth—the birth of evil—was staged. Caliban furiously rejects Prospero's attempts to teach (i.e., subjugate) him, rapes Miranda, is captured, escapes, and engages in an orgy (including sex with his mother). Prospero is captured and raped. Ariel's arrival disperses Caliban and the other rapists, and after some improvisation Miranda and Ferdinand marry. Various characters speak lines of what was once Prospero's epilogue. At the end, there is no change of light, and no curtain. This description, necessarily brief, perhaps is long enough to support the view that seventeenth-century (per)version by Davenant and Dryden has its modern equivalent.

In 1990 Brook again staged *The Tempest*, this time in Paris at his International Center for Theatrical Creations. Brook did not hop on the colonialist interpretation (Prospero as exploiter) that has dominated most productions since Jonathan Miller's; Brook's Prospero was dark-skinned, the West African actor Sotigui Kouyate, and his Caliban was a white man. Dennis Kennedy in *Looking at Shakespeare* gives us a glimpse of what must have been an extremely interesting production:

A few bamboo sticks became the sinking ship, the surface of the water for a drowning sailor, and a cage for Ferdinand. [Kennedy provides a photo showing how three or four poles, some ten feet long, each held at angles by two or three men, represented the foundering ship.] The essentially metaphoric design was joined by occasional witty metonyms, like the model of a ship worn as a headpiece by Ariel in the opening, or the scene in which Gonzalo, sitting on the floor, was surrounded by miniature castles, created by green-clad stagehands who inverted flowerpots filled with sand. (Page 283)

If we turn to television and screen versions, we find there is not much of interest. The BBC television version (1979) is competent but unexciting. Michael Hordern had played a low-keyed Prospero with the Royal Shakespeare Company in 1978, and he pretty much repeated the interpretation in the BBC version. Many viewers find that the strongest passages are the scenes of Caliban (Warren Clarke), Trinculo (Andrew Sachs), and Stephano (Nigel Hawthorne).

One noteworthy film version—or, rather, not a version but an analogue—is Peter Greenaway's *Prospero's Books* (1991), with John Gielgud. Gielgud speaks virtually all of the lines of all of the parts, the idea being that he, or, rather, Shakespeare, is creating the play. (Some distinguished actors are in the film, but except for Caliban they can't do much with their roles.) The film begins with Prospero entering a pool in what seems to be a Roman palace. Refreshed, he begins to compose the play while a boy on a swing above the pool urinates on a floating ship. Water (the source of life) is important throughout, as are books, including *A Book of Games*, *A Book of Utopias*, and of course *The Book of Water*. At the end of the film, Prospero breaks his staff and drowns his books, but Caliban rescues two of them, a large folio volume (the complete plays except for *The Tempest*) and this last play of Shakespeare's, *The Tempest*, which in fact appears as the first play in the folio of 1623.

Bibliographical Note: Many of the titles recommended below, in Suggested References, Section 4 (Shakespeare on Stage and Screen), include brief discussions. The following titles offer extended comments on particular productions. On Beerbohm Tree's *The Tempest*, see Mary M. Nilan, *Shakespeare Survey* 25 (1972), and on Peter Hall's 1973 production with Gielgud, see *Peter Hall's Diaries,* ed. John Goodwin (1983). For a small book with good comments on several modern productions, see David L. Hirst, *The Tempest [Text and Performance]* (1984). Peter Greenaway discusses his film in an illustrated book, *Prospero's Books: A Film of Shakespeare's "The Tempest"* (1991).

Suggested References

The number of possible references is vast and grows alarmingly. (The *Shakespeare Quarterly* devotes one issue each year to a list of the previous year's work, and *Shakespeare Survey*—an annual publication—includes a substantial review of biographical, critical, and textual studies, as well as a survey of performances.) The vast bibliography is best approached through James Harner, *The World Shakespeare Bibliography on CD-Rom: 1900–Present.* The first release, in 1996, included more than 12,000 annotated items from 1990–93, plus references to several thousand book reviews, productions, films, and audio recordings. The plan is to update the publication annually, moving forward one year and backward three years. Thus, the second issue (1997), with 24,700 entries, and another 35,000 or so references to reviews, newspaper pieces, and so on, covered 1987–94.

Though no works are indispensable, those listed below have been found especially helpful. The arrangement is as follows:

1. Shakespeare's Times	6. Shakespeare's Plays:
2. Shakespeare's Life	General Studies
3. Shakespeare's Theater	7. The Comedies
4. Shakespeare	8. The Romances
on Stage	9. The Tragedies
and Screen	10. The Histories
5. Miscellaneous Reference	11. *The Tempest*
Works	

The titles in the first five sections are accompanied by brief explanatory annotations.

1. Shakespeare's Times

Andrews, John F., ed. *William Shakespeare: His World, His Work, His Influence,* 3 vols. (1985). Sixty articles, dealing not only with such subjects as "The State," "The Church," "Law," "Science, Magic, and Folklore," but also with the plays and poems themselves and Shakespeare's influence (e.g., translations, films, reputation)

Byrne, Muriel St. Clare. *Elizabethan Life in Town and Country* (8th ed., 1970). Chapters on manners, beliefs, education, etc., with illustrations.

Dollimore, John, and Alan Sinfield, eds. *Political Shakespeare: New Essays in Cultural Materialism* (1985). Essays on such topics as the subordination of women and colonialism, presented in connection with some of Shakespeare's plays.

Greenblatt, Stephen. *Representing the English Renaissance* (1988). New Historicist essays, especially on connections between political and aesthetic matters, statecraft and stagecraft.

Joseph, B. L. *Shakespeare's Eden: the Commonwealth of England 1558–1629* (1971). An account of the social, political, economic, and cultural life of England.

Kernan, Alvin. *Shakespeare, the King's Playwright: Theater in the Stuart Court 1603–1613* (1995). The social setting and the politics of the court of James I, in relation to *Hamlet, Measure for Measure, Macbeth, King Lear, Antony and Cleopatra, Coriolanus,* and *The Tempest.*

Montrose, Louis. *The Purpose of Playing: Shakespeare and the Cultural Politics of the Elizabethan Theatre* (1996). A poststructuralist view, discussing the professional theater "within the ideological and material frameworks of Elizabethan culture and society," with an extended analysis of *A Midsummer Night's Dream.*

Mullaney, Steven. *The Place of the Stage: License, Play, and Power in Renaissance England* (1988). New Historicist analysis, arguing that popular drama became a cultural institution "only by . . . taking up a place on the margins of society."

Schoenbaum, S. *Shakespeare: The Globe and the World*

(1979). A readable, abundantly illustrated introductory book on the world of the Elizabethans.

Shakespeare's England, 2 vols. (1916). A large collection of scholarly essays on a wide variety of topics, e.g., astrology, costume, gardening, horsemanship, with special attention to Shakespeare's references to these topics.

2. Shakespeare's Life

Andrews, John F., ed. *William Shakespeare: His World, His Work, His Influence*, 3 vols. (1985). See the description above.

Bentley, Gerald E. *Shakespeare: A Biographical Handbook* (1961). The facts about Shakespeare, with virtually no conjecture intermingled.

Chambers, E. K. *William Shakespeare: A Study of Facts and Problems*, 2 vols. (1930). The fullest collection of data.

Fraser, Russell. *Young Shakespeare* (1988). A highly readable account that simultaneously considers Shakespeare's life and Shakespeare's art.

―――. *Shakespeare: The Later Years* (1992).

Schoenbaum, S. *Shakespeare's Lives* (1970). A review of the evidence and an examination of many biographies, including those of Baconians and other heretics.

―――. *William Shakespeare: A Compact Documentary Life* (1977). An abbreviated version, in a smaller format, of the next title. The compact version reproduces some fifty documents in reduced form. A readable presentation of all that the documents tell us about Shakespeare.

―――. *William Shakespeare: A Documentary Life* (1975). A large-format book setting forth the biography with facsimiles of more than two hundred documents, and with transcriptions and commentaries.

3. Shakespeare's Theater

Astington, John H., ed. *The Development of Shakespeare's Theater* (1992). Eight specialized essays on theatrical companies, playing spaces, and performance.

Beckerman, Bernard. *Shakespeare at the Globe, 1599–1609* (1962). On the playhouse and on Elizabethan dramaturgy, acting, and staging.

Bentley, Gerald E. *The Profession of Dramatist in Shakespeare's Time* (1971). An account of the dramatist's status in the Elizabethan period.

———. *The Profession of Player in Shakespeare's Time, 1590–1642* (1984). An account of the status of members of London companies (sharers, hired men, apprentices, managers) and a discussion of conditions when they toured.

Berry, Herbert. *Shakespeare's Playhouses* (1987). Usefully emphasizes how little we know about the construction of Elizabethan theaters.

Brown, John Russell. *Shakespeare's Plays in Performance* (1966). A speculative and practical analysis relevant to all of the plays, but with emphasis on *The Merchant of Venice, Richard II, Hamlet, Romeo and Juliet,* and *Twelfth Night.*

———. *William Shakespeare: Writing for Performance* (1996). A discussion aimed at helping readers to develop theatrically conscious habits of reading.

Chambers, E. K. *The Elizabethan Stage*, 4 vols. (1945). A major reference work on theaters, theatrical companies, and staging at court.

Cook, Ann Jennalie. *The Privileged Playgoers of Shakespeare's London, 1576–1642* (1981). Sees Shakespeare's audience as wealthier, more middle-class, and more intellectual than Harbage (below) does.

Dessen, Alan C. *Elizabethan Drama and the Viewer's Eye* (1977). On how certain scenes may have looked to spectators in an Elizabethan theater.

Gurr, Andrew. *Playgoing in Shakespeare's London* (1987). Something of a middle ground between Cook (above) and Harbage (below).

———. *The Shakespearean Stage, 1579–1642* (2nd ed., 1980). On the acting companies, the actors, the playhouses, the stages, and the audiences.

Harbage, Alfred. *Shakespeare's Audience* (1941). A study of the size and nature of the theatrical public, emphasizing the representativeness of its working class and middle-class audience.

Hodges, C. Walter. *The Globe Restored* (1968). A conjectural restoration, with lucid drawings.

Hosley, Richard. "The Playhouses," in *The Revels History of Drama in English*, vol. 3, general editors Clifford Leech and T. W. Craik (1975). An essay of a hundred pages on the physical aspects of the playhouses.

Howard, Jane E. "Crossdressing, the Theatre, and Gender Struggle in Early Modern England," *Shakespeare Quarterly* 39 (1988): 418–40. Judicious comments on the effects of boys playing female roles.

Orrell, John. *The Human Stage: English Theatre Design, 1567–1640* (1988). Argues that the public, private, and court playhouses are less indebted to popular structures (e.g., innyards and bear-baiting pits) than to banqueting halls and to Renaissance conceptions of Roman amphitheaters.

Slater, Ann Pasternak. *Shakespeare the Director* (1982). An analysis of theatrical effects (e.g., kissing, kneeling) in stage directions and dialogue.

Styan, J. L. *Shakespeare's Stagecraft* (1967). An introduction to Shakespeare's visual and aural stagecraft, with chapters on such topics as acting conventions, stage groupings, and speech.

Thompson, Peter. *Shakespeare's Professional Career* (1992). An examination of patronage and related theatrical conditions.

———. *Shakespeare's Theatre* (1983). A discussion of how plays were staged in Shakespeare's time.

4. Shakespeare on Stage and Screen

Bate, Jonathan, and Russell Jackson, eds. *Shakespeare: An Illustrated Stage History* (1996). Highly readable essays on stage productions from the Renaissance to the present.

Berry, Ralph. *Changing Styles in Shakespeare* (1981). Discusses productions of six plays (*Coriolanus*, *Hamlet*,

Henry V, Measure for Measure, The Tempest, and *Twelfth Night*) on the English stage, chiefly 1950–1980.

——. *On Directing Shakespeare: Interviews with Contemporary Directors* (1989). An enlarged edition of a book first published in 1977, this version includes the seven interviews from the early 1970s and adds five interviews conducted in 1988.

Brockbank, Philip, ed. *Players of Shakespeare: Essays in Shakespearean Performance* (1985). Comments by twelve actors, reporting their experiences with roles. See also the entry for Russell Jackson (below).

Bulman, J. C., and H. R. Coursen, eds. *Shakespeare on Television* (1988). An anthology of general and theoretical essays, essays on individual productions, and shorter reviews, with a bibliography and a videography listing cassettes that may be rented.

Coursen, H. P. *Watching Shakespeare on Television* (1993). Analyses not only of TV versions but also of films and videotapes of stage presentations that are shown on television.

Davies, Anthony, and Stanley Wells, eds. *Shakespeare and the Moving Image: The Plays on Film and Television* (1994). General essays (e.g., on the comedies) as well as essays devoted entirely to *Hamlet, King Lear,* and *Macbeth.*

Dawson, Anthony B. *Watching Shakespeare: A Playgoer's Guide* (1988). About half of the plays are discussed, chiefly in terms of decisions that actors and directors make in putting the works onto the stage.

Dessen, Alan. *Elizabethan Stage Conventions and Modern Interpretations* (1984). On interpreting conventions such as the representation of light and darkness and stage violence (duels, battles).

Donaldson, Peter. *Shakespearean Films/Shakespearean Directors* (1990). Postmodernist analyses, drawing on Freudianism, Feminism, Deconstruction, and Queer Theory.

Jackson, Russell, and Robert Smallwood, eds. *Players of Shakespeare 2: Further Essays in Shakespearean Performance by Players with the Royal Shakespeare Company*

(1988). Fourteen actors discuss their roles in productions between 1982 and 1987.

——. *Players of Shakespeare 3: Further Essays in Shakespearean Performance by Players with the Royal Shakespeare Company* (1993). Comments by thirteen performers.

Jorgens, Jack. *Shakespeare on Film* (1977). Fairly detailed studies of eighteen films, preceded by an introductory chapter addressing such issues as music, and whether to "open" the play by including scenes of landscape.

Kennedy, Dennis. *Looking at Shakespeare: A Visual History of Twentieth-Century Performance* (1993). Lucid descriptions (with 170 photographs) of European, British, and American performances.

Leiter, Samuel L. *Shakespeare Around the Globe: A Guide to Notable Postwar Revivals* (1986). For each play there are about two pages of introductory comments, then discussions (about five hundred words per production) of ten or so productions, and finally bibliographic references.

McMurty, Jo. *Shakespeare Films in the Classroom* (1994). Useful evaluations of the chief films most likely to be shown in undergraduate courses.

Rothwell, Kenneth, and Annabelle Henkin Melzer. *Shakespeare on Screen: An International Filmography and Videography* (1990). A reference guide to several hundred films and videos produced between 1899 and 1989, including spinoffs such as musicals and dance versions.

Sprague, Arthur Colby. *Shakespeare and the Actors* (1944). Detailed discussions of stage business (gestures, etc.) over the years.

Willis, Susan. *The BBC Shakespeare Plays: Making the Televised Canon* (1991). A history of the series, with interviews and production diaries for some plays.

5. Miscellaneous Reference Works

Abbott, E. A. *A Shakespearean Grammar* (new edition, 1877). An examination of differences between Elizabethan and modern grammar.

Allen, Michael J. B., and Kenneth Muir, eds. *Shakespeare's Plays in Quarto* (1981). One volume containing facsimiles of the plays issued in small format before they were collected in the First Folio of 1623.

Bevington, David. *Shakespeare* (1978). A short guide to hundreds of important writings on the subject.

Blake, Norman. *Shakespeare's Language: An Introduction* (1983). On vocabulary, parts of speech, and word order.

Bullough, Geoffrey. *Narrative and Dramatic Sources of Shakespeare*, 8 vols. (1957–75). A collection of many of the books Shakespeare drew on, with judicious comments.

Campbell, Oscar James, and Edward G. Quinn, eds. *The Reader's Encyclopedia of Shakespeare* (1966). Old, but still the most useful single reference work on Shakespeare.

Cercignani, Fausto. *Shakespeare's Works and Elizabethan Pronunciation* (1981). Considered the best work on the topic, but remains controversial.

Dent, R. W. *Shakespeare's Proverbial Language: An Index* (1981). An index of proverbs, with an introduction concerning a form Shakespeare frequently drew on.

Greg, W. W. *The Shakespeare First Folio* (1955). A detailed yet readable history of the first collection (1623) of Shakespeare's plays.

Harner, James. *The World Shakespeare Bibliography*. See headnote to Suggested References.

Hosley, Richard. *Shakespeare's Holinshed* (1968). Valuable presentation of one of Shakespeare's major sources.

Kökeritz, Helge. *Shakespeare's Names* (1959). A guide to pronouncing some 1,800 names appearing in Shakespeare.

———. *Shakespeare's Pronunciation* (1953). Contains much information about puns and rhymes, but see Cercignani (above).

Muir, Kenneth. *The Sources of Shakespeare's Plays* (1978). An account of Shakespeare's use of his reading. It covers all the plays, in chronological order.

Miriam Joseph, Sister. *Shakespeare's Use of the Arts of Language* (1947). A study of Shakespeare's use of rhetorical devices, reprinted in part as *Rhetoric in Shakespeare's Time* (1962).

The Norton Facsimile: The First Folio of Shakespeare's

Plays (1968). A handsome and accurate facsimile of the first collection (1623) of Shakespeare's plays, with a valuable introduction by Charlton Hinman.

Onions, C. T. *A Shakespeare Glossary*, rev. and enlarged by R. D. Eagleson (1986). Definitions of words (or senses of words) now obsolete.

Partridge, Eric. *Shakespeare's Bawdy*, rev. ed. (1955). Relatively brief dictionary of bawdy words; useful, but see Williams, below.

Shakespeare Quarterly. See headnote to Suggested References.

Shakespeare Survey. See headnote to Suggested References.

Spevack, Marvin. *The Harvard Concordance to Shakespeare* (1973). An index to Shakespeare's words.

Vickers, Brian. *Appropriating Shakespeare: Contemporary Critical Quarrels* (1993). A survey—chiefly hostile—of recent schools of criticism.

Wells, Stanley, ed. *Shakespeare: A Bibliographical Guide* (new edition, 1990). Nineteen chapters (some devoted to single plays, others devoted to groups of related plays) on recent scholarship on the life and all of the works.

Williams, Gordon. *A Dictionary of Sexual Language and Imagery in Shakespearean and Stuart Literature*, 3 vols. (1994). Extended discussions of words and passages; much fuller than Partridge, cited above.

6. Shakespeare's Plays: General Studies

Bamber, Linda. *Comic Women, Tragic Men: A Study of Gender and Genre in Shakespeare* (1982).

Barnet, Sylvan. *A Short Guide to Shakespeare* (1974).

Callaghan, Dympna, Lorraine Helms, and Jyotsna Singh. *The Weyward Sisters: Shakespeare and Feminist Politics* (1994).

Clemen, Wolfgang H. *The Development of Shakespeare's Imagery* (1951).

Cook, Ann Jennalie. *Making a Match: Courtship in Shakespeare and His Society* (1991).

Dollimore, Jonathan, and Alan Sinfield. *Political Shakespeare: New Essays in Cultural Materialism* (1985).

Dusinberre, Juliet. *Shakespeare and the Nature of Women* (1975).

Granville-Barker, Harley. *Prefaces to Shakespeare*, 2 vols. (1946–47; volume 1 contains essays on *Hamlet, King Lear, Merchant of Venice, Antony and Cleopatra*, and *Cymbeline*; volume 2 contains essays on *Othello, Coriolanus, Julius Caesar, Romeo and Juliet, Love's Labor's Lost*).

———. *More Prefaces to Shakespeare* (1974; essays on *Twelfth Night, A Midsummer Night's Dream, The Winter's Tale, Macbeth*).

Harbage, Alfred. *William Shakespeare: A Reader's Guide* (1963).

Howard, Jean E. *Shakespeare's Art of Orchestration: Stage Technique and Audience Response* (1984).

Jones, Emrys. *Scenic Form in Shakespeare* (1971).

Lenz, Carolyn Ruth Swift, Gayle Greene, and Carol Thomas Neely, eds. *The Woman's Part: Feminist Criticism of Shakespeare* (1980).

Novy, Marianne. *Love's Argument: Gender Relations in Shakespeare* (1984).

Rose, Mark. *Shakespearean Design* (1972).

Scragg, Leah. *Discovering Shakespeare's Meaning* (1994).

———. *Shakespeare's "Mouldy Tales": Recurrent Plot Motifs in Shakespearean Drama* (1992).

Traub, Valerie. *Desire and Anxiety: Circulations of Sexuality in Shakespearean Drama* (1992).

Traversi, D. A. *An Approach to Shakespeare*, 2 vols. (3rd rev. ed, 1968–69).

Vickers, Brian. *The Artistry of Shakespeare's Prose* (1968).

Wells, Stanley. *Shakespeare: A Dramatic Life* (1994).

Wright, George T. *Shakespeare's Metrical Art* (1988).

7. The Comedies

Barber, C. L. *Shakespeare's Festive Comedy* (1959; discusses *Love's Labor's Lost, A Midsummer Night's Dream, The Merchant of Venice, As You Like It, Twelfth Night*).

Barton, Anne. *The Names of Comedy* (1990).

Berry, Ralph. *Shakespeare's Comedy: Explorations in Form* (1972).

Bradbury, Malcolm, and David Palmer, eds. *Shakespearean Comedy* (1972).

Bryant, J. A., Jr. *Shakespeare and the Uses of Comedy* (1986).

Carroll, William. *The Metamorphoses of Shakespearean Comedy* (1985).

Champion, Larry S. *The Evolution of Shakespeare's Comedy* (1970).

Evans, Bertrand. *Shakespeare's Comedies* (1960).

Frye, Northrop. *Shakespearean Comedy and Romance* (1965).

Leggatt, Alexander. *Shakespeare's Comedy of Love* (1974).

Miola, Robert S. *Shakespeare and Classical Comedy: The Influence of Plautus and Terence* (1994).

Nevo, Ruth. *Comic Transformations in Shakespeare* (1980).

Ornstein, Robert. *Shakespeare's Comedies: From Roman Farce to Romantic Mystery* (1986).

Richman, David. *Laughter, Pain, and Wonder: Shakespeare's Comedies and the Audience in the Theater* (1990).

Salingar, Leo. *Shakespeare and the Traditions of Comedy* (1974).

Slights, Camille Wells. *Shakespeare's Comic Commonwealths* (1993).

Waller, Gary, ed. *Shakespeare's Comedies* (1991).

Westlund, Joseph. *Shakespeare's Reparative Comedies: A Psychoanalytic View of the Middle Plays* (1984).

Williamson, Marilyn. *The Patriarchy of Shakespeare's Comedies* (1986).

8. The Romances (*Pericles, Cymbeline, The Winter's Tale, The Tempest, The Two Noble Kinsmen*)

Adams, Robert M. *Shakespeare: The Four Romances* (1989).

Felperin, Howard. *Shakespearean Romance* (1972).

Frye, Northrop. *A Natural Perspective: The Development of Shakespearean Comedy and Romance* (1965).

Mowat, Barbara. *The Dramaturgy of Shakespeare's Romances* (1976).

Warren, Roger. *Staging Shakespeare's Late Plays* (1990).

Young, David. *The Heart's Forest: A Study of Shakespeare's Pastoral Plays* (1972).

9. The Tragedies

Bradley, A. C. *Shakespearean Tragedy* (1904).

Brooke, Nicholas. *Shakespeare's Early Tragedies* (1968).

Champion, Larry. *Shakespeare's Tragic Perspective* (1976).

Drakakis, John, ed. *Shakespearean Tragedy* (1992).

Evans, Bertrand. *Shakespeare's Tragic Practice* (1979).

Everett, Barbara. *Young Hamlet: Essays on Shakespeare's Tragedies* (1989).

Foakes, R. A. *Hamlet versus Lear: Cultural Politics and Shakespeare's Art* (1993).

Frye, Northrop. *Fools of Time: Studies in Shakespearean Tragedy* (1967).

Harbage, Alfred, ed. *Shakespeare: The Tragedies* (1964).

Mack, Maynard. *Everybody's Shakespeare: Reflections Chiefly on the Tragedies* (1993).

McAlindon, T. *Shakespeare's Tragic Cosmos* (1991).

Miola, Robert S. *Shakespeare and Classical Tragedy: The Influence of Seneca* (1992).

———. *Shakespeare's Rome* (1983).

Nevo, Ruth. *Tragic Form in Shakespeare* (1972).

Rackin, Phyllis. *Shakespeare's Tragedies* (1978).

Rose, Mark, ed. *Shakespeare's Early Tragedies: A Collection of Critical Essays* (1995).

Rosen, William. *Shakespeare and the Craft of Tragedy* (1960).

Snyder, Susan. *The Comic Matrix of Shakespeare's Tragedies* (1979).

Wofford, Susanne. *Shakespeare's Late Tragedies: A Collection of Critical Essays* (1996).

Young, David. *The Action to the Word: Structure and Style in Shakespearean Tragedy* (1990).

———. *Shakespeare's Middle Tragedies: A Collection of Critical Essays* (1993).

10. The Histories

Blanpied, John W. *Time and the Artist in Shakespeare's English Histories* (1983).

Campbell, Lily B. *Shakespeare's "Histories": Mirrors of Elizabethan Policy* (1947).

Champion, Larry S. *Perspective in Shakespeare's English Histories* (1980).

Hodgdon, Barbara. *The End Crowns All: Closure and Contradiction in Shakespeare's History* (1991).

Holderness, Graham. *Shakespeare Recycled: The Making of Historical Drama* (1992).

———. ed. *Shakespeare's History Plays: "Richard II" to "Henry V"* (1992).

Leggatt, Alexander. *Shakespeare's Political Drama: The History Plays and the Roman Plays* (1988).

Ornstein, Robert. *A Kingdom for a Stage: The Achievement of Shakespeare's History Plays* (1972).

Rackin, Phyllis. *Stages of History: Shakespeare's English Chronicles* (1990).

Saccio, Peter. *Shakespeare's English Kings: History, Chronicle, and Drama* (1977).

Tillyard, E. M. W. *Shakespeare's History Plays* (1944).

Velz, John W., ed. *Shakespeare's English Histories: A Quest for Form and Genre* (1996).

11. *The Tempest*

In addition to the titles listed above in Section 8, The Romances, and those listed in the Bibliographical Note on page 190, at the end of the discussion of *The Tempest* on Stage and Screen, see the following:

Auden, W. H. "The Sea and the Mirror: A Commentary on Shakespeare's *The Tempest,*" *The Collected Poetry* (1945). *The Dyer's Hand and Other Essays* (1968), pp. 128–34, 524–27.

Bamber, Linda. *Comic Women, Tragic Men* (1982).

Brower, Reuben A. "The Mirror of Analogy: *The Tempest,*" in *The Fields of Light* (1968), pp. 95–122.

Cantor, Paul. "Prospero's Republic: The Politics of Shakespeare's *The Tempest."* In *Shakespeare as Political Thinker,* eds. John Alvis and Thomas West (1981), pp. 239–55.

Graff, Gerald, and James Phelan, eds. *"The Tempest": A Case Study in Critical Controversy,* 2nd ed. (2009).

Halpern, Richard. " 'The Picture of Nobody': White Cannibalism in *The Tempest."* In *The Production of English Renaissance Culture,* eds. David Lee Miller, Sharon O'Dair, and Harold Weber (1994), pp. 262–92.

Hulme, Peter, and William Sherman, eds. *"The Tempest" and Its Travels* (2000).

James, D. G. *The Dream of Prospero* (1967).

Kirsch, Arthur. "Virtue, Vice and Compassion in Montaigne and *The Tempest,*" *Studies in English Literature* 37 (1997): 337–52.

Kott, Jan. "Prospero's Staff," *Shakespeare Our Contemporary*, tr. Boleslaw Taborski (1964), pp. 163–205.

Leavis, F. R. "The Criticism of Shakespeare's Late Plays," *The Common Pursuit* (1952), pp. 173–81.

McDonald, Russ. *Shakespeare's Late Style* (2006).

Neill, Michael. " 'Noises, / Sounds, and sweet airs': The Burden of Shakespeare's *The Tempest." Shakespeare Quarterly* 59 (2008), 36–59.

Orgel, Stephen. "Shakespeare and the Cannibals." In *Cannibals, Witches, and Divorce: Estranging the Renaissance*, ed. Marjorie Garber (1987), pp. 40–66.

Patterson, Annabel. *Shakespeare and the Popular Voice* (1991).

Shakespeare Survey 43 (1990).

Singh, Jyotsna G. "Caliban Versus Miranda: Race and Gender Conflicts in Postcolonial Readings of *The Tempest."*

In *Feminist Readings of Early Modern Culture*, eds. Valerie Traub, M. Lindsay Kaplan, and Dympna Callaghan (1996), pp. 191–209.

Still, Colin. *Shakespeare's Mystery Play: A Study of "The Tempest"* (1921).

Taylor, Mark. "Prospero's Books and Stephano's Bottle: Colonial Experience in *The Tempest*," *Clio* 22 (1993): 101–13.

Traversi, Derek A. *Shakespeare: The Last Phase* (1955).

Vaughan, Alden T., and Virginia Mason Vaughan. *Shakespeare's Caliban: A Cultural History* (1991).

Vaughan, Virginia Mason, and Alden T. Vaughan, eds. *The Tempest* (2011).

Wilson, J. Dover. *The Meaning of "The Tempest"* (1936).

The Signet Classics Shakespeare Series:

The Tragedies

*extensively revised and updated expert commentary
provides more enjoyment through a greater
understanding of the texts*

ANTONY AND CLEOPATRA, Barbara Everett, ed.

CORIOLANUS, Ruben Brower, ed.

HAMLET, Sylvan Barnet, ed.

JULIUS CAESAR, William and Barbara Rosen, ed.

KING LEAR, Russell Faser, ed.

MACBETH, Sylvan Barnet, ed.

OTHELLO, Alvin Kernan, ed.

ROMEO AND JULIET, J.A. Bryant, Jr., ed.

TROILUS AND CRESSIDA. Daniel Seltzer, ed.

**Available wherever books are sold or at
signetclassics.com**

S363

The Signet Classics Shakespeare Series:

The Histories

*extensively revised and updated expert commentary
provides more enjoyment through a greater
understanding of the texts*

HENRY IV: PART I, Maynard Mack, ed.

HENRY IV: PART II, Norman Holland, ed.

HENRY V, John Russell Brown, ed.

HENRY VI: PARTS I, II, & III, Lawrence V. Ryan,
Arthur Freeman, & Milton Crane, ed.

RICHARD II, Kenneth Muir, ed.

RICHARD III, Mark Eccles, ed.

READ THE TOP 20
SIGNET CLASSICS

1984 BY GEORGE ORWELL

ANIMAL FARM BY GEORGE ORWELL

LES MISÉRABLES BY VICTOR HUGO

ROMEO AND JULIET BY WILLIAM SHAKESPEARE

THE INFERNO BY DANTE

FRANKENSTEIN BY MARY SHELLEY

BEOWULF TRANSLATED BY BURTON RAFFEL

THE STORY OF MY LIFE BY HELEN KELLER

NARRATIVE OF THE LIFE OF FREDERICK DOUGLASS
 BY FREDERICK DOUGLASS

HAMLET BY WILLIAM SHAKESPEARE

TESS OF THE D'URBERVILLES BY THOMAS HARDY

THE FEDERALIST PAPERS BY ALEXANDER HAMILTON

THE ODYSSEY BY HOMER

OLIVER TWIST BY CHARLES DICKENS

NECTAR IN A SIEVE BY KAMALA MARKANDAYA

WHY WE CAN'T WAIT BY DR. MARTIN LUTHER KING, JR.

MACBETH BY WILLIAM SHAKESPEARE

ONE DAY IN THE LIFE OF IVAN DENISOVICH
 BY ALEXANDER SOLZHENITSYN

A TALE OF TWO CITIES BY CHARLES DICKENS

THE HOUND OF THE BASKERVILLES
 BY SIR ARTHUR CONAN DOYLE